"A prosecutor in a stalking case knows that the jury wants to know—Why? In *Evil Thoughts: Wicked Deeds*, Dr. Mohandie answers that question about some of the most notorious criminal cases in America's history. Just like he did in the courtroom and during investigations, Kris brings these infamous cases to life in a way that explores and fascinates. He unlocks and explains the minds of killers and stalkers. This is a book that shines a light on some of the darkest shadows that lurk in the world around us."

> **—Judge Scott Gordon (Ret.)**, Founding member, Stalking and Threat Assessment Team, LA County District Attorney's Office

"Dr. Mohandie's ability to blend his professional expertise, personal life experiences, and storytelling ability takes you into the mind of some of the most dangerous criminals this country has ever seen. *Evil Thoughts: Wicked Deeds* is a must-read for anyone who wants to immerse themselves in the world of forensic psychology through the eyes of one of the best in the business."

> **—Derrick Levasseur**, Detective, Author, and TV Personality

"Worrying about the safety of Lakers fans, players, and staff has given me many sleepless nights. I have sought out the expertise and guidance of Dr. Kris Mohandie in regards to threat assessment, but acknowledge that the risk is an everyday reality for all. This book is a MUST read as we continue to shift our collective mindset to accepting that violence can occur any place at any time. We must be prepared."

> **—Jeanie Buss**, CEO and Governor, Los Angeles Lakers

"I have worked with Dr. Mohandie for many years managing and resolving high risk hostage-taking and barricaded subject incidents. He is a true subject matter expert who I depended on when critical life and death decisions were needed during unfolding and prolonged crises. His understanding and insight into the behavior of subjects who are in personal crisis and/or predators cannot be overstated. His book shares with the reader the detailed dynamics associated with sinister behavior and crime that is captivating. It is a must read for those who have interest in the behind-the-scene work and effort done by law enforcement and mental health professionals."

> **—Michael Albanese**

EVIL THOUGHTS:
WICKED
DEEDS

ÉVIL THOUGHTS:

WICKED DEEDS

KRIS MOHANĐIÉ

PH.D., ABPP

with

BRIAN SKOLOFF

Post Hill
PRESS

A POST HILL PRESS BOOK

Evil Thoughts: Wicked Deeds
© 2019 by Kris Mohandie, Ph.D., ABPP
with Brian Skoloff
All Rights Reserved

ISBN: 978-1-64293-211-9
ISBN (eBook) 978-1-64293-212-6

Cover art by Cody Corcoran
Cover photo © ID Investigation, Discovery
Interior design and composition by Greg Johnson, Textbook Perfect

This is a work of nonfiction. All people, locations, events, and situations are portrayed to the best of the author's memory.

Post Hill Press
New York • Nashville
posthillpress.com

Published in the United States of America

For my mother, Linda Merle Roberts,
and father, Luc Francois Mohandie.
No mere words will ever be enough
to thank my loving parents
for all they did for me
and so many others as teachers,
and human beings.

CONTENTS

ACKNOWLEDGMENTS

There are so many people to acknowledge, who made this book possible, through their unique influence and contributions to my life and work.

First—and foremost—are my mother and father who—as teachers—emphasized education, learning, questioning, and being literate. Mom introduced me to reading, and those Hardy Boys books! She worked hard to raise two boys as a single mother, yet touched the lives of so many. Dad rose from his impoverished life in the small village of Saint-Francois, Guadeloupe, against the odds, and immigrated to the US as a teenager, to pursue education and a better life.

My grandmother, Irene Roberts, always believed in me, and through her love and example made the impossible always seem possible. Her words and wisdom have simultaneously confounded and inspired me to this day. I often reflect upon her deepest message of the faith she held so dear: "I am in this world but not of it."

I was fortunate to have so many wonderful mentors, whose lessons continue to teach even after their passing. Dr. Marty Reiser gave me the chance, taught and coached me, then entrusted me to take on greater responsibilities. I will be ever indebted and thankful for all he has done for my career. Dr. Chris Hatcher built upon Dr. Reiser's thorough introduction to the world of police psychology, and spent countless, exhausting hours helping me conceptualize threat and violence risk assessment, and other aspects of operational psychology. I miss them both.

Dr. Reid Meloy has been a wonderful and thoughtful mentor, and now friend. I am grateful for the chance to learn didactically, and now collaboratively throughout the years. There is no keener mind when it comes to the forensic psychological world, and I am still in awe of all he has done, and continues to contribute, to our knowledge base of the darkest and most malevolent criminals our world has ever known.

Assistant Chief Mike Albanese—who I will always think of as 10-David from LAPD SWAT—supported the development of a powerful model of crisis negotiation, from within the first and best domestic SWAT team ever created. Working on the ground floor with Mike, on cases and teaching, gave me some of the best memories I've had across my career.

I have had the honor of coming to know, learning from, working together with, and becoming friends with Dr. Mike McMains, a police psychologist and pioneer in crisis negotiations.

Thank you to John Lane, Greg Bolles, and Jeff Dunn, who each led the LAPD's Threat Management Unit, and afforded the opportunity to conduct research and consult on fascinating stalking and threat cases. Special thanks to the support throughout the years from the Association of Threat Assessment Professionals and the California Association of Hostage Negotiators. I am grateful to the courage of Lenora Claire and Kathleen Gallagher for sharing their terrifying experiences, and helping so many through their ongoing advocacy.

Beth Silverman, Rhonda Saunders, Henry Schleiff, and Lorna Thomas at Investigation Discovery, Erin Moriarty at CBS *48 Hours*, Anderson Cooper, Star Price, Scott Gordon, and Jimmy Fox: I thank all of you for the opportunities you afforded me, the cases, new experiences, and helping me grow in my career in ways I could not imagine. Each of you has been an example of a star blazing a trail, visionaries in your respective crafts, with complete commitment and absolute dedication.

Assistant Chief Frank Piersol, supporter and friend, is the innovator who oversaw the LAPD's evolution from the post-Gates era, and the expanded role of psychology in law enforcement. I am ever grateful for your mentorship, leadership, and friendship. You created so many opportunities for me, and other psychologists in law enforcement.

I am thankful to the many people who helped facilitate interviews, opened doors, and provided access to case material. And especially to the victims, and those who survived to carry the torch of their memories and legacies, and to the brave, selfless, and honest men and women of law enforcement who fight day in and day out for justice. A special thank you to the Glendale Police Department investigators of the Angel of Death task force, including John McKillop, Will Curie, and Tony Fuschia. *They* are the heroes of that case.

The late Roy Hazelwood and Robert Ressler, and John Douglas from the FBI's esteemed Behavioral Science Unit. I am grateful to have known and learned from each: great men, and fearless trailblazers.

Similarly, psychiatrist John Macdonald provided a foundation for future threat assessment thinking. Sharing time with him, years ago, in Colorado, when he was in his eighties was one of the highlights of my career—he was still curious, hungry for knowledge, and working on his next book.

Dr. Angela Donahue and Dr. Gerald Sweet have been trusted colleagues and friends throughout the years, providing invaluable input and support when I needed it most. I'd also like to thank David K., Gary F., Angela B., and Merv S. for their friendship and support throughout the years. Yes, "to thine own self be true." Bic M., thank you for your support throughout the early years of my career. Rochelle Calhoun has been a steady and loyal supporter of my career since my second year of graduate school—thank you so much! Laura K., thank you for encouraging me to embrace my personal style. A special thanks to the guys of Dexter Drive: Aaron, Matt, and Jessie.

Derrick Levasseur, my partner on two prior investigative shows, and now friend. Thank you for your encouragement, the privilege of working with you, and teaching me the small amount I know about social media. And to those great new friends and followers on Twitter, who ask the tough questions and offer the unique and sometimes humorous perspectives, your support and stimulation has been meaningful in ways I could not have anticipated.

For my literary agent Frank Weimann and especially my agent Harry Gold—I cannot thank each of you enough for believing in this project and helping me see it through. Throughout the years, Harry, you have been so supportive and I am ever grateful.

I cannot say enough to acknowledge Drew Leavens from Specialized Training Services who continues to this day to facilitate psychology training experiences that were basically unheard of when I was getting started in this field. Through Drew's trainings, special workshops, and conferences, I was able to meet and learn from many of the greats in the field. Later, Drew supported and promoted my own lectures on school and workplace violence, and mass homicide. He published my first book, *School Violence Threat Management*, painstakingly editing it, line by line, word by word. I *thought* I knew how to write, but Drew helped me take it to the next level.

A special thank you to my son, Kashmir, who has served as the most special source of inspiration in my life.

I know I've left so many out, and I don't think I've done an adequate job of acknowledging everyone, or justice to all who have done so much for me.

I am especially grateful to the Source of all. Thank you, God, for this life, the experiences you allowed me to have, the people you surrounded me with, and the flow of inspiration.

It was 1988, and I was all of twenty-four years old. I was in my second-year internship half-time, and I was also moonlighting after-hours at a private practice. At this point, I'd met a guy who dreamed of killing and was terrified of the images in his head—in retrospect, probably a budding sex killer who was trying to fight his images and urges. I'd interviewed a woman who had a genuine multiple personality disorder, from years of horrifying sexual abuse, and recently met a tragic boy who set fires and acted out, who had been kept chained in a basement, fed dog food, and used by his father and all of his pedophile friends as an object until he was rescued. But most of my work was with normal people struggling with anxiety, failed relationships, and some school misbehavior.

I received an intake sheet in my box at the private practice: "Robert P., has an Uzi, will kill people if his court case doesn't go his way." I was to see him this very day, and I really didn't know quite what to think. The secretary buzzed me later that afternoon to let me know he had arrived. I went out to the waiting room and invited him into my comfortable outpatient office.

He was about forty, married with two kids, and highly educated; he had a nice house in a suburb and was working at a local tech firm. He proceeded to tell me his story.

The company had some lucrative government defense contracts, and he had blown the whistle on some cost-overrun issues—you know, like five-thousand-dollar hammers or one-thousand-dollar toilet seats. At that point, he perceived he was retaliated against, and his employer made his life difficult and very stressful.

So much so that Robert took a week of sick leave to regroup. He returned to work and started to obsess about it. "Why should I have to use *my* sick time? This should be a workers' comp reimbursement." So he filed a workers' comp suit. All he wanted was his week of sick time back and to be left alone.

His employer made a federal case out of it, and Robert went through the adversarial questioning of his truthfulness, the legitimacy of his claims, and so forth in the pretrial proceedings. His integrity was questioned. The case was going to a final hearing. The stress had been so much for Robert that he wasn't eating, wasn't sleeping, and was infuriated. "How dare they?"

He decided what he was going to do. He made a list of all the people who had betrayed him, dirtied his image and, in his words, "destroyed" him. He then sought and purchased an Uzi on the black market, with a ton of ammunition. He told me that if the hearing did not go his way, he was going to kill all these people.

I asked him where he was keeping the Uzi. He said at his cabin.

He perceived he had been destroyed, yet he had a cabin. And a nice home. And a wonderful family. By the way, he was also moonlighting. In addition to his nice 1988 salary of one hundred thousand dollars, he was also pulling down another hundred thousand dollars a year dabbling in the real estate market.

But cognitive constriction had caused him to fixate on the questioning of his integrity and the sense of being wronged. Moral righteousness was the theme.

I was terrified, overwhelmed, and sure my career—before it had begun—was over. I was going to lose the degree I had not yet earned, would never get licensed, and didn't even have malpractice insurance yet. I said to Robert, "I'll be right back."

Now if you are ever in a therapist's office and you've just told him or her something heavy and the response is "I'll be right back," it might be a clue that something is amiss. Bless his heart, Robert stayed while I fled to my supervisor's office.

I told my supervisor the same story I just told you. He said, "I'll come with you. I think we can help him."

So we both sat down with him. My supervisor told Robert we could help him, complimented him for coming in to address this, and focused on the part of Robert that must not have wanted to do what he had been planning. The workers' comp hearing was about two weeks out. We had some time.

Robert went home that day. I met with him a few more times. He ultimately saw the big picture that his life hadn't been destroyed, that he had already made his point, and he was going to accept the outcome of the hearing, no matter what.

During our last visit, Robert thanked me. He then volunteered that he had gotten rid of the Uzi. Out on a friend's sailboat, between Los Angeles and Catalina Island, he had slipped it out of his briefcase and into the deep water of that channel.

I said, "Robert, but you paid eighteen hundred dollars for that gun. Why didn't you sell it?"

He replied, "I didn't want some crazy guy to get it."

He offered to let me use his story with his real name, even to go speak to anyone about what he had gone through. I have chosen to protect his identity here. But I am grateful for the experience, for his courageous decision, and to fate for intervening. I occasionally think of Robert, and I hope he is well, and I hope that his life has over and over again proven to him how glad he is to be alive and reinforced that he made the right choice.

It wasn't my great clinical skill that led to this positive outcome. We should have hospitalized him until he let go of his homicidal plan and impulses. We should have warned the intended victims. We should have called the police to let them know about the threats. But it was 1988, and we really didn't know what we were doing with this stuff. We did not do any of that.

I got lucky.

Later, I told my supervisor about a postdoctoral internship position at the Los Angeles Police Department; the advertisement specified to contact the Director of Behavioral Science Services Section, Dr. Martin Reiser. My supervisor encouraged me to apply. The real journey was about to begin. We all have to start somewhere.

The Human Abyss

"Yea, though I walk through the valley
of the shadow of death, I will fear no evil."

—Psalm 23:4

Over many years now, I have studied and met killers and various criminals from all over the world.

Terrible people doing terrible things. Evil thoughts, wicked deeds.

When I was six years old, I remember walking through tall grass, wet with the morning dew, in wonder at the world around me. Innocent and free. It was a world of caterpillars, lizards, snakes, and birds, and if I was really lucky I might see a woodpecker or even a hawk circling above. I'd lie on the grass and watch the clouds pass by in the blue sky. It rained a lot back then, but it was the rain of hope, and everything was beautiful and green.

I was twenty-five years old in 1989 when I earned my Ph.D. in clinical psychology.

Originally, I had been a political science major and wanted to eventually become a lawyer, but I switched over to psychology during my first year of undergraduate study at California State Polytechnic University, Pomona.

I've always been sort of lucky—right place at the right time—and compared to kids these days, not so planful. I grew up in Southern California and did not have any desire to go anywhere else to attend school. So I applied to two local schools without giving it much thought. Hell, it was 1980, and things were pretty relaxed.

At Cal Poly, I did not care at all for the political science professors or the coursework. It seemed difficult to do well or master the material if you didn't agree with their views, which in retrospect tended to be Marxist and socialist nonsense, and I had trouble tracking their often meandering logic and analyses.

If I had known more back then, I would have challenged them about violent true believers like Joseph Stalin and Chairman Mao who were armed and inspired by these ideas, and the millions who died as these philosophies were rammed down their throats at the point of a gun. Believe or die.

But I found the psychology coursework in my general education fascinating. I'd had a little taste of it in high school in a religion-and-psychology class. Learning about the human psyche, what makes us tick and why, quickly became my passion. I was seventeen and had finally figured out where I was going, at least generally, and I was all in. For the first time, I gave school my all. I knew I couldn't stop there, because if you go into psychology, you have to get your doctorate to do the really interesting stuff. There was a lot of talk about graduate school, and I applied to a few, but the one that really caught my eye was the California School of Professional Psychology—the Los Angeles campus, to be exact—in a simple ad. It was American Psychological Association-approved and, well, it was in California! It was a nontraditional professional school, the first of its kind. Less research, more emphasis on practice. I got in, and it was an amazing experience.

During those five years, I had the opportunity to complete several internships. As luck would have it, my first one was at the Anaheim Police Department counseling first-time juvenile offenders. The next year I worked in a community mental health center in Pomona, doing rotations with the severely mentally ill and the psychiatric emergency team, and performing standard outpatient work. My final year, I interned helping out developmentally disabled kids and their families. And in the midst of it, I moonlighted in a private practice in Upland, where I had my first brush with danger—that client from my prologue who was planning to commit a workplace mass murder.

Joining the Los Angeles Police Department in 1989 as an unpaid intern was the beginning of finding my true niche. I saw the advertisement for a part-time internship at the LAPD, a tiny posting on the bulletin board at my graduate school as I was approaching the completion of my Ph.D. It seemed like it might help me develop a specialty that could be useful in my future career. A simple ad, after all, had resulted in a grad school choice. And I'd gotten a taste of police culture at the Anaheim PD.

I called Dr. Martin Reiser, not knowing at the time that this was the man who had founded police psychology in the 1960s and become the first full-time staff psychologist with any police department in the country—the LAPD.

He eventually hired me as his psychological assistant. I was relieved, exhilarated, grateful, and overwhelmed. I was going to learn to do therapy with police officers, be taught hostage negotiation, go out on dangerous-incident calls, teach, maybe do some research, and receive mentoring from the very man who had developed this unique niche. Maybe I'd even be able to pay off my student-loan debt!

We worked out in the field and in the office together. I learned my craft firsthand from Dr. Reiser, and in 1991 became a licensed psychologist still working with police in Los Angeles.

I've been interested in criminality and violence ever since I can remember. I used to read the Hardy Boys mystery books as a kid, the first things that got me excited about solving crimes and understanding the makings of a criminal. I'd had an innocent, serene childhood, with warm memories of exploring the outdoors, lying in fields of wet grass, watching the clouds and butterflies drift by. But there was always that attraction to darkness. For some reason, I always wanted to hurl myself as deep into it as I could.

During my teenage years, I sensed the mounting antisocial turbulence in society. Unlike most kids, I was transfixed by deviant sociopolitical violence and criminal behavior like plane hijackings, the Jonestown mass suicides, and the activities of the Manson gang and the Symbionese Liberation Army.

I grew up in Los Angeles County as the Crips and Bloods were first forming in my neighborhood. Born Krishnan Raj Mohandie in a rough area of Altadena and looking "racially ambiguous," I experienced all sorts of colorful nicknames—sometimes as a misperceived outsider, other times as a misperceived insider.

But I survived, adjusting to the volatile world around me through my wits and my ability to talk and listen to many diverse types. I was observant, could think on my feet, and talked my way out of the gauntlet of racially charged conflicts that were part of my daily life.

By the time I joined the LAPD and began working with Dr. Reiser, his unit—the Behavioral Science Services Section—largely treated shell-shocked police officers, suffering from what was later known as post-traumatic stress disorder (PTSD); worked to hypnotize victims to enhance their memories of horrifying events; and used psychology to help defuse life-and-death hostage situations.

Hostage negotiation teams began springing up in the early 1970s after the well-publicized standoffs at Attica state prison in New York and the Munich massacre at the Olympics in Germany. It was then that law enforcement began to wonder if maybe there was a viable alternative to storming a building with guns blazing, which usually resulted in loss of life, second-guessing, and litigation.

The New York Police Department began using hostage negotiation techniques in the 1970s for garden-variety domestic violence situations, holed-up criminals, the mentally disturbed, and the like.

My chosen professional niche within the field of police psychology became operational psychology—the application of psychology to police tactical and investigative operations. And my first love was hostage negotiation, as a member of what we now call Crisis Negotiation Teams, or CNTs. The name shift reflected the reality that most domestic incidents do not involve a hostage taker leveraging for money and political change, but rather some distraught or deranged individual, often under the influence of drugs or alcohol, overwhelmed with emotions and contemplating the worst-case resolution to their life dilemma.

The LAPD hostage negotiation unit that I joined in 1989 as a college grad was only the third such agency established in America, behind New York's and San Francisco's, which put me on the ground floor of the emerging field.

I rolled out to incidents in progress watching Dr. Reiser give his real-time input to help prevent suicides and homicides. He turned me loose on my first solo assignment in 1990—a parolee with an AK-47 holding his common-law wife and child hostage. When I arrived at the scene, the first responding sergeant was screaming over the phone at the guy. It was not going well.

I applied some suggestions I'd learned from Dr. Reiser and the most recent CNT class I'd attended: "speech lower and slower," for example, and a few other basic tricks of the trade.

At one point, we heard the sound of metal clacking against teeth over the phone line as the man placed the rifle barrel into his mouth. I suggested the sergeant ask him to please take it out as we didn't want a mishap. And he did! I was thrilled.

After hours of talking, the man finally agreed to surrender. It was a terrifying yet tantalizing first real-world look into the human abyss of criminality. The suspect survived, and so did I. I was hooked.

The LAPD's first CNT was unlike the New York City/East Coast model, which separated the tacticians, or uniformed police, from the talkers—people like me.

The LAPD had already formed the first domestic SWAT (Special Weapons and Tactics) team in the world, and it was considered the best. It was founded in the 1960s under the command of Chief Daryl Francis Gates, who would later find notoriety for the failure of his paramilitary approach to policing, and for his command staff's failure to act decisively at the outset of the infamous Rodney King riots in 1992.

From the beginning, psychologists like me in Los Angeles were attached to hostage negotiation units led by SWAT teams. My role meant accessing information and providing it to the entire team on-site, known as psychological intelligence gathering.

I was to determine whether a person was "negotiable" or not—could he or she be talked off the ledge, and if so, how? In addition, I was expected to provide specific strategies and dialogue during these tense hostage situations, and to be present in order to monitor and provide real-time feedback during the negotiation process.

By 1992, at age twenty-nine, I wore three hats at the LAPD. I was a practicing psychologist treating a full slate of patients such as PTSD-afflicted police officers. Simultaneously, I was serving as a consultant to numerous units within the department, including the elite LAPD hostage negotiation/SWAT team, the threat management unit, and numerous investigative squads, like those for sex crimes and robberies and homicides. I also was serving as a training instructor, sharing knowledge about all of the above inside and outside the LAPD.

Fast-forward more than two decades and I wear even more hats. Along the way I picked up some forensic expertise and began consultation with other police agencies, as well as in the private sector regarding threat and risk assessment, including in the entertainment industry. Around 2002, it became too difficult to juggle the consultations I was doing with law enforcement agencies and private clients, work on criminal and civil cases, and a contract with the FBI in its Behavioral Analysis Program assisting around the country on counterintelligence and counterterrorism matters.

With the birth of my son, I never went back to the LAPD as an employee and officially retired from the agency in 2003.

While I am no longer employed full-time by the LAPD, I continue to work as a clinical, police, and forensic psychologist based in Los Angeles. My work takes me all over North America.

No two days are ever the same. One morning, I'm helping an entertainment client deal with a potentially dangerous stalker, and in the afternoon, a university is calling with concerns about a threatening and unstable student. A day later, I'm testifying about a sanity issue for the prosecution in a homicide trial. Within twenty-four hours, I'm review-ing materials for two other murder cases and a police shooting, then I move on to working on yet another shooting and another homicide case.

In the middle of it all, I'm getting my son up for school, making breakfast, spending some quality time with my family, making sure homework is getting done and turned in, and doing the nighttime family home routine. I'm grateful to get to do what I do, but being a parent is the best and most important role of all.

By week's end, I'm juggling a long conference call on multiple threat and risk cases with a large corporate client, while being on standby to provide testimony in a federal police shooting case. Then comes an emergency call from a university with concerns about one of its students possibly posing a campus violence threat.

I love it! I'm in my zone.

Unfortunately for the world, there is never a shortage of work in the arena of threat assessment, extreme violence, and victimology, a fancy way of referring to the social science dedicated to the study of the rela-tionships between victim and perpetrator and the psychological effects on them from their experiences. Traumatic bonding, Stockholm syn-drome, and counterintuitive victim responses are all part of victimology.

I deal with nefarious characters of all types, and work with clients including police departments, federal and international law enforcement agencies, and criminal and civil courts. I have testified more than seventy times in criminal trials and twenty-five in civil cases, given more than forty depositions, consulted to both defense and prosecution teams, and worked on numerous death penalty cases in multiple states and juris-dictions, including California, Alaska, Washington, Nevada, Nebraska, Oklahoma, and Texas, as well as Canada.

Occasionally I dabble in on-air endeavors as well, having appeared in and hosted several TV true-crime documentary-style shows, such as the Investigation Discovery network's *Most Evil* and *Breaking Homicide*.

Everything I've done, seen, and learned going all the way back to college has taught me much about evil deeds and the people in every corner of society who commit them.

My hope here is to provide an informed peek behind the curtain of criminality in a world that's getting darker and more dangerous by the day, a chance to delve into the minds of the vicious while providing insight into why these people do what they do and lessons we can learn as a society to help stop or at least reduce the bloodshed.

America has become the international capital of mass shootings, the once-shining light upon a hill now often viewed in muzzle flashes and body counts garnering headlines around the world. And even though not all events happen on American soil, it seems that our criminals have inspired many international offenders.

Mass casualty shootings occur far too regularly as demented gunmen fire on throngs of innocent people in random cities and towns across the U.S., like Parkland, Florida; Las Vegas, Nevada; Sutherland Springs, Texas; and San Bernardino, California, to name just a few.

We are no longer shocked when kids and teachers hide in closets from gun-toting predators, followed by the ubiquitous "thoughts and prayers" but very little action to stem the carnage.

Is it any surprise that the mother of a recent victim said, rather than prayers, she wants people to actually do something to stop these trage-dies from occurring again and again and again?[1]

It's gotten to the point where some believe the best solution is to arm teachers and fortify schools like military bases or prisons. Do we really want to arm teachers? Do they want to be armed? Even police officers who train extensively occasionally discharge their weapons accidentally.

How are first-responding officers supposed to know the difference between the hero teacher with a gun and the armed offender? Do we want to make it easy for a violent student to access the gun by overpow-ering an armed teacher? I don't think so. If teachers wanted to be cops, they would have gone to the academy. These solutions create more prob-lems than they solve.

---

[1] "Distraught Mother of Mass-Shooting Victim Says She Doesn't Want 'Thoughts' and 'Prayers,'" Women in the World, November 9, 2018, https://womenintheworld.com/2018/11/09/distraught-mother-of-mass-shooting-victim-says-she-doesnt-want-thoughts-and-prayers/.

Targeted, purposeful, goal-oriented and agenda-driven violence fueled by cognitive thought and fantasy in which anger and rage are converted to cold-blooded planful revenge used to be the province of the assassin.

Now we see many categories of individuals who have stepped up to the targeting platform, with a myriad of ideological and personal issues driving their plans.

Much has been learned about targeted violence, including the fact that the perpetrators typically engage in certain behavioral and thought sequences. This knowledge can help with early detection and interruption of the violence, and assist experts in distinguishing the hunters—the truly dangerous—from the howlers who may be all talk.

"Leakage" is at the top of these patterned responses and forms the foundation of "See something, say something" campaigns. Would-be violent criminals very often telegraph their plans to friends or family or on social media platforms, offering a window into their maniacal thoughts before they carry out the vicious act.

If something makes you uncomfortable, fearful, or anxious that something bad might happen, screenshot it or otherwise record it and get it to the police.

And if the first responder doesn't seem to be on board, find another one who is. Maybe it's not a real threat, but if it is, there will be no reversing it once action has been taken.

Are you afraid to report a loved one who is out of control? Do you feel that no matter what you do, it could have a bad outcome? Arguably that is telling you that the person needs intervention to keep him or her and others safe.

Do you think it is helping not to keep a potentially dangerous person and the people around that person from being harmed? Better to have some relatively minor fallout now than to later experience something permanent, a traumatic scar, another event on a landscape already brimming with blood and pain, and more graves leading to inconsolable sorrow.

No two violent criminals are the same. All have their own reasoning and rationalization for their righteous indignation, but there are at least three common threads that often string them all together: power, fear, and the need for notoriety—the yearning for omnipotence, the unbridled desire to instill and inflict terror, and the absolute goal of being remembered for what they have done.

In their minds, they're standing on a pulpit while the world is listening to their commanding sermon.

The truth is, though, with the advent of social media and its allure of instantaneous cult celebrity, for many, it's not just in their minds.

Social media stokes the inherent narcissism—the extreme selfishness and self-absorption—of many offenders who believe their agenda merits a shout-out to, and recognition by, the world, a sense of entitlement to take what is owed to them and exact their revenge.

They can now leave behind a virtual manifesto, selfies, Facebook posts and YouTube videos, so-called cyberprints of their violent pathway, visible to the masses in perpetuity, an indelible mark on the world that makes offenders feel as if they will become part of history.

In reality, they live in infamy, but they're unable to, or unwilling to, discern between famous and infamous. Oftentimes, it doesn't matter to them so long as they're remembered.

Long ago, in many cases of completed suicide, the notion of cognitive constriction (tunnel vision) that death is the solution to a person's life problems was observed. The homicidal subject shares much in common with the suicidal, and there is often overlap. Taking a life, whether it is one's own or another's, still means a life lost.

Many mass shooters take their own lives at the conclusion of the event. Death becomes cemented in their minds as the sole answer to a plethora of troubling life questions, leaving them to focus solely on the technical execution of the crime.

Many of these offenders start their journey with self-hate and a self-destructive wish, and then they come to the conclusion that those who "drove them to it" should pay the price first.

After all, is not the malignant killing of other humans a form of self-destruction?

For many, killing brings a sense of overwhelming power, and going down in a blaze of glory only magnifies their satisfaction in carrying out the ultimate attack on a mass of innocents.

Some of the most infamous serial killers believe they were called upon to commit their crimes by a greater authority or out of a so-called code of mercy. One example is Efren Saldivar, an "angel of death" who killed up to two hundred hospital patients while working as a respiratory therapist in California, largely in the early 1990s.[2] He is regarded as being among the most prolific serial killers of our time.

I interviewed Saldivar extensively and can tell you there was nothing merciful about his actions, nor did he actually live by the code he used as the impetus for his crimes. It was merely his hunger for control over life and death that consumed him more and more with each killing.

The hostage taker, by comparison, is in a different category of criminality altogether. In hostage cases, bad decisions are heaped upon worse decisions, and the offender's hopelessness and anger erupt into a frustrated life and a dramatic acting out. Police arrive quickly, and the negotiation to save lives begins. It is literally a life-and-death situation.

Stalkers, meanwhile, come in four district categories: the Intimate Stalker, the Acquaintance Stalker, the Private Stranger Stalker, and the Public Figure Stalker.

They can terrorize anyone, from the ordinary citizen who becomes the fixation of their former intimate partner to the celebrity stalked by an unstable individual who psychotically perceives a relationship where none exists. Ivanka Trump, President Donald Trump's daughter, had a dangerous stalker for years; the same man also had other victims who were unfortunate enough to cross his path and become targets of his disturbed fixations and grandiose and violent delusions.

The truth is that the average stalking victim is an everyday person—a woman tries to say goodbye or simply "I'm not interested," and the rejected man cannot handle the word "no." We live in a world of

---

[2] Paul Lieberman, "Saldivar Admitted to Possible Role in '100 to 200' Deaths," *Los Angeles Times*, January 13, 2001, https://www.latimes.com/archives/la-xpm-2001-jan-13-mn-11940-story.html

increasing entitlement, and the more pathologically narcissistic take rejection deeply to heart.

The stalker then embarks on a campaign of harassment, vengeance, and perhaps a twisted attempt to coerce the victim into a relationship. These are, in fact, the most dangerous cases, and most domestic-violence murder victims were stalked prior to the tragedy.

Delusional people have found a place to feed their psychotic misperceptions and conspiratorial thinking in the virtual world of social media. Like-minded individuals validate and encourage paranoid thought processes and embolden the criminal with groupthink.

Support for any form of deviance, even cannibalism and bestiality, can be found online. Cyberspace and social media ferment ideas that used to simply dissipate into the atmosphere; delusional, conspiratorial, and angry, disaffected individuals now have a home to stimulate their thoughts, instead of receiving corrective feedback from an in-person confidant or mental health professional.

So-called violent true believers, a term coined by my friend and colleague Dr. J. Reid Meloy in a scholarly analysis we wrote after the September 11 terror attacks, can be domestic or foreign. They commit acts of violence based on belief systems. Maj. Nidal Malik Hasan, for example, a psychiatrist no less, in 2009 shot and killed thirteen people and wounded thirty others, most of them unarmed soldiers, in the worst mass murder in American history at a U.S. military installation, in Fort Hood, Texas.

Hasan had been inspired by Islamic extremist beliefs he found primarily on the internet. He was not formally attached to any terrorist group, nor had he ever attended training to commit such a violent act. His radicalization was virtual, fed by the internet and social media, but his killing was very real and underscored that we have entered a new era in which identification with a belief system doesn't have to come from face-to-face interaction but can be achieved via computer while living in the real world.

Violent true believers identify with an extremist belief system and have accepted, indeed embraced, that violence is an essential part of achieving the goals associated with those beliefs.

The truth is that in America, despite all the attention paid to Islam, our worst and most frequent violent true believers are homegrown haters fed by fear or rejection, or by some perceived slight to their way of life. Some call themselves "incels," involuntary celibate woman-haters.

The latter was the case with twenty-two-year-old Elliot Rodger, who killed six students in a 2014 rampage near the campus of the University of California, Santa Barbara. In online postings, he railed against the women who had rejected him and the men they had chosen to have sex with instead.

In a final handwritten entry in his journal on the day of the killings, he penned, "This is it. In one hour I will have my revenge on this cruel world. I HATE YOU ALLLL! DIE." His laptop was later found by authorities open to a disturbing YouTube video he had recently uploaded, titled "Day of Retribution."

He was on a mission for payback, and no one could stop him. Rodger, however, also neatly fits into the category of a mass casualty shooter. Many of these violent offenders qualify for several categories of criminal offense.

These individuals often have another kind of duality about them. On one hand, they may be very aware that others do not agree with their dark thoughts and fantasies and thus censor much of what they share about them. But they also have accepted, usually without any lingering questions or doubts, that the evil and malignant solutions that drive them to commit such atrocities are reasonable and therefore actionable.

The often calm and matter-of-fact narrative they use to describe their ideas and impulses can be enormously unsettling.

Even among those with mental health issues, thoughtful choices and decisions are made, often with chilling deliberation. A person can be very mentally ill yet behave rationally and carry out crimes with premeditation and malice aforethought.

Regarding those with obvious mental health issues, our country suffers from the very freedoms we hold dear. We come upon situations in which we are not able to force the afflicted to get treatment, and only after a crime does the clamor begin that the person with the broken brain must receive help.

We blame the guns. We blame political rhetoric. We blame hatred, racism, and religion. But where does the blame truly fall?

In a number of cases, there is shared responsibility, to varying degrees. But free will and freedom of choice are necessary values for our democratic society to function, leaving us with a conundrum: How do we stop these violent acts before they are carried out without infringing upon the very rights that millions of law-abiding, sane citizens hold so dear?

Throughout all of my work as a forensic psychologist, I help answer some of the most pressing questions. Why did the person do it? Was it related to mental illness? What is wrong with this person? Is he or she sane? Insane? Are there understandable factors that could be used to argue for or against leniency in sentencing after a criminal conviction? Should a juvenile offender who killed at school be tried as an adult? What drives the serial killer to wreak such havoc on society?

The questions are challenging, but the work is immensely gratifying.

The field is full of experts for hire who sell and distort their opinions to fit the narratives of their clients, who are paying for someone to provide the answers they want, not necessarily the truth. These "hired guns" justify their distortion of the truth with all kinds of excuses.

We see this play out often in criminal trials, where defense and prosecution teams pit professionals like me against one another on the witness stand in what amounts to a battle of the experts, leaving jurors to determine who is more believable.

I am not that guy. I tell anyone who hires me, "I will tell you what I think, whether you like it or not."

I often think of what I do as a descent into the depths of human depravity, pain, and suffering, where most people would never allow themselves to go.

I walk through my life knowing what people are capable of and understanding that appearances can be deceiving. There are a lot of memories: the shock wave of the earth beneath me as a suicidal man hurtles from his jumping platform 270 feet high after hours of negotiation; the bitter smell of tear gas introduced into the barricaded residence of a methed-out subject when the wind shifted; the sight of a child's bloody handprints trailing downward on the sliding glass window of the room where his father hacked him to death with a machete, cut his own wrists, and set the apartment on fire.

The trail of death and mayhem has yielded a mind-expanding post-graduate education.

Thankfully, I seldom dream or have nightmares about my cases anymore, and I find safety and calm in embracing my purpose in all of it.

I wasn't dragged here. I came here of my own free will.

"A Good Day to Die"

A Hostage Taker's Last Stand

*"To die, to sleep—No more—and by a sleep to say we end
The heartache and the thousand natural shocks..."*

— William Shakespeare, from *Hamlet*

This was not the outcome I had hoped for. Not what I could have ever imagined. One life lost. One life saved. Fair trade? Lesser of two evils? Nonetheless, the innocent was freed and the criminal felled, so one could look upon this with a sense of success. I felt simultaneously triumphant and unsettled. Was there blood on my hands? Had I done my best to get both out alive? Had I done my job? This was near the start of what I had hoped to build into my life's work. And it had ended in death—albeit that of a deranged, drug-addled man on a mission, but still, a body sent to the morgue on my watch.

It was a Tuesday at about 9:30 in the morning during heavy commuter traffic in the Los Angeles area. Significant danger was brewing in the San Fernando Valley, and we had to get there fast.

As it often was, particularly in domestic-involved barricades, the clouds of death were looming.

I was already up and working when the phone rang in my Chinatown office: "Metro SWAT, West Valley Division. Negotiators requested. The suspect is a slightly built Vietnamese male, high on crack, armed with a handgun."

I quickly grabbed a notepad and a couple of granola bars, told my boss I was en route, and slid into an unmarked police cruiser, calm and steady, flying at about one hundred miles per hour.

I was super relaxed and confident, and focused my mind on the mission. *Expect success*, I told myself. Nothing less would suffice. Part of my task was to help cops determine whether an event was negotiable or would escalate into violence and lives lost—the latter assessment pushing decision makers into countermeasures to stop aggressive behavior, up to and including the use of deadly force.

Thirty-two-year-old Vietnamese refugee Tan Khuat was holed up in an apartment with a gun and his own young child as hostage. The situation was beyond tense. The sense of urgency was palpable even before I arrived on the scene.

From the beginning, psychologists like myself in Los Angeles were attached to hostage negotiation units led by men like SWAT supervisor Sergeant Michael Albanese, a tough, buffed-out Renaissance man with deep blue eyes, a clean-shaven head, and a master's degree from the University of Southern California. He was gruff but smart and glib, committed to negotiations, and I looked up to him. We had already started traveling here and there doing training presentations for the department. He was a committed family man, was honest, had an incredible work ethic, and always incorporated unique phrases from his world, which included horseback riding, fierce workouts, and suspenseful fiction.

Today, domestic hostage situations are generally resolved by either negotiation (talking), tactics (less lethal or deadly force), or a combination of both.

According to FBI data over the past twenty years, of the approximately eight thousand hostage and barricade incidents measured thus far in the United States, some 54 percent were peacefully resolved using negotiations alone. Another 13 percent were solved by a combination of talking and tactics—negotiation plus forced entry with tear gas, deadly force or other less lethal options. Twenty-one percent of the cases ended solely using tactics (weapons and force), while 3 percent of the incidents resulted in suicide or a suicide attempt. Lastly, 7 percent of hostage taking suspects simply escaped.[3]

During my travels consulting to various police agencies, I once picked up a coffee mug at the Littleton Police Department in Colorado belonging to its hostage negotiation team. Imprinted on the mug were the words "We talk 'til they drop, one way or another," with a picture of a phone on one side, crosshairs on the other. The reality is that although the team tries to resolve situations by talking, the force option is always there. The two options are not mutually exclusive and work together in support of a common mission.

It was the LAPD who pioneered the concept of cross-training and teaching officers hostage negotiation techniques based in both psychology and tactical skills and weaponry. And by October 1992, not only were the LAPD's hostage negotiators fluent in English and Spanish, but specialists also were conversant in Farsi, Arabic, French, Mandarin, and other languages.

However, the unit was still a few weeks shy of certifying their first Vietnamese-speaking negotiators when the call came in to me regarding Tan Khuat.

It immediately caused me concern.

Some feelings, ideas, and sentiments are best expressed in one's native tongue, and even if you get around that, there is something immediately comforting about knowing you are talking to someone who speaks your language. It's an instant feeling of being home, a connection, and an understanding, and it removes the stressor of trying to keep important ideas and feelings from getting lost in translation.

So much is conveyed by something so seemingly simple. Speaking a common language perhaps reflects a shared culture and similar

---

[3] "Incident Statistics," Hostage/Barricade Reporting, Critical Incident Response Group, Crisis Negotiation Unit, California Association of Hostage Negotiators Training Conference (Burbank, CA), September 7, 2018.

experiences, and may expedite rapport-building and provide relief from the fear of yet another basis for the misunderstandings that occur all too often in human interactions. On a practical basis, it prevents missing what the person is saying and why he or she is saying it. With lives in the balance, it is not the time for interpretive errors such as, "I said, 'I have a gun,' not 'I have *no* gun'!"

The first responding officers that day were met with a barrage of gunfire. They were unsuccessful in talking the suspect down. After more shots were fired, they pulled back and secured the perimeter to keep bystanders from getting hurt, and then made the call for the SWAT and Crisis Negotiation Teams to be deployed.

Khuat was a Vietnamese refugee living in the San Fernando Valley, about fifteen miles north of downtown L.A. Like many of those fleeing war-torn Vietnam, he arrived as a boat person. During his teenage years in Vietnam, he had been forced to work for the Communist government. After being imprisoned for trying to escape his work assignment under the totalitarian regime, he lived in hiding from 1978 to 1980 until his arrival in the United States in 1981, where he took the name Gene Morgan.

Once in the U.S., Khuat earned a certificate in electronics from a vocational school. After his most recent job as a sound engineer, he filed a workers' compensation claim alleging he had suffered stress due to on-the-job harassment.

During the course of his evaluation and treatment by a psychiatrist named Julius Griffin, Khuat exhibited threatening behavior and revealed that he regularly used cocaine, alcohol, and marijuana, which partly resulted in his losing his workers' comp claim.

Khuat's background and history were provided to me in exquisite detail by Dr. Griffin, who had called the LAPD to report Khuat's initial threats. I spoke directly with Dr. Griffin by phone, and in addition to receiving some great background information from him then, I asked for a copy of his report. Arrangements were made to get it to the scene.

This has always been an important role for the on-scene psychologist on a negotiation team, making such contact, when invaluable information can be obtained. I remember one guy who, distraught over a failed relationship, was threatening to jump off the CNN building at the start of the O.J. Simpson civil trial, on a hot day in January. He claimed to have a gun *and* he was threatening to jump. He refused to give his name, and given that we were face-to-face with an armed jumper, it was imperative to get some intelligence on whom we were dealing with. He gave up the name of his shrink. I called the doctor, and that resulted in our getting the suspect's identity, which facilitated a background check. There had been no prior violence to police officers, weapons registrations, or weapons history—not 100 percent reassuring but better than nothing. Turns out he didn't have a gun, and it would not have looked good to shoot an unarmed person threatening to jump off the top of one of the tallest buildings in Hollywood, let alone CNN's Hollywood headquarters. Ultimately, he was overpowered with less lethal beanbag rounds after several hours of negotiation that had led to an impasse, as he began his countdown to pull out his nonexistent weapon. He was then safely taken into custody.

When I arrived on the scene with Khuat, a violent guy who *really did* have a gun, dozens of officers held a necessarily wide perimeter that spanned from the tactical officers' inner sanctum with the greatest danger to a nearby street corner occupied by a patrol officer who had no idea what the fuck was really going on.

Thousands of citizens drove by, some miffed at the inconvenience and wishing ill will upon the source of it, while others were curious and gawked, asking questions met with empty shrugs and "Move on, please."

Khuat had financial difficulties and previous incidents of domestic violence exacerbated by his drug use. He had fallen out of favor with his family—namely, his wife, sister-in-law, and two young children. Soon Khuat had found himself living in his car.

His family situation hit rock bottom when, during a deathbed family vigil, Khuat made disrespectful comments about his brother-in-law, who was dying of AIDS. Finally, the family had had enough. Khuat had brought about shame and dishonor.

He suffered what we call the "emotional triple whammy," plagued by severe drug, family, and employment problems. In his own mind, it was all over and he was permanently checking out. Game over. And he was taking his family with him.

I contacted and interviewed relatives on the phone to obtain some further history as I worked to analyze just how to get inside his head, to possibly save his life and the life of his young hostage. They told me that, anxious to get back into the good graces of his family, he had impulsively driven from Southern California to Hazelden treatment center in Minnesota for substance abuse rehab—world-renowned, but even it cannot help the man who does not want help.

While receiving treatment, he decided after five days that rehab detention felt too much like the prison camp he had experienced back in Vietnam. He drove back to California, where his family labeled him a quitter and ostracized him. Still no longer welcome among his relatives, he desperately drove back to Minnesota only to be turned away from the facility. He returned, hopeless, desperate, and near the end of his rope.

Back in California, Khuat's life completely fell apart. He started smoking crack as murderous thoughts flooded his mind. Cocaine and other stimulants have a strong association with violent acting out, as well as suicide. He planned to perform what we call a "family annihilation." He would kill his wife, his sister-in-law (whom he blamed for his problems), his six-year-old son, and his three-year-old daughter. The ultimate end would be to take himself out. That was the plan, anyway. As his depression worsened, Khuat called Dr. Griffin, who had conducted his workers' compensation evaluation.

"I'm done," Khuat told him. "Today is a good day to die."

Khuat then informed Dr. Griffin of his lethal plan, although thankfully it didn't go so well.

Among those gathered on the streets around the area were a few of Khuat's friends and relatives, one of whom was Harold Blaisch, his lawyer in a minor car-crash case.

Khuat had made a call to a receptionist in Blaisch's office earlier that same day while he was already barricaded in the apartment.

"He said he had shot at a police car…and that if he went outside he was facing 15 years in jail," the receptionist said, according to the *Los Angeles Times*. "He said if he was going down, he wanted to take five people with him."

At the outset, high on crack, Khuat unleashed multiple shots inside the family's apartment, in L.A.'s Reseda neighborhood. His wife, son, and sister-in-law escaped unharmed, leaving behind three-year-old Janet.

Khuat then barricaded himself and Janet inside the second-floor residence, armed with a firearm and about as unstable as anyone could be, a ticking time bomb.

I reported to the makeshift command post located inside the apartment complex on Sherman Way. My first impression: a standard parking lot for a typical apartment complex in Anywhere, USA. Strip malls and sprawling apartment complexes lined the neighborhood's streets, which were densely populated with average good people making a go at it, and the incessant buzz of traffic hovered thick.

Command and negotiations were set up in Apartment 204, three doors down from 201, where Khuat and Janet were holed up. The thought occurred to me, *How far can a bullet travel through drywall here?* But I sucked it up. I guess we might be the bullet trap for the command staff.

Generally, when I show up to a standoff, I assess the situation. Is the person armed? Suicidal? Does he have a reason to live? Has he had episodes of previous violent behavior or suffered from mental illness? Is he open to dialogue?

While Khuat was inside Apartment 201 with his young daughter, he screamed through the window. He said he was armed with two pistols and hell-bent not only on killing himself but on taking "blood with me."

He was making it very clear that he had no intention of either of them coming out of this alive. My job was about to become extremely difficult.

I surmised that in his desperation, failed rehab attempts, and ostracization from his family, Khuat felt trapped and was unwilling to submit to arrest. The facts that he had found the rehab facility intolerable after only a couple days and that it reminded him of the prison camp in Vietnam were other important considerations. Jail was certainly not going to be acceptable to him either. I suspected surrender was not an option.

Our team was led by my good friend Sergeant Michael Albanese, the incident supervisor. Unfortunately, as mentioned previously, we had zero trained negotiators who spoke fluent Vietnamese, so Mike had enlisted two Vietnamese patrolmen—Long Nguyen and Doug Nguyen, not related—who, ironically, were scheduled for that upcoming negotiation training I mentioned. That's right, upcoming. So we had two untrained negotiators for an unfolding worst-case scenario.

Two Vietnamese speakers were necessary because we needed one to talk with Khuat and the second to interpret for us simultaneously. Time was not on our side.

One of the many misconceptions regarding SWAT teams in action is that they anxiously want to "go tactical" with guns blazing, bursting through a door and taking the suspect or suspects out. That's generally untrue; thoughtful cops rarely choose, except as a last resort, to put themselves or others in harm's way. That said, if they need to go tactical, they're more than capable of resorting to deadly force. Here my strategy, with the help of Long and Doug, was to talk to Khuat in his native language in order to form a bond between him and his Vietnamese countryman. To get him to feel like there was hope, and to try to lessen his homicidal resolve and intent into more of a sense of calm and thoughts that he had other, nonviolent options.

I had an indirect but personal stake in all this madness. I was in the second year of a relationship with a Vietnamese woman who was my wife-to-be and the future mother of my son.

I'd been around her family a lot, a seasoned clan of immigrants who also had weathered the same horrible conditions of fleeing a war-torn country. Being around her family, I was exposed to how they talked and the dynamic inside a Vietnamese-speaking household where the parents spoke only their native tongue and the kids were expected to learn and speak English, so they could help interpret. This assignment was hitting pretty close to home.

So there I was with these two young Vietnamese patrol officers, both admirable guys with eyes as big as saucers as they were being thrown into the deep end of an intense life-and-death crisis negotiation situation. We proceeded with our operation as Sergeant Albanese, undaunted, pulled up a chair and spoke sternly to the officers. He didn't pull any punches.

"Okay, here's the deal, guys. You're going to call this guy up, talk to him, and you're going to do exactly what we say. And don't fuck this up!" They didn't realize it, but this was Sergeant Albanese's way of being light-hearted and humorous.

I wasn't nearly as optimistic.

After listening to Khuat's initial ranting and raving and reckless gun-shots, I felt we would be damn lucky to extract young Janet out of this situation alive. So much for the optimism of the drive. But I pulled the pessimism out of my bones and moved past it while making a mental note of these feelings I'd been taught to attend to.

Hopelessness was what I was sensing, and it was not mine nor was it going to become mine, no matter what. After I had spoken with Dr. Griffin, we had begun the process of "trapping" Khuat's phone, which meant shutting down his service in Apartment 201 and issuing only a direct line to the command post so that Khuat couldn't make calls to anyone else. The only people he could talk to were us. We owned the phone.

Back in those days, you could do that. These days you try, but it's a real challenge with all the devices and social media access points. Control is compromised if pilgrims to the operation offer their input, or someone who was part of the original problem exacerbates it by intruding into the mix.

The media soon began to arrive on scene, clambering for position with their cameras to capture the unfolding drama.

"You guys really need to move yourselves down the road," we advised them. They pushed back, complaining that cops were always trying to keep them from getting the story.

"Okay, suit yourself," we said.

Then, as if on cue, Khuat stormed out of the apartment and shot a couple of rounds toward the gathering reporters. From that point on, we had complete compliance from the media and could focus on the task at hand. More than one officer, in the serious mood of the moment, had a chuckle at their expense.

Meanwhile, we prepared for war and attempted diplomacy. The tactical SWAT team had stationed a sniper on the roof of the opposite building complex, camouflaged under a "hide," which in this case was a tarp used to conceal the sniper's position and presence. An Emergency Entry Assault Team was set up on either side of Apartment 204.

We immediately had one major logistical problem. On the opposite rooftop, a tree was blocking the sniper's view of Khuat's front door. That meant sending somebody to fix a rope to the tree. Luckily, the tree was flexible enough to pull down, giving our sniper a clear line of sight. It took a while, but talking to Khuat, keeping him busy, provided just that opportunity.

Negotiation involves a lot of things. In the best of all possible worlds, we get everyone out alive. But the key goal is to lessen the risk to innocent bystanders and victims. The bad guy…well, he might not be so lucky.

Now it was time to begin bargaining for little Janet's life.

Once we had set up phone communication, Khuat's dialogue with Officer Long Nguyen was not encouraging. Khuat vehemently regretted not killing the family members who had escaped. Plus, he was adamant about shooting Janet and himself. Then he hung up the phone. We switched to a bullhorn as he unexpectedly emerged from inside the apartment and began making weird jungle-like noises.

A number of the officers stationed on the perimeter were Vietnam vets, and Khuat's outrageous banter took many of them back to their combat days in the jungle.

"Come and get me, you guys!" he shouted, a wiry guy filled with drug-induced defiance.

"Five hundred of you guys! Come and take me on, you fuckin' guys! Let's see what you've got," Khuat taunted. "Bring me all your fuckin' FBI, CIA! Fuckin' c'mon, man! Let's go!

"I got da baby! I got da baby! I'll fuckin' kill her! You guys wanna come shoot me? Go right ahead!"

Khuat's bravado, mixed with his guttural, often incoherent ramblings, set the hair on the back of my neck up on end. He clearly had a death wish, and throughout the entire incident, he never once referred to his child by her name.

He was grandiose, thinking he could take on five hundred officers and that the department would even consider sending that many resources to deal with him. And the FBI and CIA? Well, they had no interest in this case. But that is a cultural piece of this equation. Back in Vietnam, "officer" is more of a generic term used to describe all sorts of law enforcement, usually lower-ranking.

As events unfurled, I realized that perhaps Khuat was not going to negotiate. Worse, he did not relate to his daughter in a personal, human way but instead objectified her as "the baby." *It's only a matter of time*, I thought, *before he kills his daughter and himself, or forces the police to shoot him—so-called suicide by cop.*

Officer Long Nguyen called him again as Khuat reiterated his threats to kill and shoot it out with police. He told Long he wasn't going to jail and laughed inappropriately, a clear sign of instability and one that gave me pause.

But soon Khuat began to refer to Long as his "brother in law enforcement."

That could only be good. But was it good enough? Could we avoid bloodshed?

Long spoke in Vietnamese while Khuat responded in English. Now Khuat seemed to be bonding with the officer.

While Long spoke, I passed him notes. "Keep talking to him like that, Vietnamese—he is responding. Lower and slower. Call him your brother too. Tell him, 'You and I both know we don't want that.... Let's figure this out together. No big deal, brother.'"

We were careful not to say anything of a threatening nature or divulge details that might tip him off that he could be taken down by our sniper at any moment. *Maybe there is hope*, I began to think.

A few hours passed, and all we wanted was a peaceful resolution. But if he was not willing to talk resolution and resolve things without violence, and remained fixated on murder and suicide, then we needed to stall and buy time.

Still, I was dead calm. My emotions could not take over. I was thinking clearly and stayed focused on the task. The key to succeeding as a police and forensic psychologist is being able to remain immersed in the present, setting aside all other distractions with just one goal to achieve.

Remaining cool and composed and professionally diligent are among the top tools of the trade. It's a mindset, a sort of meditation-like state one must take on, unflappable and focused. I've always been good at it.

We especially wanted his daughter to be safe and comfortable. But Khuat remained threatening and menacing.

"This is going to end. I'm gonna take blood with me and your best guys," he shouted.

At the moment, the time factor was working out okay for me and the team. We were working to build a relationship with the suspect. But it would soon have a negative effect on Khuat. He was fired up and grandiose, consistent with the cocaine and crack that he'd been freebasing. But we also were fighting against that very chemical battle inside Khuat's body. Stimulants have the strongest association with violence.

My experience in negotiating with drug users is that they're unpredictable and dangerous, traits that become worse as they begin coming down. That's the hazardous timetable we are on. While Khuat was in the midst of experiencing his jittery drug-enhanced violent impulses, we knew the downside would soon come when he began to crash without being able to keep his high going with more cocaine.

Soon, he was bound to feel more depressed, more despondent, more hopeless. But Khuat, as we found out, was a smoker, which was a mixed blessing in that he now wanted cigarettes. That would buy us more time. Maybe it would even take the edge off. Or it might create an opportunity. Other than cigarettes, Khuat didn't want anything. Not food. Not alcohol. Nothing. He only wanted to die and take his daughter with him.

Another common misconception in crisis negotiation is that when a suspect makes a demand in a hostage incident, you immediately grant it. That's untrue. Gratification only sets up more grandiose behavior. In addition, it starts a complicated process of delivering those items safely, something that is extremely dangerous when the suspect has guns.

We arranged to get Khuat some cigarettes delivered outside his door. He wanted an entire pack. We settled on three cigarettes. Sure, we could have given him a whole pack, but we wanted him to keep coming back asking for another smoke. Without realizing it himself, he would become more and more dependent on us to satisfy his needs and wants, while we were buying time. And we had eyes on him from all directions, watching closely how he retrieved those cigarettes. If he had to be taken out, that might be the best ploy to distract him and separate him from his daughter.

The cigarettes were delivered, and our sniper was ready for Khuat to emerge from the room. So what did Khuat do? He came out with Janet held in front of his face as a human shield. *Who does that with their own flesh and blood?* I asked myself. *Informative. He's not particularly attached to her. He's already dehumanized her. Fuck.* As he leaned down, gun in his hand, he picked up the cigarettes. Had he come out without Janet, it would have been game over. The police would have swooped in for an arrest from their assigned posts, with the sniper ready to use deadly force if he resisted. But that's not what happened.

Back on the phone with Long, Khuat knew he was going to jail— rather, he knew he was *not* going to jail, because any confinement was intolerable to him. I told Long to tell him that maybe we could get him into a facility that offered treatment. Given the history, this was probably not a good option, but we had to try it. Khuat kept going back to his desire to commit suicide. We continued talking as things started going around in circles. I sensed that we had reached an impasse. It was becoming increasingly clear that this conflict might not be resolved through negotiation. Khuat's death wish was hardcore.

Even when Khuat stopped talking, he would leave the phone line open, just setting it down on speaker, so we could still hear him monologuing to his daughter, explaining how he was going to kill both of them. It was a very unsettling dialogue. Who talks that way to his own flesh and blood?

Although the officers at the command post were still optimistic that we could wear him down, Sergeant Albanese and I felt otherwise.

"You have to give us the green light to go tactical," Albanese told me.

Then command called me into the room.

"All right, Doc. What's the deal here? What's going on?"

They wanted my opinion as to whether Khuat was "negotiable" or not. This was a first-time experience for me. Before this case, I had responded to the killing of police in the line of duty, to other, more negotiable hostage and barricade incidents, and had spent time counseling distraught and suicidal officers.

There had been another case in which an offender, barricaded alone in a motel room after killing his wife, had forced a confrontation with the SWAT team, resulting in a shootout and his violent death in a haze of tear gas. However, this was the first hostage incident with actual negotiations I was involved in and in which I was beginning to sense that the situation could be resolved only through deadly-force tactics—a sniper-initiated assault to end Khuat's life.

Is it ethical to use psychology to end a life? Is it ethical *not* to use it when an innocent child's life hangs in the balance? I know there are certain desk-jockey psychologists who might judge me for using my expertise in a manner that leads to death. I say, go back to your Monday-morning quarterbacking and making excuses for all kinds of violent offenders. We had an innocent child to save.

Nothing in college or grad school had prepared me for this moment. My LAPD hostage negotiation training helped, but mostly it was the times I'd gone out with Dr. Reiser and having a strong moral compass that prepared me to offer this on-the-spot opinion that would lead to the ultimate decision. Always call it as you see it. That has been my mantra during my entire career, and I don't give a fuck who is paying me. You hire me, and I'm going to tell you what I think. No matter the outcome.

This was not an issue of personal introspection: *What am I becoming? What is happening to me? Will my career survive this test?* None of the above. I was locked in the present and hoping that we would get out of this mess without little Janet's murder.

Sergeant Albanese envisioned a couple of scenarios. One was two dead bodies—Khuat's and the three-year-old girl's. The other, if we succeeded, meant getting the girl back unscathed, with Khuat being the only death. One dead or two?

The commanding officers were hesitant. This was not long after the Rodney King riots rocked Los Angeles. I stepped up to say my piece with certainty. That was my job.

"Gentlemen, Tan Khuat is not negotiable. We've tried everything. He's high. He's coming down. He's getting more depressed. He's menacing. He's got a strong homicidal-suicidal plan. He's got guns and ammo and a history that precludes him from being talked to."

I took a deep breath and laid out my conclusion.

"In my opinion, Khuat will surely kill his daughter, and he will facilitate killing himself, which could also include police officers. This will not end peacefully."

The main impetus behind my decision was that we were seeing no change in his resolve to carry out his murderous plan.

The commanding officers huddled while Long, Doug, and I continued to fight the good fight on the phone with Khuat. Even though the authorization to use deadly force had been given, to exercise the fatal green light, we had to keep talking in case there was still the slight chance of an eleventh-hour save. We always hoped for that. We also didn't want to tip Khuat off as to what was about to come, so we continued talking through his demands.

"More cigarettes. I want a pack this time."

Khuat also wanted a face-to-face meeting with Officer Long Nguyen, his Vietnamese "brother" and new friend. I immediately put the kibosh on any such contact. That stuff, when a negotiator foolishly walks out unarmed into a deadly situation, happens only in the movies. It is considered a definite don't in this business. In the real world, officers get killed doing that.

"I want last meal. The baby gonna take a nap. I'm gonna eat and then we gonna do this thing."

Khuat's mental state was rapidly deteriorating.

But talk of food was a good sign. With that, we could buy ourselves more time.

"But I want Burger King, not McDonald's. *No McDonald's!*"

We generally spend a lot of time on food orders, going through the details. It's a great stalling technique. You can grind out a food order for twenty minutes or more.

"Do you want fries with that? Cheese? Onions? How do you want that cooked? We also have to find a Burger King."

Khuat was emphatic. No McDonald's. And he wanted Pepsi, not Coke. Negotiating the food process ate up almost another hour. Everything had to go through the command post for approval, and while the logistics may sound simple, they're not. We still had to deliver the food in a way that no one would get shot.

Khuat's Burger King order was relayed to a nearby patrol officer standing on a street corner—that same one who'd had no idea what the fuck was going on and how important he had become. The officer was specifically instructed to go to a Burger King. However, there on the corner stood a McDonald's.

Fuck SWAT. I'll just go to McDonald's, the officer thought. *A burger's a burger.*

Perhaps the officer did not fully understand who the food was for, and I suspect he thought going to McDonald's was much more convenient.

Meanwhile, Khuat was getting impatient.

"Where's my goddamn food? I'm getting hungry. Where's my Pepsi? Where's my last meal?"

The food finally arrived, only it was McDonald's! My heart sank. We couldn't even get the fucking food order right! What was Officer Nguyen, the negotiator who had now created a relationship with Khuat, going to do? Blame it on the chaos and confusion—"Those friggin' white folks, they screw everything up"?

I told Long to own up.

"I'm so sorry," he told Khuat. "They messed up and got McDonald's. I know you're hungry. We can still try and get you Burger King."

"No. Fuck it. I just eat this."

"Have it your way," I responded sardonically under my breath, recalling Burger King's advertising slogan. I was keeping calm by any means possible.

Next, a clever and safe food-delivery method had to be determined. Room service was not coming around anytime soon, so the tactical guys decided to put the food on a desk chair with wheels and pull a rope so that the meal would arrive in front of Khuat's door.

"Why can't you just walk it to the door?"

We assured Khuat that nobody was coming near him. We didn't want to risk confrontation. We just wanted to get him his food. Khuat was quite amused at the moving-chair trick that delivered his food. On the open phone line, he assured us that Janet was alive and sleeping.

"I won't wake her up right now," he said. "I'll wait until she gets up and then we do this thing. Nobody better shoot me."

At the eight-hour mark, this was the moment of truth. Khuat's time was up. He was to come out and grab the food as we watched and listened in deafening silence.

Then came the big moment. There was movement. The door opened. As Khuat walked out, we waited for the sniper shot. It was the longest four seconds of my life.

We were supposed to hear the pop of a gun, and then an officer's voice proclaim, "Code four, suspect in custody, victim rescued."

Instead, there was a single rifle shot as Khuat scurried back inside the apartment. Khuat had come out holding his gun, and as he bent down for the food, the sniper's bullet, instead of landing right between his eyes, pierced his ear. What had sounded like a second gunshot was the door slamming behind Khuat as he retreated into the apartment.

The wound put him in shock and made him even angrier. "You see that? They fucking shot me!"

The next sounds we expected to hear were more rounds going off inside the apartment as an angry Khuat shot his daughter and then himself. My heart was pounding in my chest, and I could hear the blood pumping in my ears.

Thump. Thump. Thump.

However, plan B came into play, in a moment that seemed like an eternity. Mike Albanese often said during our presentations, "We are the last phone call. We have the wherewithal to stop behavior. Our mission is to save lives, and we have absolute reverence for human life." No truer statement has ever been made, and the LAPD SWAT team, the first of its kind in domestic law enforcement, is *the* best. The Emergency Entry Assault Team—heroes who regularly put themselves in harm's way to protect the innocent and keep us all safe, and who here were poised on the left and ready on the right—stormed the apartment. Khuat made a hasty retreat to the bathroom. Over the phone, we heard the sound of glass shattering as the team kicked in the bathroom door. Khuat lay in the bathtub with Janet on his chest as a shield. Two officers were set up on either side of the bathroom door. With a .357 Magnum pistol to his daughter's head, Khuat shouted as he rose out of the bathtub.

"I kill baby, I kill baby, I kill baby!"

"Don't you fucking kill her!" an officer yelled back.

Not the most graceful dialogue, but enough to draw Khuat's non-verbal behavior, automatically and subconsciously, to the source of the words. Khuat moved his head slightly just as the officer fired one precise round from his shoulder weapon into his left eye socket. He dropped the baby just as a second cop ran in. Janet didn't even hit the ground. He caught her like a hot potato, then zipped her out of the room. She was tossed from officer to officer with nary a scratch on her.

In an instant, Khuat was dead.

His relatives were downstairs. They thanked us profusely for saving Janet and weren't the least bit upset that Khuat had been killed. In fact, they were glad to be rid of him, happy he was dead. Me? I was relieved that Janet was alive and well. The real heroes: that sniper on the roof and those SWAT cops who had breached the apartment door, entered an uncertain hell, and extracted an innocent life from the grip of otherwise certain death.

When food arrived later, we were all starving. It had been hours since any of us had eaten. I didn't feel so good after eating my burger. October 20, 1992, would be the last day I ate red meat. It felt strange participating in the taking of a human life, especially when the life belonged to a man who reminded me of my own extended family. This was the first incident in which my expertise was used in the taking of a human life. It would not be the last.

Looking back on 1992, I see there was so much death and violence around us. The L.A. riots, police suicides, dead suspects, line-of-duty deaths, and now this. I was just twenty-nine and immersed in more carnage and chaos than most psychologists see in an entire career.

But I also had a moment of clarity. I had gone—and would go—where I was needed without hesitation. Khuat's death proved the intensity of my commitment to my work and brought home the fact that these events were very real and that my words, my opinions, had consequences.

The cost of failure in this case had been death. But the cost of this child's life also had been death. It was a reality I would learn to come to grips with; I would come to understand that losing a life is sometimes worth saving a life. Today I know the price paid on that day was worth it. I wonder about Janet today as I watch my own son grow older. What is she like? What was she told? Is she okay, and is she living a full and purposeful life? I don't think at all about Tan Khuat except as the obstacle to her future. I hope Janet is well and leading a prosperous life, filled with love, dreams, and hope.

The valuable lesson I learned that day was that not all incidents are negotiable, and sometimes the acceptable outcome is the lesser of two evils. It's up to me to call it as I see it.

I told myself to embrace it, to own it, and that I was one of the few who could do this. But it is a burden I carry, a burden that comes with the job.

In hindsight, there is only one thing that should have been done differently: use two snipers in case one missed.

The Hunters

Serial Killers Among Us

"And I looked, and behold a pale horse; and his name that sat on him was Death, and Hell followed with him."

—Revelation 6:8

As I mentioned previously, I was an avid reader of the Hardy Boys mystery books as a child. I wanted to solve the unsolvable cases.

It's one of the things that got me into my current profession, though instead of going into law enforcement, I was drawn much more toward understanding the minds of villains than chasing them down and arresting them.

I wanted to become more of a detective of the brain, digging deep into their psyches to understand what makes them tick.

At about the age of ten, I read *The Hooded Hawk Mystery* in the Hardy Boys series, a story of how the young sleuths receive a trained peregrine falcon as a gift that swiftly brings down a pigeon carrying two precious stones. The retrieval of the gems leads them into a kidnapping-for-ransom case that enthralled my adolescent mind.

I worked in the pet business as a kid and always gravitated to the more extreme, predatory creatures. I kept razor-toothed, carnivorous piranhas and electric eels as a teenager. I was drawn to sharks and lions and birds of prey, fascinated by their killer instincts.

As an adult, I have taken to falconry as a hobby. Odd as it may seem to some, given that I spend my days helping catch and comprehend human predators, I'm fascinated by the falcon's predatory purpose. It is not to maim or mutilate for the enjoyment of killing; rather, the falcon hunts to eat, to live, to exist. It does not waste or kill for the thrill.

It represents raw, natural, acceptable killing power in the cycle of life, a will to survive against all odds.

It is a reminder of the purpose of nature when it comes to killing versus the perversion of it in our species.

There *is* a place in the natural order of things for killing. To harness and observe with my bird some of that raw power up close on a daily basis is pretty cool. It's a little dangerous too, as the scar one half millimeter above my left eye reminds me every time I look in a mirror. An error on my part, and Zeus' talon nearly blinded me. It wasn't personal; he simply wanted to land.

In the falcon, one of the smartest and most effective killing machines in the animal kingdom, there is a natural purpose that is juxtaposed with the wickedness among some of those in our own species. I find this contrast comforting.

Efren Saldivar is no goddamn falcon. By comparison, he's a sheep—but he is no less lethal than the sharp-taloned creature that lands on my arm by command.

It was 2002, shortly after Saldivar pleaded guilty to six murder counts. The deal with prosecutors would spare him the death penalty.

He'd be locked up behind bars for the remainder of his existence, six consecutive life sentences.

It had been a long, arduous, and painstaking path to get there, to get this monster off the streets, out of the hospital where he had preyed on society's most vulnerable victims—the sick and elderly, in a place where people went to be helped, not killed. Pretty outrageous, really, a predator lurking and hunting among the flock of compassionate angels that day in and day out ease human suffering.

But now I would get to study him in greater detail. Look him in the eyes. Try to learn something that could help prevent this from happening again. He had nothing to lose at this point after giving up his right to an appeal.

And my job, after all, in part is to save lives by gaining a better understanding of those who take them.

Saldivar had spent nine years meandering the halls of a suburban Los Angeles hospital while working as a respiratory therapist. It was a time period during which he would cement his reputation as being among the most prolific serial killers in history.

As if that were something to be proud of. But a lot of them are. Narcissism is a common personality feature among serial killers.

Dubbed an "angel of death" with a so-called "magic syringe," he often clocked the graveyard shift, finding himself alone and largely unsupervised in the sprawling Glendale Adventist Medical Center, a faith-based health-care facility about ten miles north of downtown L.A. just off the Ventura Freeway.

Not the best place for a guy with a need to prove himself and a willingness to do so by playing God.

"Lights off and quiet." That's how Saldivar described his work hours, in a virtual living boneyard of unsuspecting victims.

At times, he claimed he killed out of mercy, relieving the suffering of the old and ailing.

But he was no fucking angel, and he certainly showed no mercy. His victims died in an agonizingly painful way, stuck in their bodies unable to move, their cognitive functions fully intact but their bodies paralyzed by the drug he injected them with while their lungs stopped sucking in air.

They were powerless to do anything but slip into oblivion. It was like drowning in their own beds, eventually leading to cardiac arrest and lights out. Death did not come calmly.

This person is a monster, but one hidden behind the mask of a soft-spoken, seemingly well-mannered average young man, someone you wouldn't even notice on the street and, for a while at least, someone who didn't hover over a hospital bed with a syringe in his hand.

I spoke softly and calmly with him ("low and slow"), sitting in a stiff, hard-backed chair in a tiny box of a secure prison room not long after he was sentenced.

"Let's get started. How did you end up here?"

"Misjudgment," Saldivar told me, chuckling nervously as he sat slumped in his chair wearing an orange prison shirt with a low-hanging crew collar, a faded white T-shirt underneath squeezed tightly around his neck.

He stared blankly at times, looking up and down and around the room as if perplexed by some of my questions, trying to find the right words to answer in a way that would satisfy both him and me. His matter-of-fact tone was noteworthy.

"That's the thing; I can't remember the thought process that I went through.... Something inside me wanted to release a lot, not a lot, but a few of these people—well, through the years it becomes a lot, but a little at a time—of their terminal status."

He still maintained the persona of someone who actually thought he was doing God's work, good deeds for the dying, an almost Jack Kevorkian-like person who euthanized his victims out of a sense of humanity. Kevorkian, in fact, was something of a hero to him. Some of these guys often try to rationalize their behavior, and Saldivar did that and then some.

"To me it was something that didn't seem wrong."

His wire-rimmed glasses sat perfectly on the bridge of his nose; his black hair was neatly slicked back. To the average person, Saldivar wouldn't look like a killer. And that's partly what made him so deadly for so long.

He then coolly began to recount the first time he took a life. It was 1989. He was nineteen years old and new to the hospital.

It was near midnight. The facility was practically empty. The family of a cancer patient on his floor was in their loved one's room saying their final goodbyes.

Saldivar recalled that the doctor soon arrived and removed the patient from life support, signed off on the death certificate, and then left the room. But the man continued to breathe, his chest heaving up and down.

"I go, 'Oh, this is strange,'" he told me, again with a freakishly nervous smile on his face.

"And the nurse was like, 'Do something, stop that, stop that.' And since I was new, I said, 'Well, this is the real world. Is this what's expected of me?' I don't want any trouble. I already liked the place. So I did what I had to at the moment."

He was speaking not apologetically but as if he were some sort of savior who had to do something for the sake of the family and a nurse in need. A dark knight in shining armor.

"I thought about the family, after they said their goodbyes. He's still breathing!"

Saldivar's eyes widened creepily, excited at the thought of what he had done, recounting it in detail as if it had just happened, but this event had taken place nearly fifteen years earlier.

"How's that going to affect them? How's that going to look on the doctor who signed the death certificate without actually doing what he was supposed to, and personally checking that there's no heartbeat?" he recalled thinking.

"And so I thought of that. And the way the nurse told me, it was like…no big thing. And so I assumed that this is the real world. It's not classroom anymore, so I better get with the ball."

He said he used some tubing in the room to finish the man off, attaching it to the patient in a way that would recirculate carbon dioxide, then stood there and watched him suffocate. *What kind of person does that?* I wondered, then associated it silently with the same kind of kid who pulls the wings off a fly or uses a magnifying glass on an anthill—repeatedly, with zeal.

"I'd say it definitely changed me."

"How did that change you?"

"I don't know. But I felt something."

An epiphany, an awakening, a switch turned on, I thought, knowing this first act would only feed his desire to kill more.

He took a long pause to think about his next words carefully, then laughed softly.

"Like a loss of innocence of some sort."

I've seen this kind of epiphany in other cases. A moment when the killer, who had previously only dreamed of carrying out such acts—the acts contained in a safe little compartment in his mind—realizes these are no longer just intangible thoughts. The genie is out of the bottle, and there is no way to put it back in. This kind of switch goes only one way—on. In my experience with this kind of offender, there is no off switch until the killer is captured or dead.

Saldivar went on to explain how his killing method evolved over the years; he settled on a drug called Pavulon, which he would scoop up around the hospital and tuck away for when he needed it.

Pavulon, or pancuronium bromide, is an extremely potent muscle relaxant once used as one of three drugs to carry out lethal injection of condemned prisoners: sodium thiopental to induce unconsciousness, Pavulon to cause muscle paralysis and respiratory arrest, and potassium chloride to stop the heart. As part of a cocktail, Pavulon is not cruel or unusual; it causes a peaceful slipping away. But on its own, it leads to suffocation with full cognitive awareness—a quiet but torturous death, the storm of death panic contained by the person's immobility. One of the worst ways to die.

"What was your understanding of how the Pavulon would cause the death?" I asked him.

"It would put them into respiratory arrest immediately. And from there, cardiac arrest was imminent."

Saldivar said that by 1994, he had "released" more than sixty patients in this manner and "lost count" after that. He kept killing for at least three more years.

We believe the actual number is likely in the hundreds. Some serial killers meticulously track their numbers, their "conquests," while others, like Saldivar, approximate. In their own way, both types show their callous disregard for humanity. One keeps score as if he is a video game player racking up points or a hunter collecting trophies, while the other thinks so little of the individuals that he doesn't keep track at all.

In March 1998, after authorities received tips about a man with a "magic syringe" at the hospital, Saldivar came in for questioning.

Polygraph examiner Ervin Youngblood and Glendale police detective Will Currie didn't have to do much to get him talking—and confessing.

It was during that first interrogation that Saldivar mentioned using the drug Pavulon, something that would eventually lead to his undoing.

But he also spoke of many more deaths he contributed to by purposefully not providing adequate treatment, such as not performing CPR when a patient was dying.

"Could that be more than one hundred patients?" Youngblood asked during that first face-to-face.

"I believe so," Saldivar said. "Anywhere from one hundred to two hundred."

"Okay. Definitely under five hundred?" Youngblood prodded.

"Oh, yeah. Definitely," Saldivar replied.

While authorities had no evidence that any coworkers had assisted Saldivar in the killings, he told them that some had indeed been aware of what he was doing and even encouraged him to continue. This perception of an imagined audience of fans is likely just that, imaginary and self-serving to provide him with even more of a sense of purpose—and rationalization for his homicidal compulsion.

"We didn't pick anybody healthy...who had a future," Saldivar told Youngblood.

"It became a joke, and that was my way of handling the guilt."

By the time the hours-long interrogation with authorities ended, Saldivar had gone into so much detail, he figured he'd already said plenty.

"I think that's enough to lock me away."

Unfortunately, he was released soon after for lack of evidence, then recanted the entire confession. There was yet to be a body confirming his claims, what is referred to as "no corpus" or "corpus delicti"—a lack of facts and circumstances constituting a prosecutable breach of the law.

Afterward, Saldivar told the media in televised interviews that the investigators had duped him into believing they already had all the evidence needed to convict him. It was a ridiculous lie, as any review of his confession made perfectly clear.

He also claimed he fabricated the whole tale because he had been feeling suicidal but hadn't had the guts to take his own life. He'd wanted to go to prison. He'd wanted the death penalty. But he'd changed his mind once reality had begun to set in.

And so he took it all back. Here in California, despite there being nearly 750 inmates on death row, Saldivar's claim that he fabricated this story to commit suicide by a false admission was particularly weak, given that inmates here stand a greater chance of dying of natural causes, due to appeal after appeal and obstructions to implementing the death penalty from the anti-capital-punishment lobby.

As we sat talking about the murders a year after his conviction, I recalled a book he mentioned that he had read as a teenager: *On a Pale Horse*, by Piers Anthony, a fantastical tale about a man who accidentally kills Death and therefore must take on his duties.

"You are the new Death," Fate tells the man in the book. "This is the way it is done. He who kills Death becomes Death."[4]

Saldivar immediately became excited by that thought in the book.

"So it's a story about this guy taking this job he has no choice to take, and how he goes about collecting souls of people that are dying," Saldivar explained, noting he had read the book when he was sixteen years old. He was now thirty-two.

His memory of the story was crisp, as if it were a sermon that played over and over in his mind throughout the years, a guidebook that would carry him along his poisonous path, an identity he imagined himself to be fulfilling, providing a purpose for his crimes.

He went on to recount more of the story in perfect detail, smiling and laughing demonically under his breath.

---

[4] Piers Anthony, *On a Pale Horse: Book One of Incarnations of Immortality*, (New York: Random House, 1983).

The devil eventually comes to visit the man, Saldivar recalled, but the man pushes him away.

"His hand goes in, actually pulls out the devil's soul. And he realizes the devil doesn't have power over him. He's just as powerful over the devil…and so that puts the devil in check."

In fact, it was Saldivar who believed he was putting the devil in check.

While he said the book didn't necessarily influence his own taking of lives—"subconsciously, maybe"—I knew it was among the key drivers that had drawn him to think he was a merciful taker of souls, a story that had a huge impact on him and his need for power, for omnipotent control over life and death.

Whom we look up to as our heroes, fictional or otherwise, says a lot about who we are, who we want to become, and what we might be willing to do. He *identified* with the theme of this book, the persona of this character, and it would eventually become his perceived burden to carry, not of misfortune but of responsibility.

It was a role he could adopt when he was feeling impotent, lost, depressed, or powerless. And eventually opportunity collided with this well-worn mental trail. Now he was Death unhinged.

The killings would become his antidote for his sense of inadequacy, providing meaning to his otherwise meaningless life.

I was involved in the investigation from beginning to end, with the privilege of working with the Glendale Police Department and other law enforcement agencies to help crack the case.

It would prove to be a much lengthier, more intense commitment than I imagined as I walked in for the first briefing at the 1940s three-story blue house that authorities had been given to set up the task force headquarters, just across the street from the hospital.

My understanding was that the house had been provided through the kindness and commitment of the hospital administration to support the mission of laying this horrifying nightmare to rest.

I walked into the main meeting area, a living room with spartan yet comfortable seating, a simple table, and a whiteboard with scores of names in dry-erase black marker scribbled across it, a partial list of the dead from just one year. It was a daunting sight.

I really had no clue at the time as to the length of this tortuous journey that we hoped would eventually put Saldivar away for life or send him to the death chamber.

I remember getting the call that a search warrant was going to be executed at Saldivar's parents' house, where he lived.

It was a modest home with minimal furnishings in a typical working-class neighborhood. His room was small, with access to a very basic bathroom. I was struck by the simplicity and austere nature of the entire household. It was dark and depressing, and seemed even more so with the knowledge that this was the home of a killer we had to catch.

Religious books and materials consistent with his parents' Jehovah's Witnesses faith punctuated the place.

The conflict inherent between their faith and Saldivar's serial homicides, and what we would discover under his bed—a massive pornography collection (some one hundred videos)—stood out to me.

It was such a religious place, yet such indoctrination had not inhibited his sexual or killer impulses. Could they actually have contributed to them in some way? I was profiling this man with every step I took and every piece of evidence collected.

As a police psychologist, I was looking for anything that could shed light on his motivations. The religious aspect of this household and Saldivar's stated belief in a moral code that justified his killer conduct—was there a connection?

Was it the source of his twisted moral compass, the need to believe in something and to have purpose, but the inability to embrace the values his family had attempted to set for him?

Was it the rejection of some medical interventions within the faith that had gotten all twisted up in his mind? The answers might never present themselves, but it is in the questioning that sometimes a pathway becomes clearer. Why?

What *wasn't* discovered in his home was the very thing we'd hoped to find: Pavulon, or any other such drugs that could have been used to kill.

Authorities did find something oddly striking, though: a printout of a lung test. Written on it where the patient's name normally would be were the words "Saldivar, Efren Hey You."

The doctor listed? "Kevorkian, Jack."

But it still wasn't enough even to keep him in custody.

Nailing Saldivar partially came down to numbers: an inconceivably high body count—more than one thousand, a figure that matched roughly how many patients had died during Saldivar's tenure there dating back to 1989.

That was eventually whittled down to 171, after cutting out many of the deaths from years earlier and trying to gain a tighter focus on the fresher cases that could yield more damning clues.

The next number was 117, the bodies that hadn't been cremated. We'd have no luck proving murder with just ashen remains. Body tissues had to be tested for the presence of traces of the chemical byproducts, and even that was sketchy. Prior to this case, Pavulon and another substance he sometimes used, succinylcholine, were viewed as very difficult to detect. On top of that, investigators had to make sure the person had never been treated with either of those drugs.

By March 1999, about a year after Saldivar had initially confessed—and soon after recanted—we'd narrowed our number down to twenty.

A month later, cops obtained another warrant to dig up the bodies.

Twenty bodies to exhume. Twenty bodies to examine. Twenty bodies that would either make or break the case.

It was a grueling, methodical, and scientific search for just the right remains, just the right time frame, just the right evidence needed to arrest and convict.

We knew Saldivar had likely killed hundreds of patients, but we had to home in on the ones that would corroborate our theory beyond a shadow of a doubt.

Throughout the painstaking investigative process, as we worked to chip away at the numbers, I hit the road to interview other notorious "angels of death." We needed to learn more about their motivations, their modi operandi, how they chose their victims and why. It would eventually help us get to the twenty.

Members of the task force had already reached out to other jurisdictions that had dealt with these types of serial killer cases. It became clear that we had to narrow down the pool of so many hospital deaths during Saldivar's work there. To do that, I needed to understand his motivations. Did he really have a code he applied to his choices of whom he'd decide to kill? I had to learn more.

So I suggested that I research other cases with an emphasis on behavioral dynamics, motivation, and lessons we could learn. We had to test our theories of the crime in order to eventually convince a jury of Saldivar's guilt.

We were basically looking for needles, or "magic needles," in a haystack. I figured the best way to get at some of these answers was to go to the sources—other murderers who claimed they killed for the same reasons as Saldivar.

I headed off to a state prison in Lebanon, Ohio, to meet with Donald Harvey. Harvey was serving multiple life sentences after pleading guilty in 1987 to killing thirty-seven people, mostly while working as a nurse's aide at hospitals in Cincinnati and Kentucky.

He also had been dubbed an "angel of death" and later told us he had actually killed eighty-six chronically ill patients starting as far back as 1970 as a way to end their suffering.

Unlike Saldivar, who specifically chose a drug that he hoped would mimic what could be seen as the natural death of an already dying patient, Harvey used arsenic and cyanide, even rat poison, sometimes slipping it into the food he fed them. He also suffocated some patients by simply removing their oxygen or putting a pillow over their face.

Harvey was eventually caught after an astute medical examiner got a whiff of cyanide while performing an autopsy on one of the deceased patients. He would later acknowledge that the thrill of the kill came from his deep desire to decide who lived and who died.

A charming, glib character, he had a noteworthy psychopathy and lack of remorse when I visited with him in Ohio.

He was excited to tell his story, and shared it with a sense of flamboyance and bravado.

Harvey had been a big fan of Agatha Christie's detective novels since he was a child, many of which featured murderers who used poison to carry out their kills, something that struck me as eerily similar to Saldivar's obsession with *On a Pale Horse*.

Also, much like Saldivar, Harvey had initially confessed and then recanted, and his first homicide was by suffocation.

Two guys who had confessed and recanted? That was also an interesting correlation. Suffocation is a simple method but hands-on. These two guys were not tough, strong men who could overpower a struggling victim fighting back but instead preyed on the weak.

Any defensive effort they would have to overcome could not be strong. Even so, suffocation is more personal and confrontational than either of these two personalities would be comfortable with, especially in the long run. Thus, there was a need for the method to evolve into something more passively aggressive.

Harvey also made it clear that he had strayed from his so-called code. He once tried to poison a neighbor who was making waves about his theft of shared electricity, and he even poisoned people who were not going to die. He also poisoned his gay lover so that he would not be able to leave him, keeping him sick and dependent, but not killing him.

Hardly a humanitarian motivation. And I suspected that the impulse to kill—once gratified—would demand satisfaction based more on opportunity than on any claimed code.

Harvey would die in prison in 2017, several days after being attacked and beaten in his cell, not an uncommon death for a serial killer. It happened to Jeffrey Dahmer, too. There is power for the guy who takes out the uberkiller within the prison milieu.

I also visited with Richard Angelo, a New York nurse who, like Saldivar, used Pavulon to induce cardiac arrest in multiple patients.

But unlike Saldivar, whose goal was to kill, Angelo hoped to revive his victims and play hero. Unfortunately for him and some of his victims, that didn't work out so well.

"I wanted to create a situation where I would cause the patient to have some respiratory distress or some problem, and through my intervention or suggested intervention or whatever, come out looking like I knew what I was doing," Angelo told investigators during his confession. "I had no confidence in myself. I felt very inadequate."

Impulsive, anxious, and self-doubting, he had a strong need to prove himself.

He also appeared to have episodic bouts of depression and difficulties with social interaction.

Indeed, during my time with him, I noted his sense of neurotic anxiety even so many years after his killings. He was a brooding, pessimistic guy who was highly self-critical and relied on his hero fantasies to relieve his negative mood states.

Unlike Harvey, who definitely enjoyed the spotlight and receiving credit for his misdeeds, Angelo was much more self-effacing and appeared genuinely regretful—a guy who wanted to do the right thing but just couldn't quite get it right. Believe it or not, he had been an Eagle Scout.

And the usual heroics of being in health care were not sufficient to remedy his broken sense of self.

He wasn't psychopathic, but his feelings of inadequacy had set him on a path of horrible judgment that resulted in the multiple killings. He needed to prove himself. He needed to be the hero. He needed the excitement of an emergency room during a code situation. It seemed to me on many levels that he was similar to Saldivar.

Saldivar didn't want the loud fanfare, but he did enjoy having become the dark entity of Death whose task was to relieve suffering—which made him, at least in his own mind, a necessity, an integral part of the hospital's "helpers."

To hear him tell it, he *helped* that physician who had erred on the death certificate!

The choice of Pavulon was eerie and speaks to the drug's power to induce defenselessness in those injected with it, making it naturally attractive as a weapon of choice to nonconfrontational types like Saldivar and Angelo. It was no coincidence.

Angelo's undoing would eventually come in a similar fashion to Saldivar's, with the exhumation of bodies and toxicology tests showing the presence of Pavulon in patients who should never have received the drug.

At thirty-three years old, Angelo was convicted in 1989 of second-degree murder, manslaughter, criminally negligent homicide, and assault. He was sentenced to sixty-one years to life in prison, and when I interviewed him he was locked up at the Clinton Correctional Facility in Dannemora, New York.

Back in California, the case against Saldivar ground on.

I returned with a better understanding of the true nature of these so-called angel-of-death killers. They are not humanitarians. They kill whenever they get an opportunity, and their code is not one of mercy but instead merely opportunity without confrontation.

Once they start, they don't stop.

So in Saldivar's case, we didn't need to look just at the deaths of patients with DNR (do-not-resuscitate) orders or the terminally ill on his shift, but basically any death—and maybe even more so, those who *hadn't been* expected to die.

This was somewhat counterintuitive, I know, given his stated motive—or rather, his perception of his motive—that he merely was helping those already dying leave this life for the next. But the takeaways from my interviews with Angelo and Harvey, and from my review of many other cases, suggested we needed to open our minds to other avenues.

Eventually, after multiple examinations and toxicology tests on the twenty bodies that were exhumed in Saldivar's case, we were able to find traces of Pavulon in six of them.

Six out of twenty? Are you fucking kidding me? We never expected that many hits. And there were even three additional bodies that were considered wobblers, meaning the findings were not definitive enough to present in court.

To me, the implications were astounding. Were we *that* good or lucky to identify so many? Or is the deadly truth that there were *so many more* murdered that it was easy to get these hits?

I suspect the answer is: all of the above.

Now it was finally time to hold Saldivar accountable for his crimes—at least a few of them. Let me be clear. I believe he has never been held accountable for the unnamed many who fell to his "magic syringe" and murderous hand.[5]

The truth is, it would be a whole lot easier on everyone—surviving family members and the overtaxed judicial system—if the hammer of justice could be delivered swiftly on the basis of these six cases. Another confession with this handful of known hits, and it potentially would be "game over."

Now there was an arrest to be planned, an interrogation to be strategized, and hopefully a final confession from Saldivar if all went well.

So we on the task force assembled and got our game plan together.

It was meticulously orchestrated, a strategy based partly on my psychological assessment of Saldivar and his crimes. I laid it out for the cops in crisp detail.

The time of day for the arrest was important—early, before any distractions could derail it. Maybe before he'd eaten. Take him down before he'd gotten to work. Remove him from any audience or anyone else who might continue to buy into the bullshit he'd been telling himself for years, that he could beat this.

Stop him on the freeway, have his car towed away, let him feel the world crashing down on him.

His involvement had likely faded from his memory, as much time had passed. Deep down inside, though, he still had fear, because he knew what he did. And we would soon let him know that nothing had stopped, that Father Time had caught up and it was over. The inner truth would erupt inside him and induce hopelessness.

---

[5] CBSNews.com Staff, "Hospital Worker Admits 40–50 Killings," CBS News, March 27, 1998, https://www.cbsnews.com/news/hospital-worker-admits-40-50-killings/.

The psychology of the arrest was everything, and we brainstormed it down to the last detail. "Efren, it's over. You know it. Deep down inside, you've always known this day would come. We are here to talk about the why."

We got him just as planned.

It was a purposefully long ride to the police station with Saldivar cuffed in the back of the car. The air of finality hung chokingly thick, asphyxiating any hope that remained in his mind that he would ever be free again.

Detective Currie, the cop who had elicited Saldivar's first confession (later recanted), and another detective were at the station as Saldivar was brought in. The strategy was well-scripted. I was in a nearby room with the other detectives watching a live video feed from the interrogation room, ready to provide any needed input should the questioning somehow get derailed or benefit from some adjustment.

It didn't take long for Saldivar to create a near impasse with Detective Currie over the prior confession.

Saldivar needed to have his moment. It was clear if he had it, he would give a full confession again. A quick time-out was taken, and Currie took a step back. He needed to focus on winning the war, not this bullshit battle.

Why eventually led to how, when, and where, and Saldivar's final chilling admission.

With dual confessions now and the bodies to back them up, Saldivar's fate was sealed.

At nearly fifty years old, Saldivar remains locked away at the Substance Abuse Treatment Facility and State Prison in Corcoran, California, with no chance of ever being free again.

Mark Twain wrote that "of all the animals, man is the only one that is cruel. He is the only one that inflicts pain for the pleasure of doing it." Some of the most infamous serial killers in history lived by this creed. Saldivar, despite his proclamations that he killed out of mercy, was really no different.

Taking lives feeds these killers' grandiose and insatiable desire for omnipotence, but the satisfaction after some kills is short-lived. During the cooling-off period, the urge to kill builds again. And it must be fulfilled.

For other serial murderers, killing gives their otherwise worthless lives meaning in a world where they feel as if they don't fit in.

In either case, their secrets fuel their sense of power and superiority. The longer they get away with their crimes, the more formidable they feel, and their scorn for the perceived inept authorities who pursue them multiplies. This often leads to more brazen acts and greater risk-taking.

But don't be fooled by the Hollywood stereotypes like Hannibal Lecter, the cunning, calculated evil geniuses of the big screen who always outsmart authorities with their intellect and devious, well-thought-out plans.

These are largely not the serial killers among us. I've studied them my entire career.

Just the moniker "serial killer" has somehow over the years created a mystique with the impression of a powerful predator at the top of the food chain, a real-life bogeyman with off-the-charts intelligence who hunts and kills humans like prey.

It is an image embraced by the media, guaranteed to generate headlines, intrigue, and often movies and television shows.

Admittedly, when I began studying them, reading books by well-known FBI profilers like John Douglas, Roy Hazelwood, and Robert Ressler, then eventually interviewing several notorious offenders in prisons, I too was fascinated and taken in by the allure of the wicked.

But at a certain point, as I was immersed in this world of nightmares, it became something else entirely. The mystique evaporated. These people are the worst of the worst, killing for sport and power. They are bottom-feeding scum who steal from society in the most vulnerable of moments and then, often in the end, game the legal system to cowardly keep from being held accountable with a death sentence of their own.

Serial killers rarely want to become the victims. But they are at the top of the list when it comes to capital punishment consideration, mercy be damned.

Most are fully aware of what they are doing and why, how wrong it is, and would never even come close to being considered legally insane. They kill because they want to, often because it turns them on, literally—in a sexual way. Sex and violence are frequently intertwined.

Within this group, there are all kinds of twisted sexual desires known as paraphilias, or deviant patterns of arousal. There are cannibals who consume their victims, like Jeffrey Dahmer, who between 1978 and 1991 killed seventeen males in a horrific manner. Rape, dismemberment, necrophilia, cannibalism—they were all key components of his modus operandi.

These are the sadists, those who take great pleasure from inflicting pain, punishment, and humiliation on their victims, enjoying the suffering as they go about it. Ted Bundy, who eventually confessed to killing and raping at least thirty women, John Wayne Gacy, who was convicted of thirty-three sex-related killings, and Dahmer are all of this ilk.

Others are driven by the power and control to take human life without any overt sexual arousal. So-called angels of death would fall into this category, as well as those who may claim to have a philosophical, political, or social agenda.

I call them "so-called" angels of death because the label mistakenly gives the appearance that they are simply helping the terminally ill die, performing some sort of humanitarian public service. In Saldivar's case, there were plenty who did not fit the so-called code (self-proclaimed guidelines of acceptable victims); some of them had just pissed him off because he thought they were milking the health-care system.

The reality is that serial killers usually stray from their code, kill people who were not going to die, induce suffering in the victims and their loved ones, and are motivated by purely selfish reasons.

Philosophically driven killers include the likes of Theodore J. Kaczynski, dubbed "The Unabomber." He also fits neatly into the category of a violent-true-believer murderer, which I'll get to later.

Kaczynski, a hermit who lived in a remote cabin in the Montana woods and railed against modern technology, mailed or hand-delivered at least sixteen explosive devices to universities, businesses, homes, and public offices across the country from 1978 to 1995, killing three people and injuring more than two dozen.

The truly mentally ill, those among this set of killers who are delusional, claim to have been told to take lives by voices in their head or other external forces that they misinterpret as guidance to kill. That said, even with mental illness, these people are rarely judged to have been insane at the time of their killings, and face trial for their crimes instead of being locked away in a mental health institution.

Take Herbert Mullin, for example, who killed thirteen people between 1972 and 1973; he was delusional in his belief that human sacrifice was needed to save California from a cataclysmic earthquake. Despite such an eschewing of all tenets of reality, Mullin was found fit for trial, guilty, and sane—and was eventually sent to prison for his crimes.

Patrick Kearney was a true monster and sexual sadist. Along with his lover, he kidnapped and tortured between twenty-one and forty-three teenage boys, raping and mutilating them, then dumping their bodies unceremoniously along highways like human garbage.

He wouldn't talk about his crimes to me, and came across as very psychopathic and narcissistic. Looking into his eyes was like staring into an abyss; he had a predatory gaze of terrifying emptiness. He seemed to have no remorse, and I wondered what he was thinking about me as I sat with him. No matter how experienced a psychologist one is, one never truly knows what lies in the depths of these killers' menacing minds.

Another monster I met with was "The Skid Row Slasher," Vaughn Greenwood, who killed eleven known victims and left evidence that he may have drunk their blood at the scenes. He was quiet and strange and refused to say much to me when I spoke with him, other than to try to debunk the criminal profile developed during the investigation of his case.

"They said I was white and impotent." He was, in fact, African American.

I was much younger and brasher then and just couldn't resist a retort on my way out of the room. "I guess the profile was batting five hundred," I quipped.

Racist serial assassin Joseph Paul Franklin was also a violent true believer who murdered, by his count, twenty-three people between 1977 and 1980 in an effort to cleanse society of Jews and blacks, the sorts he believed were lesser races that needed to be exterminated. He looked with disdain upon the perverted typical serial killer, bragged about his body count, and wanted credit for cases he had not even been charged with. Yet he was terrified of the death sentence he himself faced, going so far as to practice some degree of numerology in his correspondence with me, and seeing as a bad omen the last three letters of my last name, "die."

When he brought that up to me, I told him the original French version of my name—my dad was born in the French Caribbean colony of Guadeloupe—was Mohandir. From that point on, that's how he referred to me. It helped develop rapport.

I also evaluated Lonnie David Franklin Jr., "The Grim Sleeper," for his death-penalty trial in 2016.

He had raped and murdered at least twelve female victims beginning in the mid-1980s and spanning more than two decades in and around the Los Angeles area, dumping their bodies in alleys and garbage bins. Authorities believe he could actually be responsible for more than twenty-five killings. Franklin earned the nickname "Grim Sleeper" due to a hiatus in the murders between 1988 and 2002.

His was the first successful murder case prosecution by the brilliant Deputy District Attorney Beth Silverman using familial DNA, a process in which authorities compare, through databases, genetic material found at crime scenes, looking for close matches that would lead to family members whom investigators could interview to narrow down their target search. In Franklin's case, as the trail went cold, cops did just that and got a partial match to a man arrested in 2008 for firearms and drug offenses. It turned out to be Franklin's son and eventually led detectives to their killer, who lived near where many of the victims' bodies had been dumped.

At the time, police called the new technique revolutionary in crime-solving, more so even than fingerprint analysis. Los Angeles Police Chief Charlie Beck called it "a landmark case."

"This will change the way policing is done in the United States," Beck proclaimed.[6]

Franklin took no responsibility whatsoever and tried to claim he'd just coincidentally had consensual sex with multiple victims who later ended up dead at the hands of someone else.

Michael Hughes was another Los Angeles–based predator whom I evaluated for his trial, in 2012. The then-fifty-six-year-old serial rapist and murderer was eventually sentenced to death for killing three women between 1986 and 1993. He had already been serving life in prison without the possibility of parole for four previous killings in the area.

With the exception of Joseph Paul Franklin, who considered himself a "multiple slayer" and was offended at the thought of being lumped in with the likes of those deemed to be serial killers, these offenders were primarily rapist-murderers. They fit the prototypical public perception reflected in the Ted Bundy, Richard Ramirez ("The Night Stalker"), and Dennis Rader ("BTK," for "bind, torture, kill") types.

Then there are those angels of death—who are quite prolific in their body counts, as evidenced by Efren Saldivar—with the power needs simply expressed by the repetitive taking of human lives. There is no known sexual component with them, just the sheer thrill of the kill.

Perhaps it would be most useful to think of three broad categories of serial killers with the understanding that no two are exactly alike but do often present with similar characteristics.

There are those who kill repeatedly in a sexualized violent manner, like Kearney; killers who simply take lives for a variety of power-based needs that are not sexualized, like Saldivar; and offenders like Mullin who kill repeatedly based upon psychosis, a mental disorder in which the culprit's thoughts and emotions are so impaired as to leave this person far removed from any sense of reality.

So what is a serial killer? One definition is a person who kills three or more victims with a cooling-off period in between. But what of the

---

[6] Lauren Effron and Barbara Garcia, "Cops Trying to Taint Jury Pool 'Grim Sleeper' With Photos Attorney Charges," ABC News, December 17, 2010, https://abcnews.go.com/TheLaw/grim-sleeper-serial-killer-victim-photos-released-los/story?id=12424559.

person who is stopped prior to being able to meet the criteria of that definition? The requisite fantasy life and urges are there, but the achievement or fulfillment of those desires is thwarted. What should we call those people?

I do not propose to answer that question, as there is really no single interpretation or category to put those people in, but clearly there are many who are interrupted before they can get up and running. And they are just as dangerous as the ones who fulfill their twisted fantasies.

We also have to keep in mind that, regarding the offenders who have been caught and convicted, there are quite often many more victims who died at their hands that they will never be held accountable for. Saldivar is among them. And there are so many more.

Complicating the situation is that many of these killers enjoy misleading authorities in the hope of maintaining their platform of power. They also like to brag. That's probably why so many of them ultimately do confess. Their narcissism demands credit, and their sadistic needs are fed by the secondary trauma to the populace when they tell their stories.

So the true extent of their damage and harm is likely understated and will largely remain unknown forever—meaning that these infamous serial killers throughout history have murdered many more people than we will ever be able to calculate. Further, much of what we know about serial murders comes only from those who have been caught. Is this a different population of offender than those who have not been caught? Those who have gotten away with it, continued to do it, or for whatever reason stopped or went on a hiatus may represent a more complex group of individuals. It is crucial to consider they may differ in a number of important ways from those who have been captured and convicted. But we only know what we know.

Frightening as it may be, the great likelihood is that there are many more who walk among us unknown, who keep killing to this day and will ultimately take their crimes to their graves, living free from prosecution and incarceration until their own deaths. In fact, estimates by experts conclude that there are anywhere from several dozen to several thousand uncaptured serial killers operating in the United States at any given time.

Research indicates that the U.S. has more serial killers than all other countries combined.[7] I do not doubt the veracity of this claim, because America seems to be a leader in all things violent, but again, keep in mind that the data is based only on known cases, killers who have been caught.

A handful of factors may help explain why we here in the United States suffer from so many of these demented demons. Publicity stokes the fantasies of developing deviants, and nowhere in the world is crime so glamorized as in the United States, where Hollywood movies depict these sorts as infamous legends. And the availability of extreme, sexually violent stimulation and support for it are highly prevalent in cyberspace, again poisoning those vulnerable to this incitement. But this is not unique to America; it's just more commonly glamorized in free societies.

Studying and learning about serial killers help us understand that we need to do a better job of creating a world that develops in our youth a strong empathic capacity, encourages humility, and instills the value of loving, intimate connections with our fellow human beings. But their violence also reminds us that there are wolves who live among us. We need to still retain our vigilance, trust our instincts, set boundaries, and be mindful of the situations we place ourselves in. Scary and unfortunate but true.

Efren Saldivar took advantage of the system to avoid the very fate he so mercilessly meted out to his victims—the needle that would have been used to kill him had he not pleaded guilty to avoid the death penalty. It was a cowardly move, and one seen in so many other captured serial killers who take lives under the auspices of power and control, then try to maintain that power by saving their own lives in end.

Saldivar never did quite see the maliciousness of his ways. After taking so many lives, he still looked upon his killing spree in an almost childish, matter-of-fact way, seeking out humor to assuage his inner guilt. It was clear in a letter he wrote to me in 2003, about a year after being

---

[7] M. G. Aamodt, *Serial Killer Statistics,* September 4, 2016, http://maamodt.asp.radford.edu/serial%20killer%20information%20center/Serial%20Killer%20Statistics.pdf.

incarcerated, in which he returned to his memories of the book that I believe was, in part, the impetus for his cruel future path.

"Hey Kris, I hope this missive should find you in good health. I too am doing as fair as can be expected," he wrote. "You know, I find myself with curiosity to share with you." He went on to mention a television commercial he had seen advertising an upcoming episode of the cartoon comedy series *The Simpsons*.

"Well that episode is inspired by that book you questioned me on 'Upon a Pale Horse' by Piers Anthony where the main character happens to kill the incarnation of Death and is required to assume that vacated celestial position of Death," he wrote. "It appears that somebody over at *The Simpsons* also read that book and found it funny just as I did.... Can you imagine what buffoonery and hijinks that Homer will create wielding such tremendous responsibility?

"Good thing it's only a cartoon."

The Columbine Effect

An Examination of the School Shooter

"Fame without achievement."

—Kris Mohandie and J. Reid Meloy
(from "Violent and Suicidal: Contemporary Trends,"
Keynote presentation to the annual Association
of Threat Assessment Professionals Conference, 2009)

"Isn't it fun to get the respect we're going to deserve? We don't give a shit because we're going to die doing it." The world owes them, and they're justified, taking pride in their lack of compassion.

It was a chilling postscript left behind on videos recorded in the weeks leading up to what would become a horrendous watershed event in American history—the Columbine High School massacre on April 20, 1999.[8]

Seniors Eric Harris and Dylan Klebold had prepared for months. They stockpiled firearms and ammunition. They made crude bombs

---

[8] "Transcript of the Columbine 'Basement Tapes,'" transcribed and annotated by Peter Langman, Ph.D., July 29, 2014, https://schoolshooters.info/sites/default/files/columbine _basement_tapes_1.0.pdf.

from gasoline, propane tanks, and metal pipes. They would be ignored as outcasts no more. They would live—and die—in infamy.

We call this phenomenon fame without achievement. The young people in this category feel insignificant in their daily lives, accomplishing very little while wandering aimlessly in a realm on the outskirts of any sort of societal uniformity, never quite fitting in and with no real aspirations for the future. They have an insatiable desire for recognition, and they are characterized by grandiosity, a lack of empathy for others, and a hostile sense of superiority dripping with entitlement—blossoming narcissists.

They find the cheater's way to be remembered in their desperate grasp for fame. It's the ultimate last word.

"Directors will be fighting over this story. I know we're gonna have followers because we're so fucking God-like," Klebold said in one of the videos discovered by investigators after the killings. Thankfully, I don't think any directors did.

The pair first mentioned a killing spree in their November 1997 writings, and referred to the chosen date as "NBK Day," a reference to the 1994 film *Natural Born Killers*, directed by Oliver Stone. It wasn't the first time the film had been idolized by school shooters.

The film was inspired by the real-life exploits of Bonnie Parker and Clyde Barrow, two notorious Depression-era criminals responsible for the killings of at least thirteen people until their own deaths during a shootout with authorities in 1934.

Murder was portrayed in *Natural Born Killers* as sporting, fun, and sexy, and in the film, news coverage transformed these fictional characters into instant celebrities. Art imitated life. Life imitated art. And so it goes, back and forth.

In Columbine, we saw the cycle continue with life imitating art once again. This shooting is not dissimilar to many of the more recent school shootings. There is a virtual pandemic ravaging the hearts and souls of our children—a disease that I hope can one day be cured, an optimistic but unlikely goal under current conditions.

Harris and Klebold's goal was to become famous by murdering up to 250 students at their school in a commando-like raid of indiscriminate rage and viciousness that people would talk about—even emulate—for years to come. Thankfully, like many of these events, it didn't quite go as planned. It was supposed to be a bombing with explosions in the school cafeteria that would kill and maim dozens, sending throngs of students running toward them, where they would await with guns ready to shoot them down one by one. But the bombs did not detonate. So they set about on their rampage with the firearms they had brought along, eventually killing thirteen people and injuring twenty-three more before taking their own lives. It was horrendous, of course, but it could have been so much worse.

Exactly why they did it has been debated for years. It's clear they felt wronged, shunned in all sorts of ways by their families, by classmates, by the stuck-up kids who surrounded them daily, by society in general. But there also is a fair amount of bullshit in this explanation.

Closer inspection finds that they dished it out probably more than they ever took it. They were provocative, intolerant, and judgmental, and when their peers took exception to it and gave it back to them, these thin-skinned, spoiled, overindulged young narcissists were offended. These were not abused, deprived, suffering kids at all.

Narcissists and other individuals with personality disorders rarely see their part in their interpersonal conflicts and life difficulties. It's all about the blame they externalize. There is no room for anyone else's feelings or thoughts. In their minds, Harris and Klebold had no future. They invested in death and fantasized about the notoriety they would gain from implementing their dark impulses and urges. They fed their egos with blood.

Harris and Klebold shared these fantasies with each other, bonded by a phenomenon Dr. J. Reid Meloy refers to as "clandestine excitement"— the thrill of a forbidden secret, another layer of control woven into the power-driven idea of "If you only knew." Their only hope was to achieve immortality through violence and death.

"If you could see all the anger I've stored over the past four fucking years," Klebold said in the videos. We would later refer to this practice as "injustice collecting," something many mass shooters and would-be killers do to stoke their internal rage—rage that is then converted into a cold-blooded plan for premeditated murder.

The feeling of rage is accompanied by a sense of power, and the feelings of supremacy and dominance associated with the imagined violence are the antidote for their underlying sense of powerlessness, or maybe even just a general sense that they deserve more of everything, including supplication, although they have done nothing to earn it.

These killers not only convert their anger to revenge, but they also fantasize well in advance, mentally rehearsing the carnage they hope to one day carry out in real life. By the time they enact their fantasy, they've killed dozens, maybe hundreds of times before, in the dark abyss of their minds, sometimes for years. Hence the common recounting of these horrifying attacks from survivors that the killer "seemed so calm," that he "didn't say a word," that he "seemed like he was just going on autopilot."

Harris ranted about revenge in his written journals, opining angrily about all of those mindless souls walking the Earth and getting even with the people who had wronged him: "If you pissed me off in the past, you will die if I see you. Because you might be able to piss off others and have it eventually blow over, but not me. I don't forget people who wronged me."[9]

This says a lot about what was wrong with Harris—his inability or unwillingness to let go of perceived slights, another key hallmark of the eventual school shooter. Klebold, too, had felt wronged in so many ways. He recalled how his popular and athletic older brother always made fun of him, along with all of his brother's friends: "You made me what I am."

Blaming others is another common dynamic of shooters, helping them justify the turning of violence outward against the people they deem responsible for creating the monsters in their minds.

---

[9] "Eric Harris's Journal," transcribed and annotated by Peter Langman, Ph.D., October 3, 2014, https://schoolshooters.info/sites/default/files/harris_journal_1.3.pdf.

Columbine wasn't the first school shooting, by any means, but it served to shock the national conscience because it occurred in a largely white upper-middle-class suburban Colorado town, one just like any other fine suburb. Prior events had occurred in places like Paducah, Kentucky; Pearl, Mississippi; and remote Bethel, Alaska. But Columbine, just outside the Denver metropolis? It shattered the myth, perpetuated by artificial and contrived class distinctions, that there is some invisible line that separates and protects some of "us" in the U.S. from some of "them."

If it could happen there, it could happen anywhere.

The attack continues to inspire new generations of would-be killers—many of whom weren't even alive at the time the bloodbath took place—and became the lightning bolt that announced the current school-shooter epidemic we now find ourselves living in. To this day, I consult on cases in which teenagers—even adults—idolize these two homicidal maniacs, frequenting websites devoted to their cause, pining to have sex with them, wishing they could have joined them on that fateful day, wanting to visit their graves.

In the ensuing years, through the explosion of social media and the internet, the Columbine massacre has influenced an entirely new crop of violent perpetrators and is emblazoned in the cultural script of our troubled children as a way to achieve instant notoriety.

The big end. Getting even. A bloody curtain call.

But let's take a step back. Way back. To rural Michigan in 1927.

It was here in the tiny village of Bath, not far from the state capital of Lansing and with a population of just about three hundred people, that America suffered what remains the deadliest school massacre in U.S. history, though one rarely ever mentioned anymore, given the rapid pace of repeated school shootings all over the country in recent years. And it was so very long ago now, coming up on a hundred years ago.

Farmer Andrew Kehoe was the school board treasurer and a former village clerk in this tranquil speck on the map. It was a place where students came from around the region, swelling the daytime population to twice the real census; they were the children of other farmers, many of whom had known one another for years. The Bath Consolidated School had been built about five years earlier, to replace a smattering of one-room schools that dotted the surrounding bucolic countryside.

It was 8:45 in the morning on May 18, the last day of classes for the year, when an explosion ripped through a three-story structure. The blast could be heard for miles around. Kehoe had planted the bomb in the basement. He had spent the better part of that spring in the bowels of the school booby-trapping the building.

When asked what he was doing in the basement, he had offered the explanation that he was trying to save the school money on electrical contracting work. Why would anyone not believe him? Why would anyone suspect that he was up to no good? There never had been an episode of school violence in America. Not like this.

Survivors and first responders would later describe the carnage as something they'd never envisioned, even in their wildest nightmares. Children were partially buried in the rubble with bloody limbs protruding from the mounds of broken red brick and snapped planks of wood.

There is nothing glamorous, cool, or worthy of notoriety here or in any of these cases. These are cowardly, craven, homicidal sucker punches.

As members of the community rushed to the scene, arriving to find the unimaginable, Kehoe pulled up in his truck full of dynamite, stepped back, and fired his rifle at the cache of explosives inside his vehicle. The innocent, traumatized people around him didn't know he was the offender, that he had returned to the scene of the crime. A malfunction had kept an additional five hundred pounds of explosives on the property from detonating. If they had detonated, he would have killed every single student and staff member at the school.

It is hard to imagine this statement in the context of the death that did occur, but, like Columbine, it could have been much worse.

Maybe Kehoe returned to see what had gone wrong with his plan and, frustrated, did what he could with what he had left.

Boom!

That second monstrous fireball took three more lives, including those of the school superintendent, a bystander, and Kehoe himself. When the smoke eventually cleared, forty-four people had been killed, thirty-eight of them students, and dozens more had been injured. One of the victims was Kehoe's wife, who was later found at his burned-down farmhouse not far from the school. He had killed her shortly before going to the campus, and burned to the ground every building on his property. It was scorched earth: He knew he was never coming back.

Over the ensuing years, there have been similar bifurcated events, in which the murderer begins the killing at one location—usually his home—then continues to a different location to fulfill his ultimate plan.

After the Bath bombing, everyone tried to make sense of the tragedy. Newspapers labeled Kehoe a maniac in front-page headlines across the country.

"Twisted Brain of School Official Caused Tragedy."

"Maniac Dynamites School."

"He was notified last June that the mortgage on his farm would be foreclosed, and that may have been the circumstance that started the clockwork of anarchy and madness in his brain," *The New York Times* wrote.

Reports indicated that Kehoe had grown angry over increasing school taxes and had some problems with a few fellow school board members, but to this day, no one knows exactly why he did it—though he did leave behind a message. A sign was later found hanging on a fence at his property with five perfectly stenciled, painted-on words:

"Criminals Are Made, Not Born."

Again, "It's your fault." Do you hear the familiar battle cry of the narcissistically aggrieved as they wage their cowardly unilateral assault on the unaware? It is a common thread seen in all school attacks of today.

In hindsight, one could make several correlations between the Columbine attack and Kehoe's bloody bombing. They both follow what is now a recognized pattern: anger at perceived slights. A brittle ego. An entitled mind that holds on to resentments and seethes with hostility. And key, the blaming of others.

Dylan Klebold told the world in one of his videos, "You made me what I am." Kehoe's fence post sign is thematically no different—in essence, "It is your fault. You deserve what I did." Kehoe didn't have a video camera. He didn't have social media. He used some paint and a fence for his message, but there is really no difference. Same shit, different asshole.

The Bath bombing remains an outlier of sorts, but it was a harbinger of things to come. Over the ensuing decades, escalating in the 1990s, school attacks have become unfortunately more and more commonplace, carried out with guns—not bombs—and leaving behind body counts that keep growing exponentially. And they are now largely perpetrated by students against students.

The disturbing reality is that children who had not even been born when the Columbine attack occurred, and even youths in other countries, refer to this event when planning and carrying out their own massacres. Even more disconcerting is that in a very real way, the Columbine offenders actually achieved one of their goals: notoriety. We call this the Columbine effect.

At least seventy-four known murder plots have been inspired by Columbine worldwide. Fifty-three were interrupted by law enforcement, while twenty-one attacks occurred, leaving at least eighty-nine dead and 126 wounded, with nine of the attackers taking their own lives.[10]

Fatal Columbine-inspired plots have also occurred in Finland, Germany, Canada, and most recently Brazil, while plans have been uncovered and thwarted virtually everywhere throughout the United States and the industrialized world. The number of foiled attacks is well over one hundred, I assure you, having worked on a half-dozen interrupted cases just since these statistics were compiled in 2015.

The would-be perpetrators often reference the writings and videos of Harris and Klebold, consider them heroes or martyrs, seek to one-up them, visit their graves and the campus, choose the anniversary date of the Columbine shootings for *their* day of violence, and fantasize that they are simpatico with these long-dead murderers. The history of Columbine

---

[10] Mark Follman, "Inside the Race to Stop the Next Mass Shooter," *Mother Jones*, November/December 2015, https://www.motherjones.com/politics/2015/10/mass-shootings-threat-assessment-shooter-fbi-columbine/.

has become virtual required reading if one is really going to consider doing something similar.

Twenty-three-year-old student Seung-Hui Cho killed thirty-two people on the campus of Virginia Polytechnic Institute and State University, commonly known as Virginia Tech on April 16, 2007.

"I didn't have to do it. I could have left. I could have fled," Cho said in a video he mailed to NBC News before the attack.[11] "But now I am no longer running. If not for me, for my children and my brothers and sisters.... I did it for them," Cho said, also referring to "martyrs like Eric and Dylan." And like them, Cho killed himself before authorities could arrest him.

Steven Kazmierczak, a former graduate student at Northern Illinois University, walked into the institution's auditorium with a shotgun and several handguns and opened fire on February 14, 2008. The twenty-seven-year-old killed five and wounded more than a dozen others before taking his own life. Police reports indicated that Kazmierczak had previously "examined the methods" of the Columbine shooters and that he had been "fascinated" by them and other mass killings.

In one of the more shocking school attacks in our nation's history, on December 14, 2012, twenty-year-old Adam Lanza killed twenty-six people, mostly young students, at Sandy Hook Elementary School in Newtown, Connecticut. He also killed his mother prior to the attack, then committed suicide as authorities closed in.

According to one of the final reports on the case by law enforcement, Lanza had "an obsession with mass murders, in particular the April 1999 shootings at Columbine."[12] Cops said they discovered at his home hundreds of documents, images, and videos related to the Columbine shootings, including what appeared to be a copy of the police investigation into the Colorado attack.

---

[11] M. Alex Johnson, "Gunman Sent Package to NBC News," NBC News, April 19, 2007, http://www.nbcnews.com/id/18195423/ns/us_news-crime_and_courts/t/gunman-sent-package-nbc-news/#.XTYZL5NKhAY.

[12] "Newtown Gunman Adam Lanza Had 'Obsession' with Columbine," BBC News, November 26, 2013, https://www.bbc.com/news/world-us-canada-25097127.

Lanza's mother was a gun enthusiast and would often take her son to the shooting range to practice, despite knowing about his obsession with death and violence. He would end up using her own gun to kill her, and other firearms to kill the children.

More recently—and equally as horrifying—is Nikolas Cruz's 2018 Valentine's Day attack on Marjory Stoneman Douglas High School in Parkland, Florida. Authorities said Cruz, who was nineteen at the time, also had researched the Columbine killings prior to the assault with an AR-15 rifle that left seventeen dead.

Also similar to Columbine, Cruz left behind videos full of self-loathing and an obvious desire for fame. "My name is Nik, and I'm going to be the next school shooter of 2018," he said gleefully. "When you see me on the news you'll all know who I am.... I am nothing. I am no one. My life is nothing and meaningless.... I live a lone life. Live in seclusion and solitude. I hate everyone and everything."[13]

Well, there is partial truth in those statements. Actually, what *he did* to elevate his status and be remembered was nothing and meaningless. Murdering innocent people in cold blood does not radiate purpose and status upon him. The lives of the lost are what deserve honor, remembrance, sorrow, and the illumination of greater purpose. That and what the survivors have done in the ensuing years are the only meaningful things in the whole equation.

And the list of school shooters goes on and on. Just as workplace shootings are now commonly referred to as "going postal," these individuals are "going Columbine." Clearly, the event has become something bigger, a permanent scar on our national psyche.

I've lectured extensively across North America about school shootings, threat assessment techniques, and how we as a society can try to put an end to the carnage. I even wrote a book, *School Violence Threat Management*, back in 2000. And while I wish I could say our efforts to protect young people and staff members at our educational institutions

---

[13] Michael James, "Parkland's Nikolas Cruz Made Chilling Videos Before Shooting: 'You're All Going to Die,'" *USA Today*, May 30, 2018, https://www.usatoday.com/story/news/2018/05/30/parkland-killer-video-im-going-next-school-shooter/657774002/.

from these deadly incidents have been universally successful, that just isn't the case. We continue to see the bodies of our children pile up and troubled youths turning the fantasies of their twisted minds into reality with the squeeze of a trigger. Our lives are getting deadlier by the day with the ease of access to high-powered rifles like the AR-15, which is becoming the go-to gun for mass shooters of all types.

I've studied these offenders for nearly twenty-five years and have spoken face-to-face with a handful of school shooters as they sit in prison, where they will remain for much of their lives or while awaiting their date with the executioner. Ironically, I learned the most from one who didn't kill anyone, during an incident about a decade prior to Columbine. His case would foreshadow the rising threat of missed opportunities, pariahs lashing out at society, firearm accessibility, the influence of books and movies, troubled childhoods and parental neglect—all of the now-often found components of the school shooters of today.

Strikingly, I had never heard of his case, probably because much of my own research was focused on shooters who actually killed—but I was clearly missing something. While I was conducting a school violence threat management training workshop for some school personnel in Los Angeles, a teacher came up to me and asked if I'd heard of the case of Jeffrey Cox. She had been his classmate at San Gabriel High School in Southern California at the time of the 1988 event. This incident occurred in my own backyard just a few miles from my house. I had to find out more. It was one of the early ones, and it was intriguing.

And the more I read about it, the more I knew I had to try to find him and talk to him. He was the real beginning of what was to come. Cox was eighteen years old when he barged into his fourth-period humanities class carrying an AR-15 rifle he had purchased just days earlier when he reached the legal the age to buy it himself. He was there initially to take hostages.

He didn't really have a plan. He thought he might die. Maybe kill someone. Maybe get away with a big bounty of cash like his hero D.B. Cooper, who in 1971 hijacked a plane leaving from Oregon and forced it to land in Seattle, where he freed the passengers in exchange for two hundred thousand dollars in cash. Once the plane took off again, he parachuted out with the ransom money and has never been seen again.

Cox was obviously a bit conflicted. "I had a message I wanted to get across," he said after his arrest, "of unmasking people, of disrobing the images everyone puts on, of making people real. I still think I had the right idea. But that was the wrong way of doing it. It was very foolish."[14]

I met with him at an Arizona prison in April 2001. I'll come back around to this later, why he was locked up in Arizona after finally getting out of prison in California. It is, indeed, a tragic tale of a kid whose life took a terrible turn with one bad decision that led to others.

As I sat across the table from this young man who had made so many mistakes in life, it was hard not to pity him. The prison sounds of voices yelling, cell doors slamming shut, and keys jangling on the uniforms of the correctional staff provided a reality check: This was a maximum-security hellhole.

I liked him. He was smart, witty, glib, and thoughtful. He'd had many years to contemplate his decisions. He had clearly made some bad choices but also had been dealt a tough hand. He could have been helped, like so many others, but it just never happened. So many missed opportunities.

"In reference to the 1988 incident, if you could just tell me what happened," I asked him softly, like I was speaking to my own son.

"Well, it happened in April, and in November of '87, I had had kind of a bout with suicide and had been playing a little Russian roulette, and one of my classmates told my high school guidance counselor. She was concerned, called me in, and at that time...after a few hours, I was put in a suicide prevention ward at USC Medical Center. And at the time, I just...there were a lot of kids in there who had real problems. I was just a knucklehead. And it was disturbing. And so...I got out and, of course...I decided to just be a real idiot."

The November incident Cox referred to saved his life in one sense but then sent him on a mad spiral that would eventually lead him to carry out his own school siege. He was depressed and feeling alienated and

---

[14] Jesse Katz, "A High School Gunman's Days of Rage," *Los Angeles Times*, January 14, 1990, https://www.latimes.com/archives/la-xpm-1990-01-14-ga-143-story.html.

alone while at a party at a friend's house, and began playing Russian roulette with a .357 Magnum. He put a bullet in the chamber. Of course,
one obvious question is, how is it that a .357 Magnum is accessible in
a home with no parents around while kids are partying? I suspect the
reader knows the answer to this question.

Click. Click. Click.

The bullet never fired, but he would soon find himself in a hospital
bed in the psychiatric ward of the Los Angeles County+USC Medical
Center. Fortunately, one of the kids had told a school counselor, and one
thing led to another. There, doctors worked to get inside his head, to
diminish his suicidal thoughts. He would miss the next two weeks of his
senior year at San Gabriel High School trying to get well.

Or maybe not. Maybe his agenda all along was to figure out a way to
save face, protect his ego in front of his peer group. It was embarrassing
to him to be in suicide lockup.

We know now that commonalities exist in suicidal and homicidal
minds. The same circumstances that lead a person to consider suicide
also lead to homicidal impulses, making suicidal individuals likelier to
harm others than nonsuicidal people. Cognitive constriction, a perceptual narrowing of surroundings and relationships and an inability to see
other solutions to problems can lead the person to somehow conclude
that homicide is the answer. These people experience an emotional state
of hopelessness in which they see no light at the end of the tunnel.

The adolescent mind is particularly vulnerable to this sort of
thinking—the crossover from suicidal to homicidal—as the brains of
adolescents are more malleable to outside forces and peer pressure, and
many adolescents lack the more well-formed ability of adults to come to
more reasonable conclusions based upon consideration of alternatives
and outcomes. That is not to say all do—I have met plenty of teens who
have the capability, but for one reason or another, they just don't give a
shit about the impact they have on others and embrace dark impulses.

Cox would eventually be sent home from the hospital, but what he
took away from his time in the psychiatric ward was obviously not what
was intended. One might argue that the effect was in fact iatrogenic.

It all began with a single book, *Rage*, that was provided to him to read by a nurse in the facility. One of novelist Stephen King's earlier works—he actually wrote it while still in high school in 1965—it was published about a decade later under King's pseudonym, Richard Bachman. The cover of the book is menacing, with a picture of an angry student sitting on a schoolroom desk staring indignantly at the reader.

Above the picture are words that would foreshadow so many events to come: "His Twisted Mind Turned a Quiet Classroom Into a Dangerous World of Terror."[15]

The tale is about a young man named Charlie Decker who gets called into the principal's office of his high school after threatening a teacher, and ends up getting expelled.

Decker goes straight to his locker and retrieves a gun, kills two teachers, and takes his algebra class hostage. A standoff ensues, and the students soon begin suffering from a sort of Stockholm syndrome, identifying more with their captor than with the authorities trying to end the standoff.

Decker proceeds to make certain demands of the police officers, threatening to kill students if they don't comply. He is eventually shot by the police chief but survives his wounds, and is later found not guilty by reason of insanity and committed to a psychiatric hospital.

The tale ends with Decker addressing the reader: "That's the end. I have to turn off the light now. Good night."

King reportedly reached out to his publishers and let the book go out of print in 1998 after a series of school attackers said they drew their own inspiration from the story, like Cox.[16] In 1989, for example, a seventeen-year-old Kentucky student held his classmates hostage for nine hours in an apparent attempt to act out scenes from *Rage*. In 1996, a fourteen-year-old boy in Washington state apparently inspired by the book shot and killed his algebra teacher and two classmates. And a year

---

[15] Richard Bachman, *Rage*, (New York: New American Library, 1977).

[16] Tyler McCarthy, "Why Stephen King's School Shooter Book 'Rage' Is Out of Print, and A Copy Costs $500," Fox News, May 14, 2018, https://www.foxnews.com/entertainment/why-stephen-kings-school-shooter-book-rage-is-out-of-print-and-a-copy-costs-500.

later, another Kentucky student opened fire on a prayer group at his school, killing three people. A copy of *Rage* was later found in his locker.

In a 2013 essay titled "Guns," King said he wrote the story during a time when the world was very different. "I suppose if it had been written today, and some high school English teacher had seen it, he would have rushed the manuscript to the guidance counselor and I would have found myself in therapy posthaste," King wrote. "But 1965 was a different world, one where you didn't have to take off your shoes before boarding a plane and there were no metal detectors at the entrances to high schools."

King said that the book was an honest portrayal of the "unpleasant truths," the horrors and emotions, that permeate the minds of many high schoolers even to this day. But he pulled it out of publication "because in my judgment it might be hurting people, and that made it the responsible thing to do," King wrote, while also taking the opportunity to address the need for gun control in America. "Assault weapons will remain readily available to crazy people until the powerful pro-gun forces in this country decide to do a similar turnaround. They must accept responsibility, recognizing that responsibility is not the same as culpability."

King went on to explain further and touched on some key themes that we psychologists know now to be true about what really does instigate school shootings. "It took more than one slim novel to cause [the shooters] to do what they did. These were unhappy boys with deep psychological problems, boys who were bullied at school and bruised at home by parental neglect or outright abuse. My book did not break [them] or turn them into killers; they found something in my book that spoke to them because they were already broken. Yet I did see 'Rage' as a possible accelerant, which is why I pulled it from sale. You don't leave a can of gasoline where a boy with firebug tendencies can lay hands on it."

What a thoughtful, responsible man—gun industry, take note.

Indeed, Cox was no doubt broken and simmering with discontent, and the book ignited a fire inside his head. It had an immense impact on him. He could relate. Cox, like Decker, felt he had no future.

Hopelessness was tearing him up inside. People needed to know what they were doing wrong, that they had caused this to happen.

"It held an interesting premise that, you know, this kid would detain his classmates and then kind of take the opportunity to tear down a lot of the superficial walls that everybody puts up while they're in high school, the cliques and all the bullshit everybody's gotta go through," Cox told me. "And I had decided it sounded like a pretty good idea."

Jeffrey Cox was born to Jerry and Barbara Cox, whose marriage began to crumble from the moment his mother became pregnant with him. They soon separated.

His father was a landscape architect whom Cox would describe as a man of strict discipline who saw great promise in his son, even making him dress up for school in button-downs, slacks, and fancy shoes. He expected Cox to be getting straight A's and one day attend an Ivy League school.

But as Cox explained it, that wasn't really who he was. He never saw himself living a traditional nine-to-five life or working a suit-and-tie job, but he did his best to put on a show for his dad, whom he lived with until he was about fourteen.

With his mother, a bank manager who worked late hours, Cox felt ignored at times. At other times, he said, she would lash out at him angrily for no reason at all. He was stuck between his parents' two worlds and conflicting views of the young man he was supposed to grow up to be. It was an incredibly confusing time for him. So he sought acceptance for who he was in other places. He made new friends with the popular crowd and partied with them late into the night. He was just searching for, well, himself.

But none of it would stop his downward spiral. He was lost.

"So I waited until I was eighteen, because I couldn't buy a gun," he told me during our prison interview. "And I turned eighteen on the eighth of April, went out and bought an AR-15 and a lot of ammunition, and decided that I was going to do this."

And do this, he did.

It was April 26, 1988, when Cox arrived on the campus of San Gabriel High School ready to carry out his plan. His semiautomatic rifle was too big to fit in his duffel bag, so he carried it in a box, with the bag containing what he called "miscellaneous crap"—some books, tapes, radios—slung over his shoulder.

Just outside the classroom door, he pulled the rifle out from the box and loaded it with ammunition. "Someone else opened it to exit, and I…can't even remember her name but I asked her to step back in. She did," he told me, his eyes shifting down to the floor and a concerned look on his face, as if almost embarrassed by what he was about to tell me next.

"The teacher immediately asked me what was I doing, what's going on. And I told her, 'Uh, we've got a hostage situation.' And she got very upset, and I asked her to leave. I didn't want her there. And she refused, and I threatened one of the students that was a few feet away of me in the front row. So she left."

Students began to frantically run to a door at the back of the room. Cox aimed his rifle at the ceiling and fired off a shot.

"People stopped running. Everybody froze…. I remember someone called the room on the interschool phone, and I picked it up and whoever it was, was telling me that there was a situation and you needed to get all your students out of the classroom and this and that, and I told them, 'This is where the situation is,' and I hung up."

He paused and shook his head back and forth, closing his eyes with a look of shame on his face.

"And then I remember blathering on about something, about how easy it was to get a gun and how it wasn't right or something like that, and people started asking me questions: 'What's going on?' and 'What's happening?' I don't remember everything specifically, but I do remember that I had said if I was going to start shooting people, I'd start with people I didn't know. Like that would make it more comfortable for me."

The entire ordeal lasted less than two hours, during which time he demanded one million dollars and explained he wanted to flee to Brazil, while just rambling about all the other reasons he was doing this. The situation came to what Cox would later call an anticlimactic end when he was rushed by students and tackled, then held down while heavily armed police officers flooded the room and took him uneventfully into custody. During the struggle, he tried to shoot again, but somebody's clothing got stuck in the rifle's action.

"What was your plan?" I asked him.

He looked around the room, his eyebrows raised, his lips clenched together. "Ah, the plan. Yeah, I thought at first I wanted to kill myself right in front of everybody. I thought, you know, we do this whole little afternoon of chitchat, work all these problems out, and then in this grand operatic moment I, *beeesh*, blow my brains out, right? What do I got to lose?

"And then I started thinking, *What the hell, I'll ask for money and I'll be the guy who got away with it…the D.B. Cooper of my time*…. I would figure out a way to get out of the room, and I think I was pretty much playing it by ear at that point."

It was clear that Cox really had no plan at all. He was just a super-smart but screwed-up kid who had made a ridiculously bad choice and was lucky to even still be alive. His world had just shrunk so much that he had descended to a place where he felt he had no other options, nothing but to at least be remembered for something, anything.

"Everyone else was going to go on and be doctors and lawyers…and I was going to go on and be anonymous. Just another schnook. And I couldn't deal with that," he said with a nervous chuckle. "That would have taken a little too much introspection, and I was not at all prepared to do that. *The more you think about it, the more you realize that you had it all. And why did I blow it? So I could piss my dad off? That's great.…* That's what I was saying to myself. And so I figured, you know, it wouldn't be such a bad thing. I'd be remembered. There'd be a certain grim happiness to that, I guess. Nobody would forget—forget me. Yeah, it's a little selfish, but what the heck. I was a kid."

And a kid he was. Looking back now, I see that he realized something that became profound to me in my studies of other school shooters, a way of thinking we see in nearly every single case, whether the shooter lives or dies in the end. He saw the world in only black or white. There was no gray.

"We never think that there's anything but the two choices in front of you, and at the time that's what I thought.... I thought this was my only option, that it was my only choice. This is what I have to do," he told me. Not only was the world black and white, but there was the ever-present idea of an unstoppable forward motion once the plan was set into place, what we refer to as a sense of inevitability.

No one ever asked him about the radios—they attributed his having them to his just being a stupid kid. But one of the radios was actually supposed to be for him to communicate with a friend outside the siege zone. In fact, at least a half dozen of his friends knew what he was planning to do, and that he had obtained a rifle. Not one of them stepped forward to share information.

Cox was sentenced to five years in prison but was released in 1990 after having been given credit for time already served behind bars leading up to and throughout his trial. Not long after his release, he fell in with a bad crowd, obviously having been influenced by some of the most hardened criminals during his time in prison and looking yet again for a way to fit in. This time it was a seedier peer group.

He ended up participating in a 1992 drug-dealing-related killing with several other men in Arizona. He was caught with the man's body in pieces in his refrigerator. Cox was sentenced to seventeen years in prison for second-degree murder. He was released in 2010.

I recognize that given Cox's repeated criminal forays, the second one a horrendous murder, he's a pretty flawed character. But what I learned from him has become a centerpiece of my teachings across the country about school shooters and what we as a society can do to prevent them. What we can do to help these kids before it's too late—like it was for Cox?

I know for many, especially the victims of their viciousness, it's hard to look upon these killers with pity. And truthfully, some just don't deserve it. But as I've studied them more and more, digging extensively into their backgrounds, their upbringing, their relationships with their peers, speaking face-to-face with the ones who have survived, it has become clear that there are numerous variables that play a role in school shootings.

Sometimes we as a society must also bear some of the responsibility. Why do we have guns everywhere and sell them seemingly to anyone? And many times it's the parents who shoulder the heaviest burden. Did they abuse? Did they enable? Did they ignore? Were they just not there? Did they leave their guns out for easy access?

Even Eric Harris and Dylan Klebold were not completely lost causes before they carried out the Columbine attack. While clearly evil in their intentions, they telegraphed so much of their plans in advance that had we known then what we know now about these sorts of kids, that assault may very well have been prevented.

Klebold's mother, Sue, wrote about the shooting in a 2009 essay published in *O, The Oprah Magazine*. "Dylan changed everything I believed about myself, about God, about family, and about love," she wrote. "Once I saw his journals, it was clear to me that Dylan entered the school with the intention of dying there."[17]

While she may not have known his specific violent plans, there were multiple flags she was aware of, including a violent paper he had turned in a few weeks prior to the massacre, and the fact that Dylan had asked her for a gun as a Christmas present. This was in addition to the trouble he got into junior year of high school, which included vandalizing a locker with anti-gay graffiti, hacking the school computer system to gain access to student locker combinations, and breaking into a van.

Sue Klebold complained that the school's consequences may have "alienated him." On the heels of that prior acting out, including the diversion program, she asked Dylan, "Do you need counseling?" His response was, "No, I will prove to you I'm fine." She said that her "denial factor was very big," and that if someone had come to her with details about the violent plans, "I probably would have thought my kid was not capable of this." Clearly, she was out of touch, minimized what was going on with her son, partially blaming the school for causing his alienation,

---

[17] Susan Klebold, "I Will Never Know Why," *O, The Oprah Magazine*, November 2009, http://www.oprah.com/omagazine/susan-klebolds-o-magazine-essay-i-will-never-know-why.

as opposed to the absence of parental structure, boundaries, and limits. Her one admission of error was that she should have listened more.[18]

In his 2012 book *Far From the Tree: Parents, Children and the Search for Identity*, Andrew Solomon recounts how Sue Klebold, upon learning that her son was among the shooters, prayed that he would take his own life. "I had a sudden vision of what he might be doing. And so while every other mother in Littleton was praying that her child was safe, I had to pray that mine would die before he hurt anyone else," she told Solomon.[19]

She would later go on to write her own book, *A Mother's Reckoning: Living in the Aftermath of Tragedy*, with the stated goal of providing insights to help other families recognize when their own child is in distress. Having heard her speak recently, I am not convinced she truly comprehends all she missed and the structure she failed to provide, but the message of what a parent has to live with when their kid does something terrible is undeniable.

And so with what we know now about the Columbine effect comes a greater responsibility for us all to pay attention, to intervene, to come to the rescue of all of our children, the would-be victims and shooters alike. And regarding the would-be shooters thwarted at the precipice, that often amounts to some hard choices and questions: Does society need to be protected from them? For how long? Is what's wrong with them even treatable? In my experience, so-called treatment focuses on traditional variables and ignores important issues more directly on point, like have you moved the teen from enjoying that violent movie in his head, shifted his choice in heroes, addressed his addiction to imagined power, somehow gotten him to start giving a shit and stopped his injustice collection?

Too often the reports are: "Johnny is getting along great in the juvenile facility. He hasn't had any fights here. He's going to groups." But

---

[18] Sue Klebold, "My Son Was a Columbine Shooter. This is My Story," Association of Threat Assessment Professionals Annual Training Conference, August 14, 2019.

[19] Andrew Solomon, *Far From the Tree: Parents, Children and the Search for Identity*, (New York: Scribner, 2012).

nowhere is anyone asking or talking with him about the variables that directly relate to his risk. Hardly reassuring.

But at the end of the day, who is really responsible? How about this: the offenders and those who enabled them—because they *wanted* to do what they did.

As mentioned, a little over a year before Harris and Klebold committed the Columbine shooting, they had been arrested for breaking into a van, resulting in charges for theft, criminal mischief, and trespassing. Afterwards, they had been deemed rehabilitated, worthy of redemption, and "diverted," including to some community service, counseling, and treatment. Rest assured, private lawyers advocated for leniency and the expungement they ultimately received for their first brush with the law. Where is the accountability for *these* individuals, who collectively blessed them as cured and rehabilitated and pled for leniency, as fingers of blame were pointed at the police and school after the shooting?

While all school shooters don't draw their inspiration directly from Columbine, we still see thematic similarities soundly rooted in the usual hateful desperation of young people who want to die and to take people with them, to punish those who they perceive have driven them to their actions. Many shooters display a similar sense of hopelessness and rejection, of being outcasts among their peers, bullied or ignored, and feel the need for notoriety in the absence of social bonds. Forging these dynamics is a simmering anger and rage, converted to a plan of retaliation.

Evan Ramsey is just one more example of someone who could have been stopped.

On February 19, 1997, in the rural Alaskan town of Bethel, Ramsey, age sixteen, walked into his high school with a shotgun. In just fifteen minutes, he fatally shot the principal and another student and wounded several others.

Compared to Jeffrey Cox and some of the others, Ramsey had an extremely troubled childhood. But in a different way. There is not just one violent pathway. Cox's parents were well-intentioned but preoccupied; Ramsey's were very damaged, and the replacements were perhaps even worse.

In 1986, his father, Don Ramsey, incensed at the publisher of the *Anchorage Times* for withdrawing a fuming political advertisement he had paid them to print, stormed the building and shot the place up. No one was killed, but he went away to prison for ten years.

The family soon began to fall apart. Ramsey and his two brothers watched their mother lose herself in an extended drunken binge; they felt as if she had chosen alcohol over them. The boys were taken away and spent years shuffling between foster homes, where Ramsey claimed to have been beaten and sexually abused.

He was bullied repeatedly in school and initially reported these attacks but was told by the adult administrators, he said, to just ignore it and suck it up. It would all eventually stop, they told him. But it never did. What he actually so desperately wanted was an adult—someone, anyone—to help him deal with his despair and depression. To stop the bullshit he was being subjected to. But no one ever intervened.

He eventually ended up living in the home of Sue Hare, the school district's superintendent. Guilt-ridden years after the attack, she would tell the *Anchorage Daily News* that she truly believed Ramsey was a victim.

"If people want to feel sorry for someone, I recommend Evan," Hare said.[20]

Ramsey began the siege at the school with the intention of killing himself, but he later had a change of heart. It was not the first time he had thought of suicide. He had attempted to kill himself on at least one prior occasion, walking into an Alaskan river with the intent of drowning, but was dissuaded by people who witnessed his act.

His violent intentions were serious. He obtained the gun from where it sat, out in the open, in the family's entryway. Everyone has guns in Alaska. But Ramsey was the wrong kid to be allowed such easy access.

"I felt a lot of anger. I did not know why people picked on me. I wondered why," he said in a low, sad voice during a prison interview with me in 2001.

---

[20] Lisa Demer, "Evan Ramsey's Tattered Life Filled Him with Rage. Then He Brought a Shotgun to School," *Anchorage Daily News*, February 18, 2017, https://www.adn.com/alaska-news/2017/02/18/evan-ramseys-tattered-life-filled-him-with-rage-then-he-brought-a-shotgun-to-school/.

"Describe that mental picture of your plan," I prodded.

"Me going to that high school, doing something to scare everybody, kind of get everybody to leave me alone."

Ramsey even told a few other kids of his plans prior to the attack, but he says they only encouraged him, never attempting to talk him out of it. When he told them he wanted to kill himself, they told him to kill the people who had messed with him instead, that this would earn him respect. They even showed him how to use the gun. When he showed up at the school, firearm in hand, a small crowd of kids had gathered to watch, aware of the plan. Not one of them had informed an adult.

In fact, two of the boys who knew of the plan, including the one who had taught him how to shoot the gun, were later charged in juvenile court as being accessories to Ramsey's crime.

It was toward the end of the siege at the school, after he had already shot people, that Ramsey realized he did not want to die. He ran toward the school library as police arrived on the scene. He fired some shots, and cops shot back.

"I don't want to die!" Ramsey yelled before throwing down his shotgun and surrendering.

He is now serving a 198-year sentence and won't become eligible for parole until 2063, when he would be eighty-two years old. Ironically, he is locked up in the same prison where his father was incarcerated. Full circle.

He was obviously an extremely troubled kid.

"A few days before the crime, what were your thoughts?" I asked him.

"That all the pain and suffering would end."

Ramsey's case had all the signs and themes of other school shooters— prior thoughts of suicide, worthlessness, easy access to a gun in the home, a sense that this was the fault of others, family dysfunction, and violence being the answer to all his woes.

Today, these sorts of thoughts resonate even more, specifically in the post-Columbine world, where angry, disaffected, social-media-immersed youths who feel like nothing yet feel entitled to everything come to believe that a gun is the answer, that killing is the solution to all their problems.

And part of the problem in America is that so many people have guns—that we lack the courage to recognize that firearm access is what makes the difference between a casualty and a fatality. Dr. Meloy and I tracked a number of school violence events in China. In China there were many casualties but very few fatalities. Why? No guns. The attackers used hammers and knives, and the victims could strike back defensively—as they did—with rakes and other implements.

In fact, the Chinese government was budgeting for rakes or other tools as their go-to defensive weapon of choice for their schools. Rakes. When violent offenders don't have guns in their hands, you can defend yourself with a rake.

Repeating the words of the Second Amendment will never bring back the dead or assuage the pain of the grieving, but the money from pro-gun lobbyists will still line the pockets of—and help secure elections for—so many politicians who sell their influence to the detriment of the greater good of society. The same gun-control debate continues to this day, while politicians, their hands dirty with National Rifle Association payoffs, continue to obstruct the enactment of meaningful solutions for keeping guns out of the hands of the unfit and dangerous.

On the other side of the debate, the American Civil Liberties Union, for example, and so-called civil libertarians impede meaningful change by fighting against restrictive confinement options, such as forced institutionalization, for even the most violent of criminals, claiming that would be a violation of their civil rights. Weighing in recently on the gun debate, the ACLU opposed—that's right, opposed a law that would have flagged individuals too impaired due to their severe mental illness to manage their own Social Security benefits, arguing that a disability shouldn't allow the automatic denial of any constitutional right.[21] So if

---

[21] German Lopez, "Yes, Congress Did Repeal a Rule That Made It Harder for People with Mental Illness to Buy a Gun," Vox, October 3, 2017, https://www.vox.com/policy-and-politics/2017/2/3/14496774/congress-guns-mental-illness.

you are so sick you cannot manage your Social Security benefits, you should be trusted with a firearm? Does that really make sense?

But where is the voice for the right to life, liberty, and the pursuit of happiness for the dead and injured at the hands of these maniacs? We simply have to do more to try to prevent these school shootings, and part of that starts with good, common-sense gun-control measures that would help keep firearms out of the hands of these kids.

But that's just a start. Even more important is for us, as a society, to begin to pay more attention to our youth. Don't get me wrong; many of them, most of them, even though they are just teenagers, should be held accountable for their crimes, because even in their emotional state, they largely knew the difference between right and wrong. But in this day and age of social media—Facebook, YouTube, and the like—most of these school shooters telegraph their intentions long before they carry out their plans. Sometimes it's a cry for help, and other times it's the loud and repetitive declaration of a one-sided war, a fatwa that too often goes unnoticed or ignored by those around them.

One Finland school shooter posted more than seventy YouTube videos in the months prior to his mass homicide, including on the day of the incident, indicating his plans. A year later, another Finland school shooter was targeting his college. This time the YouTube postings were reported, and the police visited him but felt they did not have enough to remove his guns or hospitalize him.

He assaulted his school the next day.

Let me be clear. My goal in studying and teaching school threat assessment is not merely to save future victims but also to help save the would-be killers from themselves. As parents, teachers, and peers, it is our responsibility to take notice, to pay more attention, to interfere, to have uncomfortable conversations, to not turn a blind eye and hope for the best, thinking that disturbing behavior is just a typical teenage phase.

We can no longer afford to do so. It is time to see something, say something, because most school shooters engage in leakage—talking about their plans beforehand. Once plans are reported, knowledge-able professionals in law enforcement can detect if there is pathway warning behavior, such as weapon-seeking, fixation (being stuck on the ideas that retaliation and violence are the answer to their problems), energy-burst warning behavior (preparing and rehearsing thoughts and actions), and last-resort warning behavior (expressing desperation and setting dates and times for irreversible mayhem). These variables are all highly associated with most, if not all, school shootings and other kinds of school violence.

After so many recent school shootings, a movement has begun to grow among survivors, victims' family members, and even law enforcement, pleading with the media not to glamorize these killers, claiming it only emboldens future shooters seeking out the same notoriety. Don't name the killers. Don't publish their pictures. Don't even talk about their crimes and motives. Focus on the victims.

While I agree, to a point, that there is a correlation between media coverage of killers and the sensationalizing of their lives and crimes and the acts of future school shooters, I think we do ourselves a disservice by not explaining their motives, upbringings, thought processes, and behaviors prior to the killings.

While we certainly don't want to glamorize them, we can learn and share what led them to carry out the killings so that we are better aware of the signs to look for in order to maybe interrupt the next one. If we don't become more present as a society in the lives of these troubled youths, the next school shooting will be just a repeat of the previous one, with the same trail of impending doom having gone unheeded.

Maybe Jeffrey Cox could have been saved. So many victims could have been saved. Other killers could have been saved. Cox wished that someone had just stopped him, told him how crazy his plan was, told him he could have a life just like anyone else. He said he told several friends of his plan but no one interfered—again, there were so many missed opportunities that we continue to see in school shootings.

"I think I would have liked to have been dissuaded. I know I would have liked to have been dissuaded, but nobody ever did," Cox told me. If someone, anyone, would have been more tuned in to Cox, his depression, and his failure to follow through on risk-reduction plans like therapy—what he did might have been avoided.

And in Cox's case, perhaps the next terrible decision—involvement in that murder in Arizona—might also have been averted. "I realize now, you look back and you realize," Jeff told me, closing his eyes tightly, breathing a sigh of exasperation with himself, *"Jesus, how stupid can you possibly be?"*

I say, to put it bluntly, how stupid can *we all* possibly be?

Death Is a Duty

The Violent True Believer

"A movement is pioneered by men of words, materialized
by fanatics, and consolidated by men of action."

—Eric Hoffer, from *The True Believer:*
Thoughts on the Nature of Mass Movements

Timothy McVeigh had finally had enough.

Enough of the government's killing its own people in places like Waco and Ruby Ridge. Enough of the political elite's trying to tamp down Americans' freedoms, trying to gut the Second Amendment, trying to take away the very rights this country was founded on. He imagined himself the first hero of the second American Revolution.

It was time to act. On April 19, 1995, he drove a rental truck full of explosives to the front of the Alfred P. Murrah Federal Building in Oklahoma City and casually walked away. Minutes later, the blast ripped the building to shreds, killing 168 people, including nineteen children, and injuring more than 650 others. His mission was accomplished. Until the terror attacks on September 11, 2001, this was the worst episode of mass homicide on American soil.

He was later executed for his criminal actions.

Syed Rizwan Farook and his wife, Tashfeen Malik, stormed the Inland Regional Center in San Bernardino, California, where dozens of employees of the county Department of Public Health were having a Christmas party in a rented banquet room. These employees provide services to developmentally disabled citizens.

The married couple came armed with multiple high-powered weapons on that Wednesday, December 2, 2015, and in the chaos that ensued, killed fourteen people and wounded twenty-two others.

Farook was a U.S.-born citizen whose parents had emigrated from Pakistan; he worked as a San Bernardino County health department employee. Malik was a Pakistani-born lawful permanent resident of the United States. She declared allegiance to the Islamic State on Facebook just before the shootings began. While authorities believe Farook and Malik were self-radicalized through the internet, the terror group didn't take long to seize some of the credit, proclaiming the two as "followers of the Islamic State" who carried out the attack as willing "soldiers."

Both of them died in a shootout with police.

Cesar Altieri Sayoc was an ardent supporter of President Donald Trump who had seized on the president's angry rhetoric during his 2016 presidential campaign. It was everything he wanted to hear, and his support was solidified even more during Trump's inauguration speech announcing to the nation that "the forgotten men and women of our country will be forgotten no longer."

Sayoc felt he was among the forgotten and that he finally had someone in his corner. He railed against former President Barack Obama and Oprah Winfrey on Twitter and Facebook with racial epithets, threatened former Vice President Joe Biden, and praised Trump and conservative causes.

It would soon be time to take action himself, to fight back for the president against all who opposed him. Authorities say Sayoc mailed sixteen improvised explosive devices targeting thirteen people toward the end of 2018, attempting to create an atmosphere of fear and intimidation for all those he felt had wronged Trump. The targets included Trump's favorite adversaries: Biden, Obama, Hillary Clinton, CNN, and a number of other former and current Democratic officials, donors, and members of Congress.

Luckily, none of the devices detonated and no one was hurt.

When Sayoc was arrested by the FBI in South Florida on October 26, 2018, agents found Sayoc's white van plastered with stickers praising Trump and condemning liberals. One sticker had the crosshairs of a rifle over an image of Hillary Clinton.

Joseph Paul Franklin remains to this day among the most prolific racially motivated serial killers in America. He worshipped Nazis and the notorious Red Brigade of Italy, a militant left-wing organization that gained notoriety in the 1970s for kidnappings, murders, and bombings. He was particularly impressed with the original Ku Klux Klan, which was founded in the 1860s as a violent terrorist organization to overthrow the government, often targeting African-American leaders. The original Klan didn't fuck around with bullshit rallies as their primary activity—they were violent and used physical assault and murder to pursue their objectives.

Franklin joined the third incarnation of the Ku Klux Klan for a few months but soon decided its members were too soft—all talk and not enough action. Protesting and sitting around complaining, as he saw it, just didn't cut it. They had strayed from the objectives of their forefathers.

There needed to be more killing, and his mission was to hopefully incite other like-minded racists to take violent action. And he was one hell of a frightening criminal, having killed twenty-three people, by his count, between 1977 and 1980 in an effort to cleanse society of Jews, mixed-race couples, and black people—he believed Jews and blacks were lesser races that needed to be exterminated. A fan of Charles Manson, Franklin hoped to instigate a race war that would create a whites-only nation and rid society of what he saw as nothing more than vile vermin.

At first glance, these criminals appear to have absolutely nothing in common. An antigovernment bomber. A pair of Islamic extremists. A politically driven whack job. A racist bent on serial murder.

But a deeper dive into their motivations reveals a strikingly similar pattern. All of them were driven to kill based on a profound belief in their own evil ideologies. To each of them, killing was a justifiable act of self-defense or a means of advancing their cause. They targeted and killed with a purpose.

It is that underlying theme that brought my fellow forensic psychologist Dr. J. Reid Meloy to coin the term "violent true believer" in a post-September 11 terror attack analysis we co-authored with some other colleagues.

The definition we came up with for what we now in the profession call the VTB is "an individual who appears to be committed to an ideology or belief system, whether secular or religious, that advances the killing of themselves and/or others as a legitimate means to further a particular goal."

Part of the term originated from the 1951 book *The True Believer: Thoughts on the Nature of Mass Movements* by American philosopher Eric Hoffer, a work that takes readers into the minds of fanatics and is a penetrating study on how one becomes such an individual.

Hoffer observed that "a movement is pioneered by men of words, materialized by fanatics, and consolidated by men of action."[22] His insights are so on point, brilliant, and erudite that the original thought Dr. Meloy and I had was to label these individuals simply "true believers."

But there were developments since the publication of Hoffer's book, new murderers, and we were in the immediate and shocking aftermath of mass homicide in the thousands brought to our soil on September 11 by Islamic extremists.

The level of violence was incalculable.

Dr. Meloy decided that a more descriptive term was needed to convey the true nature of these criminals; hence he added the word "violent" to "true believer," and the term "violent true believer" was born into scholarly and practical use—in our post-September 11 article—for identifying and studying this growing trend of fanatical homicide.

The VTB can come from all walks of life, and the desire to kill is fueled by a variety of religious, political, and racial philosophies. These

---

[22] Eric Hoffer, *The True Believer: Thoughts on the Nature of Mass Movements*, (New York: Harper & Brothers, 1951).

philosophies are more often than not rooted in a misperceived and misinterpreted set of ideas that eschew all reason and rationale in pursuit of the achievement of one fixed goal, however misguided, and these people are steadfastly committed to their beliefs while ignoring any objections or alternative opinions. They are closed-minded to the nth degree.

These are extremely dangerous individuals or groups who cannot be swayed by facts or figures and are driven solely by a deep, disturbing desire to kill in the name of whatever belief system they become so poisoned by.

But we cannot explore these violent ideological mindsets of today without first acknowledging those of the past, including religious and philosophical fanaticism that has led to millions of deaths. Violent true believers are not new and, in fact, have led churches, armies, and the bloodiest revolutions throughout history, killing in the name of whatever ideology they embrace.

So many people have killed and been killed over centuries in the name of God and Allah. The crucifixion by the Romans of Christians who refused to acknowledge pagan gods or the emperor's divinity, the stoning of nonbelievers, the Inquisition, the execution of "witches" during the Salem witch trials, and the Crusades are just a few examples.

We see such religiously motivated murders today in the form of Islamic extremism, like the actions of the San Bernardino attackers, and horrendous killings carried out worldwide in the name of Allah and the Koran.

To be clear, religious ideology has been one of the most fundamental justifications for violence throughout history. It is nothing new. On my office bookshelf, I've got a slew of violence-themed books—*Casebook of a Crime Psychiatrist*, *Mindhunter*, *The Turner Diaries*—and right smack in the middle are the Bible and the Koran.

The violent true believer has existed for as long as there has been epistemology—the study of what distinguishes a justified belief system from a mere opinion—and for as long as there have been differences between people and the concomitant notion that everyone else is wrong and they are right. In short, the VTB has been around for all of history.

The presence of violent true believers is particularly prominent in the realm of the unverifiable—for example, those who draw inspiration from individual interpretations of the Bible or Koran.

The other elephant in the room is that some of the worst VTBs perpetrated their callous crimes in the twentieth century, including the likes of Adolf Hitler, who killed some six million Jews in the Holocaust and five million other "non-Aryans"; and Joseph Stalin, who killed up to twenty million in Russia as he sought to implement his vision of Communism.

Hitler's inspiration and manipulation through violence and propaganda are a disturbing reminder of the horrors that are possible when singular ideas based on unrealistic premises are inflicted upon the masses—his idea being that Jews had to be killed in order to create a better race for all of humanity, the so-called Final Solution. Hitler believed that the great racial struggle against the Jews was apocalyptic in nature and that the entire European structure and way of life could be demolished if the Jewish conspiracy to reign supreme were to go unchecked.

Enter Joseph Paul Franklin, the epitome of the modern-day racially motivated violent true believer.

His festering ideas and frustrations with the state of America culminated in an epiphany on Christmas Eve 1975 that he would pursue a mission of starting a racial holy war. His turning point was loss of residence and inability to get a job, but these factors were heaped on a lifetime of frustration and layers of hate and indoctrination in Nazi and supremacist rhetoric.

In 1976, he legally changed his name from James Clayton Vaughn Jr. to Joseph Paul Franklin—the Joseph Paul part being an homage to Nazi propaganda minister Paul Joseph Goebbels, and the Franklin part being a nod to Benjamin Franklin, whom he considered a true American.

He embraced what he believed to be his destiny and fate. "Everything we do today, I feel we agreed to do before we were born," he would later tell me.

Over Labor Day weekend in 1976 in Atlanta, Franklin stalked an interracial couple and sprayed them in the face with mace. It was his first known attack and would quickly escalate to killing, which he believed to be a much more effective way to advance his cause. He didn't want to be seen as lackadaisical in his efforts to exterminate lesser beings, and truly wanted to inspire others to murder.

He went on to bomb synagogues, kill Jews, gun down random black people with a sniper rifle, and even kill white people who acknowledged having been involved in interracial relationships.

Franklin also admitted to shooting civil rights leader Vernon Jordan and paralyzing pornography publisher Larry Flynt with a bullet to his spine, infuriated by the interracial sex depicted in Flynt's *Hustler* magazine.

He was, indeed, a true believer in that he thought that what he was doing was right, that his cause was justified, and that killing was necessary. The mongrelization of the white race had to be stopped. Racial separatism and purification—at the point of a gun—had to be achieved by inciting a racial holy war.

In the end, he was convicted of murder in multiple states and received the death penalty in Missouri for the killing of a Jewish man outside a synagogue. He was executed by lethal injection in 2013.

When I met Franklin in prison a number of years before his death, he seemed proud of his accomplishments.

"Would it be safe to say, Joseph, that you were the most prolific assassin that the United States has seen?" I asked him, adding an affirmative answer myself, placating his sense of bravado, and hoping to draw out his true feelings about what he had done: "Because I think that is true."

"You think, really?" he responded proudly, his eyes widening. "I guess you could say that. Speaking of prolific, I've looked at some of the records, some of the records they have of stuff I've done, and I'm kind of surprised at all the stuff I was doing so fast in different cities. I'd do one job, then go another place and kill a couple more people—you know, you know what I'm talking about?"

He laughed at the thought of just how good he was at killing, just how good he was at his "job" of getting rid of the blacks and Jews. He viewed killing as a task.

One thing, he told me, that he really took issue with was the moniker that had been attached to him since his arrest: "I don't consider myself a serial killer."

"What do you consider yourself?"

"I prefer the term 'multiple slayer.'"

"And the difference to you is what?"

"Well, the serial killer has that connotation of Ted Bundy and Henry Lee Lucas, whatever that whacko's name is, the crazy bastard that killed all those women down in Texas. You know, people like that, you know, sex killers. I was not a sex killer. I didn't go around raping women and murdering them. It wasn't my MO, my style."

His laid-back Southern drawl was deceptively disarming.

He felt it was wrong to lump him in with the likes of those serial killers because, well, they were crazy. He felt his mission was rooted in reality and backed up by a reasonable cause. Those folks just killed for the sake of killing. It offended him.

He was a proud "multiple slayer" fighting for a cause, not just some mindless killer, though he did take great joy in his number of kills. "I'm a little bit ahead of Billy the Kid," Franklin told me with a grin, referencing the infamous American West outlaw and gunfighter. He saw himself as an outlaw, a rebel, and later expressed some regret at having shot Larry Flynt because he viewed Flynt as a kindred spirit in his bucking of convention.

In the weeks before his execution, Franklin would begin to express regret and remorse for killings he had committed. I suspect it was all for show in an effort to save his own skin as he appealed the death penalty right up until the very last day, right up until the needle delivered upon him the same fate he had delivered upon his victims. He, like all the condemned people on death row, was afforded substantial due process, unlike those he killed.

In a telephone interview with *The Cincinnati Enquirer* just hours before his execution, Franklin said he would have liked to have apologized to the families of his victims and asked them for forgiveness. "I'd like for people to think of me as a person who is filled with a lot of love for people, not filled with hate for people," Franklin told the newspaper.[23]

He said of himself during the time of the killings: "That was not my true self.... I'm a human being just like everybody else." But he also spoke of how he considered himself a "warrior."

"I felt that, as misguided as I was, I felt I was fighting to preserve the white race." Misguided indeed. As are all VTBs, but their core belief in what they are doing leaves little doubt in *their* minds that their calling is based on a cause greater than themselves.

Some VTBs are willing to, intend to, and want to die for that cause, while others simply accept it to be *likely* that they will die as part of their violent acts. Franklin, McVeigh, and Kaczynski, for example, had no desire or intent to die; in fact, they wanted to live as long as possible to continue carrying out their "missions."

Suicide by perpetrators during a mass casualty event, like the September 11 attacks, serves to remove an element of planning that could otherwise complicate the scenario—namely, the necessity of crafting an escape or a detection-prevention plan to avoid capture.

And those who intend to die usually have an element of martyrdom or are seeking some other sort of notoriety, something they believe is diminished by incarceration in prison or a death sentence carried out on them by someone else. It represents their desire for control over the entire scenario.

The Timothy McVeighs of the world, like Franklin, have unrealistic, overvalued ideas that somehow their actions will initiate an uprising and are absolutely justified. McVeigh never intended to die, but he took solace in the fact that he would be put to death for a cause greater than himself.

For people like him, surviving the event and planning other events keeps the action going and continues to fill up their bottomless narcissistic

---

[23] Kimball Perry, "Racist serial killer: I deserve to be executed," *USA Today*, November 19, 2013, https://www.usatoday.com/story/news/nation/2013/11/19/serial-killer-deserve -to-be-executed/3641771/.

reservoir with more hate, with more attention, with more notoriety. But death is still a reward.

McVeigh maintained until the end a deep loyalty to his cause, to his "mission."

He never apologized, and in a letter to his hometown newspaper, *The Buffalo News*, he reasoned away the bombing as a "legit tactic" in response to the U.S. government's own violent acts—specifically, the FBI raids in Waco, Texas, and Ruby Ridge, Idaho, that had left dozens dead. He wrote that he was "sorry these people had to lose their lives. But that's the nature of the beast."[24]

At his execution in 2001, McVeigh didn't speak a word. Instead, he handed a copy of the poem "Invictus" by William Ernest Henley to the prison warden. "I thank whatever gods may be for my unconquerable soul," the poem reads. "I am the master of my fate: I am the captain of my soul."[25]

Ted Kaczynski was a strange guy with an unusual bitterness against technology. He seemed content to wreak havoc on that system and gain mass attention for his views but had no real end game in mind.

A Harvard University graduate with an immensely high IQ—some say it was equal to that of Albert Einstein—Kaczynski is not the typical mass or serial murderer but fits neatly into the category of a violent true believer.

Hell-bent on delivering death to support his rage against technology and all of the evils he thought it would soon bring upon society, Kaczynski, given the moniker "The Unabomber," killed and maimed for nearly two decades, mailing or hand-delivering sophisticated homemade bombs across the country that killed three people and injured twenty-four others. He may not have killed as many as the others did, but his violence affected the airline industry big-time. Don't leave your package

---

[24] Dan Herbeck, Lou Michel, Michael Beebe, and Gene Warner. "McVeigh Hints at Some Regrets," *The Buffalo News*, June 9, 2001, https://buffalonews.com/2001/06/10/mcveigh-hints-at-some-regrets/.

[25] "McVeigh's final statement," *The Guardian*, June 11, 2001, https://www.theguardian.com/world/2001/jun/11/mcveigh.usa1.

or luggage unattended. Sun Tzu said, "Kill one, frighten thousands," the goal of terror.

The FBI worked feverishly for years to track down a suspect as the nation wondered with terrifying suspense where the next bomb might hit. The big break in the case finally came in 1995 when Kaczynski sent a thirty-five-thousand-word manifesto to *The New York Times* and *The Washington Post*. In the lengthy screed, titled "Industrial Society and Its Future," Kaczynski laid out his motives for the attacks and his perverted view that modern society was being destroyed by technology.

"The Industrial Revolution and its consequences have been a disaster for the human race," Kaczynski wrote. "To those who think that all this sounds like science fiction, we point out that yesterday's science fiction is today's fact. The Industrial Revolution has radically altered man's environment and way of life, and it is only to be expected that as technology is increasingly applied to the human body and mind, man himself will be altered as radically as his environment and way of life have been."[26]

He went on to explain away his own crimes as justifiable to draw attention to his cause, again exhibiting all the attributes of a violent true believer: "There is nothing wrong with violence in itself. In any particular case, whether violence is good or bad depends on how it is used and the purpose for which it is used."

Kaczynski demanded that his manifesto be published or he would send another bomb to an unspecified destination "with intent to kill."

A fevered debate ensued within the FBI about what to do. The agents didn't want to be seen as giving in to terrorist demands. In the end, FBI Director Louis Freeh and Attorney General Janet Reno agreed to have it published in the hope that a reader might be able to help identify the author. It was a brilliant decision.

The New York Times and *The Washington Post* published the manifesto, and in the ensuing days, thousands of people came forward suggesting possible suspects. One of those who came forward stood out to the FBI task force assigned to find the bomber: Ted Kaczynski's

---

[26] Theodore Kaczynski, "Industrial Society and Its Future," *The Washington Post*, September 19, 1995.

brother, David, who not only believed he recognized some of the ramblings but also provided the FBI with other letters and documents written by his brother.

With the help of linguistic analysts and handwriting experts, authorities soon zeroed in on their man. On April 3, 1996, agents descended on Ted Kaczynski's remote, primitive Montana cabin and took him into custody. His reign of terror was over.

In the ensuing years, his brother would try to explain why he turned him in, pointing to Kaczynski's mental health issues. Various psychologists at the time of the court proceedings attempted to establish Kaczynski's sanity but largely came to the conclusion that his own unawareness of being mentally ill proved that he was, indeed, mentally ill.

Kaczynski fought that contention even at his trial, maintaining to this day that he was not, and is not, insane. He was, however, found competent to stand trial. He ended up pleading guilty to all counts in federal court in a deal to avoid the death penalty, after the judge rejected his repeated requests to represent himself, calling it "a deliberate attempt to manipulate the trial process."

The agreement meant that he would be sentenced to life in prison without the possibility of parole, and that he forfeited his right to appeal. "The Unabomber's career is over," said prosecutor Robert J. Cleary.[27]

There is no doubt that Kaczynski was sane by most legal standards. He clearly knew what he was doing, that it would harm people—indeed, that was his intention. He also knew it was wrong, and took great efforts to elude detection. His rationale demonstrates his ability to recognize the fact that others did not agree with his strategy—that is, he could see that others would find it morally wrong. His choice to inflict his personal beliefs on others was just that, his choice.

The idea that mental health issues exist among the population of violent true believers has been debated in the field of criminal psychology since we first began studying them. Early research held two opposing views: One was that VTBs must be mentally twisted, and the other was

---

[27] William Booth, "Kaczynski Pleads Guilty," *The Washington Post*, January 23, 1998, A01.

that they were basically normal and simply doing what they felt to be right, usually with the blessings of a group.

The truth is a combination of both. These individuals often have some sort of mental rift. Personality disorders or features such as narcissism and antisocial behavior are not uncommon. But what actually instigates their actions is their ideas, philosophies, and whom and what they identify with.

Islamic fanatics, with unwavering faith that Allah has sanctioned, indeed mandated, violence against infidels and with guarantees of a heavenly reward in the afterlife, continue to plot and perpetrate violence around the world. But can we really say they are mentally ill for having such a deep belief in their faith? I would argue this is possible for some but is more often unlikely.

The idea that "with God, all things are possible" is a double-edged sword. Ordinarily, faith in something greater makes the trials and tribulations of life, loss, death, and despair manageable and meaningful. But among these true believers in the religious realm who belong to or virtually identify with a terrorist organization or belief system, this spiritual plane has been exploited to unleash their darkest thoughts, with the comfort of knowing that killing is necessary and worthy of the Supreme Being's heavenly approval.

Take Nidal Hasan, the Army major and military psychiatrist previously mentioned. On November 5, 2009, Hasan shot and killed twelve soldiers and a civilian, and wounded thirty-one others, after opening fire on the Fort Hood military base in Killeen, Texas. Hasan was shot and wounded by military police and later sentenced to die for his crimes. To him, that was a badge of honor—martyrdom achieved in the name of Allah.

An American-born Muslim of Palestinian descent, Hasan was set to be deployed to Afghanistan a few weeks later with other Army Reserve units of mental health specialists who had been trained to treat combat stress in their fellow soldiers. He later told a military panel that was to determine whether he was competent enough to stand trial that the shootings were justified because those he killed were "going against the Islamic Empire."[28]

Hasan had also exchanged messages and emails with Anwar al-Awlaki, an American-born cleric believed by authorities to have been a high-level figure in the terrorist group Al Qaeda in the Arabian Peninsula. A self-radicalized fanatic with easy access to all things Al Qaeda on the internet, Hasan said he had grown increasingly angry over America's wars in Afghanistan and Iraq, and viewed them as unwarranted hostility toward Islam. He declared a jihad against the infidels.

During pretrial hearings, Hasan explained in no uncertain terms that his killings were just and that God had chosen him for martyrdom. "I don't think what I did was wrong because it was for the greater cause of helping my Muslim brothers," he said. Again, it was all about the greater cause.

Just prior to the shootings, Hasan went to morning prayers at a local mosque, then went back to his apartment, where he shredded his birth certificate and other identifying documents and gave away many of his belongings to neighbors. He felt no need for these things anymore, as he hoped he would be killed during the attack. At the onset of the attack, he shouted, *Allahu akbar,*" Arabic for "God is great."

Prosecutors told the jury at his trial that one of his motivations had been to kill as many soldiers as possible to wage jihad on the American military for what he saw as unjust wars it was participating in. This was the same military that footed the bill for his medical degree and gave him a job. Prosecutors said he did not want to be deployed, and that he felt it was his holy duty to carry out the killings.

Hasan, for his part, didn't dispute anything prosecutors contended. In fact, he served as his own lawyer and put on practically no case in his own defense. It was obvious he wanted to die for his beliefs. He made that clear during a 2010 interview with the mental health panel that was

---

[28] Manny Fernandez, "Fort Hood Gunman Told Panel That Death Would Make Him a Martyr," *The New York Times,* August 12, 2013, https://www.nytimes.com/2013/08/13/us/fort-hood-gunman-told-panel-that-death-would-make-him-a-martyr.html.

evaluating him for competency, telling the panelists that if he did end up dying by lethal injection, "I would still be a martyr."

Hasan's extremist views of Islam had begun to percolate long before the attack.

Nearly a year prior, he had sent the first of more than a dozen messages and emails to al-Awlaki, asking whether, if Muslim U.S. soldiers killed other American fighters at the behest of Allah and on behalf of Islam, would they be considered "fighting jihad and if they did die, would you consider them *shaheeds*," Arabic for "martyrs." Al-Awlaki never replied to that message, but Hasan continued down his deadly path of righteousness. Arguably the question was rhetorical; he had already answered it himself. He had even researched suicide bombing and jihadi techniques on the internet in the days and hours before the attack.

In a jailhouse interview with the Qatar-based Al Jazeera news organization, Hasan remained steadfast in his belief that the killings had been done in the name of his greater cause. Quoting verses from the Koran, he said that God would give "glad tidings to the believers who do righteous deeds, that they shall have a fair reward."

While Al Qaeda never took official responsibility for Hasan's attack, just four days after the shootings, al-Awlaki praised the man on his English-language website as having done "the right thing" and labeled him a "hero": "He is a man of conscience who could not bear living the contradiction of being a Muslim and serving in an army that is fighting against his own people.... The only way a Muslim could Islamically justify serving as a soldier in the U.S. Army is if his intention is to follow the footsteps of men like Nidal."[29]

Twisted thinking, evil thoughts. Don't sign up for the military if you have a problem with it.

Al-Awlaki was killed in a U.S.-led drone strike in Yemen in 2011, but he left behind a virtual propaganda machine, using the likes of Nidal

---

[29] David Johnston and Scott Shane, "U.S. Knew of Suspect's Tie to Radical Cleric," *The New York Times*, November 9, 2009, https://www.nytimes.com/2009/11/10/us /10inquire.html.

Hasan and others as a recruitment strategy to attract more to kill in the name Al Qaeda's perverted interpretation of Islam.

In the twenty-first century, technology has morphed the delivery system of propaganda campaigns. With a few clicks of a mouse and a few hours, extremist views can be disseminated worldwide aiming to increase followers and incite attacks. Instead of an extremist group's having to attract a potential member to a faraway physical location with the danger of exposure that could lead to a well-placed drone strike, the internet now provides that propaganda platform—and self-radicalized individuals, like Hasan, are attracted, recruited, trained, and inspired to take action.

It is high-tech, low-cost, disruptive, and extremely effective.

Similar religiously motivated self-radicalization through virtual "membership" or association with a terrorist group has been seen in numerous attacks, including the San Bernardino shootings and the Boston Marathon bombings, in which two ethnically Chechen but Kyrgyzstan-born brothers killed three people and severely injured at least 264 others.

Angry, frustrated, disaffected people craving a sense of purpose seek a remedy for their mundane lives, and to fulfill grandiose fantasies of being more than they are or ever could be. It's the fulfillment of a fantasy of omnipotence, a form of fame without achievement. It is easy for someone to kill. It is harder to live.

Eric Rudolph's killings fall into a similar category as Franklin's race-hating killings, though Rudolph's belief system, ironically, is focused on the right to life and an abhorrence of the legalization of abortion. To defend that right to life, he chose to kill. That makes a lot of sense, right? He also railed against the "aberrant" behavior of homosexuals.

Rudolph is most widely known as "The Olympic Park Bomber," having been responsible for placing a pipe bomb in a crowded area where many people from around the world had gathered for the Summer Olympic Games in Atlanta. The July 27, 1996, explosion killed a forty-four-year-old woman and injured more than one hundred people.

Rudolph got away cleanly and would go on to carry out even more bombings, one at a women's clinic in the Atlanta suburb of Sandy Springs in January 1997, and another a year later at a similar health-care facility known for providing abortions in Birmingham, Alabama. Six people were wounded in the Georgia blast; an off-duty police officer was killed and a nurse severely injured in the Alabama explosion. He also bombed a lesbian nightclub in Atlanta, wounding five people, in February 1997.

As police closed in, Rudolph fled to the mountains of western North Carolina, where he successfully hid from authorities in the labyrinth of forests and caves. He was added to the FBI's Ten Most Wanted list, with a one-million-dollar reward for information leading to his arrest.

He was eventually captured by an astute police officer who found Rudolph rummaging through a trash can outside a rural North Carolina grocery store. He pleaded guilty in a deal with prosecutors to avoid the death penalty and was sentenced to four life terms in prison without the possibility of parole.

After his guilty pleas, Rudolph issued a meandering statement accounting for his motives. It was his first public explanation for all the killings. He declared unapologetically, knowing he would be behind bars for the rest of his life, that he was "bloodied but emphatically unbowed." He gloated that the deal with prosecutors "deprived the government of its goal of sentencing me to death." It was an example of yet another thematic component of the violent true believer: needing to maintain control of his destiny until the end.

Rudolph truly believed that he was fighting "in the defense of the unborn" and was proud of what he had accomplished, writing that "abortion is murder. And when the regime in Washington legalized, sanctioned and legitimized this practice, they forfeited their legitimacy and moral authority to govern."

During the hearing in federal court in Alabama at which he pleaded guilty to all the crimes, the judge asked Rudolph if he had indeed detonated the bomb that killed the off-duty police officer and wounded the nurse.

He replied with confidence and gratification. "I certainly did, Your Honor."

As to the attack at the Olympics, Rudolph wrote in his statement that while abortion was his central enemy, he viewed the sporting event as promoting "despicable ideals" of "global socialism" while also calling it an opportunity to shame the United States for legalizing abortion. In the closest he ever came to apologizing, he called that bombing a "disaster" and noted that he had not intended to kill "innocent civilians."

What about the attack on the gay nightclub? Well, Rudolph was simply disgusted by homosexuality, explaining that it was fine with him if it was practiced in private, but to have society recognize it as a legitimate way of life "should be ruthlessly opposed" and met with "force if necessary."[30]

Violent true believers are out there right now, obsessing, growing in number, and festering in their hatred and self-justification. Online they can find so many places to validate their beliefs, and in our polarized society, the palpable hostility and loss of civility seem to embolden them.

The price of living in a free society is that people have a right to their ideas, and to promote them, to a point. We are not Stalinist Russia or Communist China. So anyone can generate ideological propaganda that inspires violent action. Our leaders are doing a piss-poor job of modeling constructive communication, and the resultant rhetoric is incendiary to those who are teetering on the edge of the abyss, hearing encouragement to action in the ugly political debates.

However different their backgrounds and belief systems are, all violent true believers are really the same: mission-oriented in their drive to kill. They hold deeply the conviction that murder is justifiable to support their cause, and they have an overwhelming desire to be recognized for what they have done. Joseph Paul Franklin is a haunting reflection of all of the above. In fact, during my prison interview with him, he was deeply offended by something outrageously unbelievable but rooted in his fervent desire to be remembered for a job well done:

"They *still* don't want to give me credit for a lot of the murders I committed."

---

[30] "Full Text of Eric Rudolph's Confession," NPR, April 14, 2005. https://www.npr.org/templates/story/story.php?storyId=4600480

The Killing Fields

Mass Casualty Shooters and Indiscriminate Slaughter

"Vengeance is mine, and recompense…"

—Deuteronomy 32:35

The bloody bodies riddled with bullet holes still lay exactly where they had been felled. The acrid and sour smell of gunfire lingered in the air. Surreal.

I was on the scene with a team of investigators from the Los Angeles Police Department just after the shootings. Ironically, at the time, we had been working on setting up a workplace violence program that could help the City of Los Angeles identify potentially violent employees and other threats before they could "go postal." It didn't come together soon enough.

As we walked through the building, police investigators sought every speck of evidence that would be needed to convict, while I inspected the scene through the lens of psychology, looking for clues that would help us determine why and how the victims had been chosen. Most significantly, there was no sign of a struggle; everything was in order, nothing disturbed but the dead, who stood no chance. Unarmed, unexpecting, ambushed by the methodical attack of a man on a mission for revenge.

Information would soon surface about the offender and his violent trajectory, but at the time, in the immediate aftermath of the killings, we were just beginning to piece it all together.

It was a hugely disturbing scene, because some of the victims' pagers were going off, the repeated sounds of beeping and buzzing piercing the otherwise eerie silence of the rooms full of death. The victims' families had heard of the attack on the news and were desperately trying to reach their loved ones.

Four of those loved ones would never respond. A Los Angeles city electrician, Willie Woods, had ferociously acted on his disdain for his supervisors by gunning them down one by one.

Woods had worked repairing police radios for about twelve years at the C. Erwin Piper Technical Center, commonly called Piper Tech, a sprawling downtown facility on Ramirez Street along the Los Angeles River just off the 101 Freeway. It was the same facility that housed the LAPD's elite Air Support Division. But this threat could not be seen from above.

Incensed at what he saw as repeated attacks on his character and work ethic in regular evaluations by his supervisors that often found him to be merely "competent" at his job, Woods finally had had enough. It was July 19, 1995, at about ten o'clock in the morning on a Wednesday, as hundreds of city workers walked in and out of the building picking up paychecks and doing their jobs.

Because he was a city employee with an identification badge, he had no problem clearing security without a check for weapons. But that wouldn't be an issue on this day anyway. For weeks, maybe months, he had been keeping his gun in his toolbox at work, an ever-present private reminder to him that he alone held the ultimate power over his destiny, and the destiny of anyone who crossed him.

What happened next was methodical, as Woods proceeded to go on a hunting expedition with the gun, a 9-millimeter semiautomatic handgun he had purchased about eight months prior. He first fatally shot at point-blank range seventy-two-year-old Anthony Gain and fifty-seven-year-old Marty Wakefield, two of his supervisors, who were sitting in their cubicles on the building's first floor.

Woods then calmly headed toward the stairwell as the room filled with the screams of terrified workers fleeing for safety. He encountered another supervisor, sixty-one-year-old Neil Carpenter, and shot him dead in a basement hallway before killing supervisor James Walton, a sixty-year-old longtime employee, in a nearby office. Three of the supervisors had signed off on the various work evaluations that Woods had become so infuriated with. *How dare they?*

A fifth potential victim encountered Woods on the stairs as he fled, recounting later to police that he thought he, too, would be killed on the spot. But Woods passed him by, explaining that the man had been nice to him, so he got to live. The killer then fled out of the building's back door, where he was arrested a short time later by police before he could commit suicide.

Woods, forty-four years old at the time of the murders, was convicted in November 1996 of three counts of first-degree murder and one count of second-degree murder. About three months later, he was sentenced to life in prison without the possibility of parole. Just before the judge handed down Woods' punishment—he could have received the death penalty—the widow of one of the victims spoke up in court, directing her disgust directly at the killer:[31]

"You will wish the jury had given you the death penalty…. You will be one of the living dead."

It was about six months later that LAPD Detective Douglas Raymond and I met with Woods at the North Kern State Prison in Delano, California. His demeanor did indeed make him seem as if he were among the living dead. He was deflated, defeated, facing the great unknown of his first criminal conviction and the prospect of spending the rest of his life locked away in a cage.

---

[31] "Electrician Gets Life Sentence in Slayings of 4 Supervisors," *Los Angeles Times*, February 8, 1997, https://www.latimes.com/archives/la-xpm-1997-02-08-me-26751-story.html.

Detective Raymond was one of the elite operators in the LAPD's Threat Management Unit. Together, we were working on a citywide workplace violence program, and such an opportunity to interview a killer was rare, because most of them take their own lives.[32]

Woods was reluctant at first, concerned that speaking openly about the crime could hurt his chances in appeals, but he soon relented, sharing with us an incredible journey through his violent thinking for about three and a half hours. Slumped in his chair, wearing a bright yellow prison shirt with a disgustingly filthy wrinkled white T-shirt beneath it, Woods talked—not much, but the information he shared was highly concentrated. While the interview lasted several hours, much of that time was taken up by Woods' simply staring off into the corner of the room, disappearing into his mind for minutes at a time between our questions and often in the middle of his own responses.

"The person who I am is different than the person who took four lives," he told us.

"The person who took four lives? How would you describe that person?" I replied softly.

"Someone that needed help," he said in a barely audible tone, not looking at me directly, his gaze distracted toward the ceiling.

"If you could redo or change anything, what would it be?" Detective Raymond asked.

"I'd walk up to Neil Carpenter and say"—Woods paused for nearly a minute midsentence—"'I resign'…and just leave." *Easy to say now, and a little late*, I thought.

He went on to recount how he wished now he had just listened to the advice of his girlfriend at the time. "If I had listened to her before this happened, it probably wouldn't have happened. She asked me to go get help. And I guess I thought I could work out things on my own. It would have just blown over, and I would be all right."

---

[32] J.R. Meloy, A.G. Hempel, T.B. Gray, K. Mohandie, A. Shiva, and T.C. Richards, "A Comparative Analysis of North American Adolescent and Adult Mass Murderers," *Behavioral Sciences and the Law* 22 (2004): 291-309.

"So your advice to somebody else who might be having trouble at work, feel like they're getting painted into a corner, would be, 'Get help'?" I prodded.

"Get help," he repeated, moving his gaze from way off in the corner of the room directly to me. "Just get away from the situation."

He recounted a childhood fraught with violence at the hands of his father, with daily beatings "as far back as I can remember." After he had two kids of his own, he said he left them in Philadelphia, fearful that he would one day become his father, delivering the same beatings on his own children that he had endured for so many years.

"What my father did to me, his father did to him," Woods told us, noting that he had to "break the cycle" by leaving his own kids. As he grew older, he developed fantasies, which he called "scripts," during which he would act out violently toward his father in his mind—sadistic daydreams of sorts. At first, these were like cartoons, the empowering animations of a child stripped of all control, trust, and safety.

As the years passed and the fantasies continued, sometimes his father would be replaced by other male figures who he felt were somehow shaming him or making him feel powerless. And the cartoonish, unrealistic imagery evolved into visceral, extremely lifelike scenarios. The characters in his scripts would eventually be replaced by his supervisors at work, and those imaginary thoughts—"like watching a movie" inside his head—would soon play out in real life. By the time of the homicides, he had killed thousands of times in his mind.

Woods lost himself in his violent fantasies. The props for his bloody movie were at arm's reach, and there was no turning back.

A few years later, in 1999, I headed up to Pelican Bay State Prison in Crescent City, California, the state's first and most notorious supermax facility, housing some of the worst of the worst offenders.

My friend and fellow psychologist Dr. J. Reid Meloy and I were going to interview "The Alphabet Bomber," who was convicted in 1980 for a 1974 attack at Los Angeles International Airport that killed three people and injured thirty-six others. He was dubbed the "Alphabet Bomber" because his taunting message to the police stated, "This first bomb was marked with the letter A, which stands for Airport... The second bomb will be associated with the letter L, the third with the letter I, etc., until our name has been written on the face of this nation in blood." The bomber claimed to be from a group called Aliens of America.[33]

The bomber, Muharem Kurbegovic had written letters to Dr. Meloy, but upon our arrival, he refused to be interviewed. I knew Woods also was incarcerated there now, so I figured we'd give meeting with him again a shot. I was interested in seeing how his demeanor had changed after a few years locked away, and with the reality now setting in that he'd never see freedom again.

We headed over to the prison library, where Woods was working that day. Feeling pretty comfortable having already interviewed Woods once, I walked right up to him. "Hi, Mr. Woods, remember me? I was hoping to catch up with you."

He just stared back blankly, a disturbing look in his eyes that should have given me pause, but I was so focused, I didn't realize how dangerous things would soon get.

I repeated myself.

"Hi, Mr. Woods, remember me?"

Still no response, just an angry glare, something seething behind his eyes, his body beginning to tense up.

"I said, 'I remember!'" he shouted at me, moving closer, his fists now beginning to clench. He had said no such thing. In fact, he hadn't said a word before that. But in his violence-ridden mind, he had made it perfectly clear.

Uh-oh. The lights were starting to go on ever so slowly for me. Fortunately, at the same time, Dr. Meloy noticed a group of other inmates gathering around us.

"Kris, we need to leave," he said, instantly removing the blinders that had me focused on Woods and not my surroundings. We got out of there quickly and, thankfully, with no injuries.

---

[33] Jeffrey D. Simon, *The Alphabet Bomber: A Lone Wolf Terrorist Ahead of His Time*, (Lincoln: University of Nebraska Press, 2019).

What struck me was how Woods' demeanor had changed so much from my first encounter with him just a few years earlier, when he was newly in prison. Now he was a menacing man simmering with anger barely contained, like the brittle surface of hot magma—that same anger that had boiled over on the day of his killing rampage.

He hadn't just snapped. They never do. He had erupted like a powerful volcano that builds up pressure until it explodes. Woods was clearly an incensed, violent man back then, and he remained so when I saw him later—just one absolutely scary guy.

He is what we call today a mass casualty shooter. This type is different than a serial killer, who carries out crimes over a stretch of time—usually with a bit of a cooling-off period between kills—or a spree killer, who typically takes multiple lives over a shorter period of time, often with a sense of randomness to the killings.

There are multiple subsets of the mass casualty shooter. Woods fits into the set of workplace mass shooters who are fixated on righting perceived wrongs against them, often with specific targets in mind. Other mass casualty shooting incidents can begin as a domestic situation, in which the shooter is going after an ex-wife or a girlfriend and ends up taking out family members and other innocent victims caught in the crossfire.

Until the mid-1900s, mass casualty shooting events were extremely rare. They just weren't part of the American cultural script. But that would all change on September 6, 1949, marking the arrival of what was to become an escalating phenomenon. In a span of about twenty minutes, twelve people were dead, and another would die later at the hospital: a pharmacist and his wife, a shoemaker, an insurance salesman, a barber, a television repairman, and a two-year-old boy were among those in the wrong place at the wrong time on that terrifying Tuesday morning.

You've probably never heard of Howard Barton Unruh. But his infamous "Walk of Death" is believed to have been America's first true mass casualty shooting, a harbinger of what is now a tragically all-too-familiar scenario: an angry, despondent individual with a grudge taking out his disdain on innocent, unsuspecting victims at the business end of a gun.

We now call this person an "active shooter"—a term that would not be coined for another fifty years or so.

It was about 8:00 a.m. in the quiet Camden, New Jersey, neighborhood of Cramer Hill. Unruh had just finished a breakfast of fried eggs prepared for him by his mother. Less than an hour later, he grabbed his Luger handgun, a prized souvenir he had brought back from his time serving overseas with the U.S. Army during the Second World War.

He filled his pockets with other guns and ammunition and calmly walked out the door.

Unruh had a thorough list of grievances he had with people in the area, slights he had perceived—some real, some imagined. He had a separate mental list of his intended targets—local shopkeepers and neighbors he believed had wronged him in some way through minor squabbles, name-calling, and the like.

He thought people made fun of him for being gay. He believed the pharmacist had shortchanged him on numerous purchases. One neighbor repeatedly complained about his loud playing of music. Another threw trash in his backyard. The nearby barber apparently had caused Unruh's cellar to flood by dumping discarded dirt in a vacant lot adjacent to his property. All of these minor issues stewed inside Unruh's brain until he hit his breaking point and, like Woods, made a conscious decision to kill.

Unruh gained his proficiency with guns during the war, where he served with an Army artillery branch. He fought in the Battle of the Bulge, during which the Allied forces, including the U.S. military, suffered more than eighty thousand causalities in their heroic fight against the Germans. He was no stranger to violent death and blood. He also served as a gunner on a tank and received commendations in battle.

He was eventually honorably discharged from the Army. No mention of mental illness was ever provided, but Unruh's brother, Jim, would later say that he came home from the war different and "never acted like his old self."[34]

---

[34] Joseph A. Gambardello and Barbara Boyer, "Mass Murderer Howard Unruh Dies at 88," *The Philadelphia Inquirer*, October 20, 2009, https://www.inquirer.com/philly/news/local/20091020_Mass_murderer_Howard_Unruh_dies_at_88.html.

Today, with all that we know about the mental states of some soldiers returning from war, it is possible that Unruh was suffering from a condition for which there hadn't been a diagnosis at the time—post-traumatic stress disorder. The typical traumatized war veteran is filled with anxiety; he desires to *avoid* reminders of combat and thus does not seek them out. But there is a small portion of the population for whom the combat experience flips a switch, unleashing a preexisting inner hell.

For whatever reason, Unruh's last acts as a free man on Earth would be to continue killing back in America. He was deranged. He wandered from storefront to storefront, killing people at point-blank range. He walked into the street and shot people dead who just happened to have been driving by in cars at the time. He shot up into windows at people who peered out in curiosity and fear at the unusual sounds of gunfire.

His target list became whomever he felt like killing.

At some point during the rampage, Unruh was shot in the back of his leg by a man who took aim at him from the upstairs window of an apartment building, but it didn't slow him down one bit. He kept shooting.

He eventually ran out of ammunition and retreated to his own apartment as police cars swarmed into the area, sirens blaring. Officers surrounded the building and just began blasting away with machine guns. Hundreds of spectators had now gathered in streets, watching the horrifying scene play out like a movie.

Oddly, during the siege, an assistant city editor at *The Camden Courier-Post* named Philip Buxton called the house on a whim, hoping Unruh would answer and he'd get a scoop. To his shock, Unruh picked up the phone.

"Why are you killing people?" Buxton asked.

"I don't know. I can't answer that yet. I'll have to talk to you later. I'm too busy now."[35]

Unruh eventually surrendered, proclaiming to a detective, "I am no psycho." He took full credit for the killings and later provided a detailed

---

[35] Meyer Berger, "Veteran Kills 12 in Mad Rampage on Camden Street," *The New York Times*, September 7, 1949.

account to police and psychiatrists who examined him, trying to understand why he had done what he did.

During one such interview, he calmly recounted his killing of the shoemaker: "I had leveled the gun at him, neither of us said nothing, and I pulled the trigger.... He had a funny look on his face, staggered back, and fell to the floor. I realized then he was still alive, so I fired into his head."

About six weeks after the rampage, a Camden County judge signed an order declaring Unruh unfit to participate in his own defense after mental health professionals came to the conclusion that he was a paranoid schizophrenic. Only a single psychiatrist at the time, W.H. Minford, spoke up to say that he believed Unruh was competent to take part in his defense at a trial.

To lock him up in a mental institution without his ever having to face the consequences of his actions "would be regarded as psychiatrists coming to the rescue," Minford wrote. "The trial should be a full-dress affair," he continued, "and there are possibilities that legal and psychiatric practitioners may learn from this unusual and interesting case."

In the end, however, Unruh would never see a trial. He was soon transferred to a section for the criminally insane at Trenton Psychiatric Hospital, where he remained for sixty years as case number 47,077 until his death in 2009 at the age of eighty-eight.

It is doubtful that Unruh would have been found insane in most states today, given the fact that the burden of proof is on the defense to show "beyond a preponderance of the evidence"—likelier than not—that because of a mental disorder, the person did not know or appreciate the nature and quality of the crimes, or that the person was unable to distinguish right from wrong, morally or legally. The mental health establishment in the 1940s and '50s called a lot of things schizophrenia that were simply cold-blooded, what we know today as being psychopathic.

Violent psychopaths know that what they are doing is wrong. They just don't care; it is all about them and their impulses.

Was there evidence of delusions and hallucinations? It does not appear so, but did Unruh have grudges? Absolutely. Did he know he was killing? Well, he prepared his weapons. He planned it all out and appeared purposeful and goal-oriented. Did he know the police saw it as wrong? Of course he did.

Seventeen years later, in 1966, an ex-Marine named Charles Whitman would usher America into a frightening new realm of mass indiscriminate killing with more powerful weaponry. He had no specific targets, unlike Unruh. Just a desire to take as many lives as possible.

Whitman's assault was America's first mass shooting to occur after the television became a fixture in American households, leaving behind the era in which only radio and newspapers published a day later brought the news to the masses. It was a shocking, watershed event fed by the new American mass media and embedded in the explosion of American cultural transformations during the 1960s.

It was a collective traumatization of the American psyche, representing the loss of the dream of idealized innocence and safety. And this was compounded by the images that were being broadcast of the bloody and endless Vietnam War, student demonstrations, and civil rights unrest.

It represented a disturbing new reality.

Around midday on August 1, Whitman, an expert sharpshooter, gathered up his guns and ammunition, along with a high-powered hunting rifle equipped with a scope. From atop a clock tower on the campus of the University of Texas in Austin, he proceeded to carry out a killing rampage the likes of which this country had never seen.

At the conclusion of his ninety-six-minute reign of terror, thirteen people were dead and more than thirty lay bloodied and injured on the surrounding streets and in the courtyard below. Another victim would succumb to her wounds a week later. And in 2001, another victim died from a kidney condition that officials determined was the result of being shot by Whitman three decades prior, making the total fifteen dead.

Whitman was eventually killed by several police officers who finally made it to the killer's perch on an observation deck 230 feet above the ground. They shot him dead on the spot.

Prior to the campus killings, Whitman had stabbed to death his wife and his mother. This type of bifurcated event, in which the killer begins murdering at one location and then proceeds to the "main stage," is something we often see now in similar mass shootings and spree killings. Some kill initially to spare loved ones the fallout from their actions or other events, and others are just going down their list, which includes different people in different places.

Whitman knew something was wrong with him well before he carried out the attack, and actually sought help. He had visited multiple doctors voluntarily, explaining that he had strange feelings of rage and confusion, violent impulses, and headaches. He was prescribed a variety of medications, but nothing seemed to work.

Just about four months before the shootings, he visited yet another psychiatrist, saying he was having uncontrollable thoughts of anger and rage. He even mentioned thinking about taking a deer rifle to the clock tower and gunning people down. Nothing was ever done. No one followed up.

Prior to the attack, Whitman penned in his journals what is believed to be a suicide note. He didn't intend to live. "I do not really understand myself these days," he wrote. "I am supposed to be an average reasonable and intelligent young man. However, lately...I have been a victim of many unusual and irrational thoughts."[36]

He then referred to the last psychiatrist he had visited. "After one session I never saw the doctor again, and since then I have been fighting my mental turmoil alone, and seemingly to no avail. After my death I wish that an autopsy would be performed on me to see if there is any visible physical disorder."

As to killing his wife and his mother, Whitman explained in detail that he didn't want them to live with the shame of his actions. "I truly do not consider this world worth living in, and am prepared to die, and I do not want to leave [my wife] to suffer alone in it.... Similar reasons provoked me to take my mother's life."

Whitman's wish for an autopsy came true, and a disturbing discovery was made. A tumor about the size of pecan was found in his brain. This

---

[36] Gary M. Lavergne, *A Sniper in the Tower: The Charles Whitman Murders*, (Denton: University of North Texas Press, 1997).

led to a feverish debate among experts as to whether the lesion may have been at least partially to blame for his spiraling mental state. Some concluded it had not affected his thinking, while others found it may very well have contributed to an inability to control his emotions and violent impulses. No definitive sole cause for his mental degradation was found, however.

The vast majority of people who deal with brain tumors never hurt anybody. The tumor explanation also does not address the purposeful, goal-oriented nature of Whitman's violence, the meticulous planning, and the repeated reconnaissance visits to the tower.

At the time when experts were trying to figure out what did cause him to kill, mental illness just wasn't at the top of the list; the study of such criminals didn't focus heavily on their psychological state. Pathway warning behaviors, fixation, and leakage of violent fantasies—the stock in trade of modern threat assessment—had not yet been imagined. What did happen just days after the attack, however, has become a common refrain to this day—a debate over gun control. President Lyndon B. Johnson proclaimed, "The time has come for action." In a statement, he added: "What happened is not without a lesson: that we must press urgently for the legislation now pending in Congress to help prevent the wrong person from obtaining firearms."

A *New York Times* headline the next day read: "Johnson Urges Gun Curbs to Prevent New 'Tragedy.'"[37]

"The bill would not prevent all such tragedies," Johnson's statement continued. "But it would help reduce the unrestricted sale of firearms to those who cannot be trusted in their use and possession. How many lives might be saved as a consequence?"

New York Times correspondent Robert B. Semple Jr. summed up the effort in an ensuing article, noting that many on Capitol Hill and in other parts of Washington, D.C., were "cautious about predicting final success for a gun control bill."

---

[37] Robert B. Semple Jr., "Johnson Urges Gun Curbs To Prevent New 'Tragedy,'" *The New York Times*, August 3, 1966.

Those people "recalled that after the assassination of President Kennedy in November 1963, there was a strong drive for passage for [sic] restrictive measures," Semple wrote. "However, the drive collapsed before the powerful opposition of the National Rifle Association and other gun clubs."[38]

After the 1968 assassinations of the Reverend Doctor Martin Luther King Jr. and Senator Robert F. Kennedy, Congress did approve legislation regulating the sale of firearms through the mail. However, Johnson was none too pleased by its lack of any real meaningful impact, noting that it did not go far enough to control who owns guns. Does this sound familiar?

"The voices that blocked these safeguards were not the voices of an aroused nation," Johnson said. "They were the voices of a powerful gun lobby that has prevailed for the moment in an election year." He continued: "We have been through a great deal of anguish these last few months and these last few years—too much anguish to forget so quickly."[39]

But forget we did. And we continue to turn our backs on real solutions, with gun control still being debated today. As Johnson so eloquently pointed out then, any real change is stymied by pro-gun lobbyists and politicians unwilling to turn away the money that lines their pockets for reelection campaigns.

It would be about sixteen years later when yet another lone gunman— unemployed security guard James Huberty—unleashed his fury on other innocent victims, gunning down forty people at a McDonald's restaurant in the San Ysidro neighborhood of San Diego. It was July 18, 1984.

Twenty-one people were killed, and nineteen others injured. Huberty was shot dead by a police sniper strategically positioned on a nearby rooftop. The incident was the deadliest mass shooting by a sole gunman in the United States to that date.

---

[38] David W. Dunlap, "1966, 'The Time Has Come for Action,'" *The New York Times*, October 5, 2017, https://www.nytimes.com/2017/10/05/insider/1966-the-time-has-come-for-action.html.

[39] Joseph A. Califano Jr., "Gun Control Lessons from Lyndon Johnson," *The Washington Post*, December 16, 2012, https://www.washingtonpost.com/opinions/gun-control-lessons-from-lyndon-johnson/2012/12/16/38f3941e-47b4-11e2-ad54-580638ede391_story.html.

But it would be one-upped seven years later, in 1991, when thirty-five-year-old George Hennard drove his pickup truck through the wall of a Luby's Cafeteria in Killeen, Texas, then stepped out and proceeded to shoot and kill twenty-three people before committing suicide.

Since then, so many more mass shootings have occurred, with unfortunately even higher body counts and more critically injured. And the pace has quickened. Really, the only thing that separates the modern-day mass casualty shooter from those of the past is the weaponry and death toll. While the motives may differ, the underlying themes remain the same. And now many of these shooters seek the limelight afforded by modern mass communication and the internet, including social media.

They have a desire to inflict their wrath on the population at large, to subject the world to their misery and suffering, to fulfill their individual self-destructive destinies and suicidal impulses as the final act of their horrific violence, and to be remembered and assume their place in the gallery of the wicked.

Enter Stephen Paddock, who at the time of this book's writing was responsible for the most people killed in a mass shooting by a single gunman in America. The sixty-four-year-old high-stakes gambler took up his position on the thirty-second floor of the Mandalay Bay resort and casino in Las Vegas on October 1, 2017. Using a cache of high-powered rifles, he rained down gunfire on a crowd of some twenty-two thousand people attending the Route 91 Harvest country music festival on the Strip, killing fifty-eight and injuring nearly five hundred. He shot himself in the head as police closed in.

In methodology it was an atypical mass casualty shooting attack, though similar to Whitman's in that the killer chose to murder his victims from a distance like a sniper. Many more mass shooters of today carry out their carnage in a more intimate style of confronting their victims up close and personal.

No singular motive was ever determined for Paddock's killing rampage. He didn't leave behind a suicide note or any clues as to why he would want to kill so many random strangers. In the ensuing months, the FBI's Behavioral Analysis Unit was asked to dig into the case and provide a postmortem profile of Paddock, hoping to uncover a clearer sense of the motives that might help authorities stop the next such shooting.[40]

The experts spent a year digging into Paddock's background and poring over evidence collected from the crime scene and from his car and home. They explored, as they noted in their final report, "Paddock's developmental, interpersonal, and clinical history as they related to his decision to attack." The three-page summary released on January 29, 2019, laid out ten key findings as potential motivating factors. Among them were things the experts concluded had *not* been elements of the crime, such as evidence that the killings had been motivated by any sort of ideological or political beliefs. The summary also confirmed that he indeed acted alone.[41]

The FBI also determined that there was no single, clear motivating factor behind the attack and that Paddock went to great lengths to keep his thoughts private, sharing his plans for mass murder with not a single soul. This is uncommon among today's mass shooters. More often they telegraph their plans in advance, overtly leaving behind signs on social media or some sort of manifesto, or having discussed their plans with friends or family prior to the crime. These social media postings, manifestos, and communications are part of what clearly identifies a need to be remembered and the narcissistic craving for notoriety.

Arguably, Paddock purposefully chose such a public event, with thousands of people gathered to share in their love for music, to let loose a guaranteed shock wave to create his infamy. He didn't need to post anything publicly before the attack. His murders were the message.

"Active shooters rarely have a singular motive or reason for engaging in a mass homicide. More often their motives are a complex merging of developmental issues, interpersonal relationships, clinical issues, and contextual stressors," the FBI wrote. "Paddock was no different."

---

[40] John Wyman, Greg Saathoff M.D., and Andre Simons, "The Pre-Attack Behaviors of the Las Vegas Shooter: Key Findings from the FBI BAU's Expert Panel," Association of Threat Assessment Professionals Annual Training Conference, August 13, 2019.

[41] "FBI Behavioral Analysis Unit's Key Findings in October 2017 Las Vegas Mass Shooting," Federal Bureau of Investigation, January 30, 2019, https://publicintelligence.net/fbi-las-vegas-shooting-motive/.

While investigators found no manifesto, videos, suicide note, or the like, they did determine that Paddock had an overwhelming desire to die by suicide. "As he grew older, Paddock became increasingly distressed and intolerant of stimuli while simultaneously failing to navigate common life stressors affiliated with aging," according to the report. "Paddock experienced an objective (and subjective) decline in physical and mental health, level of functioning, and financial status over the last several years of his life. In reaction to this decline, Paddock concluded that he would seek to control the ending of his life via a suicidal act. His inability or unwillingness to perceive any alternatives to this ending influenced his decision to attack."

Perceptual constriction, as we call it, is a common theme among the suicidal and homicidal-suicidal; they believe there is only one way out. Killers and the suicidal convince themselves that their solution is the only real one. Also, like many other mass shooters and even serial killers, Paddock had a deep desire to attain notoriety and infamy, the FBI determined. To this end, the analysts believe Paddock was influenced by his own father's legacy. His father was a serial bank robber with a criminal record dating back to the 1940s, who once was on the FBI's Most Wanted list.

Benjamin Hoskins Paddock was captured in 1960 and sentenced to twenty years in prison, but he escaped about eight years later. He gained the moniker "Chrome Dome" because of how he had completely shaved his head. He wouldn't be recaptured until 1978.

The FBI noted that Stephen Paddock "was influenced by the memory of his father…Paddock's father created a façade to mask his true criminal identity and hide his diagnosed psychopathic history, and in so doing ultimately achieved significant criminal notoriety." And while Paddock had been just thirteen years old when Whitman rained hell from the clock tower in Texas, what lasting impact had that had on his psyche? Of course he had seen news of it, known of it, and logged it as a reference point. It was the origin of an idea: to be like his father but using the methods of Whitman.

The FBI opined that Stephen Paddock "displayed minimal empathy throughout his life and primarily viewed others through a transactional lens of costs and benefits," noting that his "decision to murder people while they were being entertained was consistent with his personality." From a cost-benefit standpoint, he chose one spot to maximize killing efficiency.

Also like many other mass shooters, Paddock was extremely goal-oriented and focused on task-specific objectives, devoting considerable energy to hobbies like gambling, the FBI found. "Once Paddock decided to attack, he characteristically devoted time, attention, and energy to the shooting. Paddock engaged in detailed preparations for the attack, including a year-long burst of firearms and ammunition acquisition. The planning and preparation—in and of itself—was likely satisfying to Paddock as it provided a sense of direction and control despite his mental and physical decline."

Overall, however, the FBI's findings raised interesting thoughts without exactly explaining what had driven Paddock to kill. They simply concluded that he was in many ways similar to other mass shooters.

It is important to note that he was—and is—nothing special. There have been so many mass casualty shootings over the years, I could write an entire book on the topic. One shooting after another. They seem to now come in bursts at least every few months. The genie has been out of the bottle for a while now. Mass murder can be translated to reality in a culture emphasizing instant gratification and notoriety.

As previously mentioned, Elliot Rodger is among a subset of mass casualty shooters known as "incels," or involuntarily celibates. On May 23, 2014, the twenty-two-year-old went on a stabbing and shooting spree near the campus of the University of California, Santa Barbara, killing six people and injuring fourteen others before committing suicide.

As noted previously, his hateful online postings seethed with misogyny and envy. His laptop was later found by authorities open to a disturbing YouTube video he had recently uploaded.

"Tomorrow is the day of retribution, the day in which I will have my revenge against humanity, against all of you," Rodger said calmly in the video, staring straight into the camera as he sat behind the wheel in his car. "For the last eight years of my life, ever since I hit puberty, I've been forced to endure an existence of loneliness, rejection, and unfulfilled desires all because girls have never been attracted to me. Girls gave their affection and sex and love to other men but never to me," he continued. "I'm twenty-two years old and I'm still a virgin. I've never even kissed a girl. I've been through college for two and a half years, more than that actually, and I'm still a virgin. It has been very torturous. College is the time when everyone experiences those things such as sex and fun and pleasure. Within those years, I've had to rot in loneliness. It's not fair."

Rodger represented the epitome of narcissism; entitlement; shallow, materialistic concerns and values; and externalization of blame. He viewed women as objects that existed to gratify his impulses and didn't see any role he played in his own rejection. He immersed himself in a virtual world online that supported his extreme, pathological misogynist views.

Elliot, were you a good listener? Did you genuinely care about others? Did you ever attempt to think of anyone but yourself? Gimme, gimme, gimme—a hallmark of the typical mass casualty shooter. Again, like Paddock and the rest, nothing special.

Jared Lee Loughner, twenty-two years old at the time of his killings, may fall into the category of politically motivated mass casualty shooters, though his true motives have never been determined, and he was clearly mentally unstable at the time of the attacks.

Loughner opened fire on January 8, 2011, during an event being hosted by Arizona Congresswoman Gabrielle Giffords outside a Safeway supermarket in Tucson. He killed six people, including a federal judge and a nine-year-old girl, and injured thirteen others. He shot Giffords in the head; the injury forced her to resign from Congress and left her severely debilitated.

By all accounts from family, friends, and investigators, Loughner had been suffering from a severely deteriorating mental state in the months leading up to the killings. He had also become increasingly paranoid about the government and developed an odd obsession with Giffords.

He railed about currency that wasn't backed by gold or silver (a gripe shared by alt-right and antigovernment groups), wrote about his planned assassination of Giffords, and posted comments online accusing the government of mind control. He was paranoid and stimulated by the noise of cyberspace, carried away by it.

In 2011, he was found not competent to stand trial and sent to a federal medical facility for treatment. A little over a year later, he was determined to be fit to face court proceedings, and he pleaded guilty in a deal to avoid the death penalty and instead obtain a sentence of life in prison without the possibility of parole.

Devin Patrick Kelley, by comparison, wasn't mentally ill, at least not in the legal sense. He was just an angry, bitter, violent man, a domestically motivated mass casualty shooter who wanted revenge on his estranged wife. Kelley walked into the First Baptist Church in Sutherland Springs, Texas, on Sunday, November 5, 2017, armed with a high-powered assault rifle, and opened fire, killing twenty-six people, many of them children and the elderly. He killed himself a short time later.

Authorities believe his main target was his mother-in-law, who often went to Sunday services there but happened to not be in attendance on the day of the massacre. The people he ended up killing were just random folks in prayer.

These mass killers are reacting to rejection and abandonment, choose a public location for access to the primary victims, and view their wrath as so important that simply killing the one person "responsible" for their grievance is not enough. Everyone in the vicinity is guilty by association, and collateral damage is essential to satisfying their intolerable grievance. Sometimes they even blame the other victims for supporting their primary target.

Shooters like Paddock and Kelley aren't overtly fueled by ideology. But with today's easy access to assault weapons and ammunition, the mass casualty shooter's actions represent a power-driven modern fantasy of notoriety—the voracious need for recognition, control, and dominance. But many of them do intertwine ideological issues into their homicidal plans. Some make an obtuse point against a system, society, or group they think is against them; others strike a note of terror against a political cause.

Prior to our current mass shooter millennium, with a few outlier exceptions, offenders like Paddock and Kelley would reach the end of their rope emotionally and restrict their murderous intentions to loved ones and then themselves. But today, murder doesn't end there, as the new cultural script calls for more. These templates have been forged on the covers of magazines, in the media, and in the virtual world of cyber-space. Mass media communication in the industrial world has become an accelerant for even more mass casualty shootings.

One thing we know for certain: These killers are as evil as it gets. No matter their motives. No matter their mental state. No matter their upbringing, the slights against them, the disputes with others, their financial or social problems. Truly courageous people with tenacity, humility, faith, and empathy survive and transcend these experiences and impulses every day.

But the justifications, rationales, and excuses offered and embraced by these offenders, and their fixations, make sense to them, and they are good with their actions. Pure evil. They often count their kills as conquests and view them as increasing their own self-worth. And whether these murderers live or die in the end, they know they've won.

For Howard Unruh, the first of the mass casualty shooters in America, however twisted his mind, he felt accomplished, at least at the time of the killings. He expressed that sentiment clearly in that telephone call with the assistant city editor at *The Camden Courier-Post*. Amid the chaos of police showering his building with gunfire, the editor asked Unruh how many people he had killed.

"I don't know, I haven't counted. Looks like a pretty good score."

Neverland

The Delusional Offender

> "Most everyone's mad here. You may have noticed that I'm not all there myself."
>
> —Lewis Carroll, from *Alice in Wonderland*

In my travels around the country meeting some of the most wicked of souls, I've also encountered the truly mentally ill, the Herbert Mullins of the world. Delusional in his belief that human sacrifice was needed to save California from a cataclysmic earthquake, Mullin methodically killed thirteen random people in a four-month stretch between 1972 and 1973.

So twisted was his mind that he thought each death was thwarting the inevitable fissure of the San Andreas Fault that would swallow up the city of San Francisco, taking thousands of lives. After his arrest, when asked why he did it, he explained: "We human beings, through the history of the world, have protected our continents from cataclysmic earthquakes by murder. In other words, a minor natural disaster avoids a major natural disaster."[42]

---

[42] Katie Dowd, "'Murder Capital of the World': The Terrifying Years When Multiple Serial Killers Stalked Santa Cruz," SFGate, April 17, 2018, https://www.sfgate.com/bayarea/article/santa-cruz-kemper-mullin-frazier-murders-12841990.php.

By the time I met with him in 1999, he'd been locked up for about twenty-six years. He is still locked away and most likely will never see freedom. For a criminal to be paroled from prison for any sort of crime, killing or otherwise, parole boards need to know that the criminal has taken responsibility for his actions, and demonstrates remorse and a convincing desire and ability to contribute to society upon being discharged. Above all, the board needs to know he will not pose a danger to the community.

Authorities must be persuaded that the criminal is no longer a threat to himself or others, and that rehabilitation during incarceration has been successful. The mind is healed. The urges to kill or terrorize are gone. The chances of a repeat of the crimes are nil. The mental twists that unleashed their darkest impulses have been resolved.

Well that's *mostly* the case. Here in California, we have some politicians who seem to have no problem letting a bunch of dangerous criminals out, and who allow anyone to waltz into our country from outside our borders without being properly vetted. These politicians refuse to comply with at least part of the law due to overly broad sanctuary city laws that block illegal dangerous individuals from being deported upon release from jail, and then these same politicians are not held accountable for the resultant crime wave and trail of death that unfold when politics trumps methodology. It is interesting to note that the same politicians who are anti-death-penalty because of the fear that innocent people will be executed often support overly broad policies that allow people to remain in our country to hurt, rape, and kill. It is a fact. Many innocent people—including police—have been killed by people who do not belong in our country and have been arrested for serious crimes on prior occasions. What is an acceptable error rate for these policies versus the death penalty, I wonder?

But I digress. I don't think that Mullin will benefit from the Jerry Browns, Gavin Newsoms, and Kamala Harrises of the world. To this day, Mullin has never met any of the parole board's criteria and likely never will. This is why I believe he should remain behind bars for the rest of his life, lest society be set upon again by a man bent on delivering death at the behest of the demons in his head.

When I spoke with him years after his kills, he spoke of much of his psychotic thinking at the time in the *past* tense. However, he remained extremely delusional—he externalized blame, minimized his crimes, and reflected upon his past delusional ideas as "hypotheses," all of which presuppose a lingering investment in his diseased thought process.

"I like to look at it as if it's only one crime spree," he told me, seemingly trying to again minimize the fact that he was a serial killer. He swirled his hand around on the table in front of him, as if sweeping up all the victims in a neat pile. One crime. Not thirteen.

So a second chance at freedom, something—dare I say?—he so desperately wants, would be a second chance to go on another spree and kill again. While his delusions may have dampened a bit after so many years, I truly believe they are largely just hibernating in the deep, dark depths of his still-broken mind.

After I set up my video camera in the visitor's room at Mule Creek State Prison in California, I waited patiently for Mullin to appear. I asked a corrections officer when he might be brought in as I fidgeted in my chair, ready to get on with the interview. Turned out that the small, weedy-looking man with missing front teeth, a receding hairline and big, round, bulky reading glasses sitting quietly next to me *was* Mullin!

That's how unassuming he is. At just five feet, seven inches tall and weighing roughly 140 pounds, Mullin just blended in like a man waiting for nothing, with nowhere to go but inside his head, quietly glancing around the room for something to fixate his eyes on.

For something to just fixate on.

He went on to provide an incredible journey into his dark and twisted thinking. Even now, twenty years after that day, thoughts of that interview sometimes creep into my mind. When I hear of other random killings that cops announce they believe might be linked to the same perpetrator—killings clearly attributable to one offender, with no discernable pattern of victim; often sloppy, frenzied, and disorganized—I think of Mullin.

I think of the terrifying reality that others just like him are still out there ready to pounce on their innocent prey, and that death could be delivered upon any one of us at the hands of a demented person at any moment, anywhere. We live in a world of illusions in which we think we have control, that if we take precautions, we and our loved ones will be safe. That's often just not the case.

The minds of delusional people, especially those who kill on command by imaginary voices or signs, or kill based on the whims of indiscernible rhythms, are inherently unnerving, largely because there often is no method to these killers' madnesses. At least not outside their own brains. Unlike more organized killers, such as Ted Bundy, who preyed on women, or Jeffrey Dahmer, who liked men and boys, the truly delusional ones, like Mullin, often don't have a specific criteria for their victims. It's just wrong place, wrong time.

This is not to say that Bundy and Dahmer didn't suffer from some sort of mental twist as well, but Mullin truly believed he was being guided by outside forces and that he was killing for the greater good—hallmarks of a delusional person in a deep state of psychosis. The Bundys and Dahmers of the criminal realm usually have personality disorders—pathological ways of viewing themselves and the world around them—typically with an emphasis upon dominance, superiority, predation, and perverse self-gratification. The Mullins of society kill for reasons other than themselves.

Speaking calmly in a matter-of-fact tone while we sat in the prison, Mullin summed it all up neatly, how others were really to blame for his killings, not him: "I believe that I'm sort of like a victim of my family and friends. They were practicing a form of killjoy sadistic witchcraft, and they caused me to be a very naive, gullible, and immature person, and then…they caused me to commit the thirteen murders."

Killjoy sadistic witchcraft, I thought—*there is no such thing*. This was psychosis, and that phrase was merely a neologism born of disordered thinking, an idiosyncratic combination of words, a classic indicator of schizophrenia and other psychotic conditions.

Mullin was born on April 18, 1947, in Salinas, California, an incredibly beautiful part of the country known as the "Salad Bowl of the World," due to its two-billion-dollar agricultural industry that supplies 80 percent of U.S. lettuce and artichokes. It's just a skip from the Pacific Ocean, one hundred miles south of San Francisco, and the birthplace of John Steinbeck. Mullin's date of birth ironically, perhaps even prophetically, coincided with the forty-first anniversary of the catastrophic 1906 Bay Area earthquake, a massive 7.9 on the Richter scale. The violent shaking could be felt all the way from Los Angeles to southern Oregon.

San Francisco's City Hall crumbled. Cable cars came to a screeching halt. And the city soon was enveloped by a raging fire that burned out of control for some four days. Roughly four square miles were leveled; more than twenty-eight thousand buildings were destroyed, and up to three thousand people were killed.

The California earthquake was a centerpiece in Mullin's eventual meltdown. Perhaps his birth on an anniversary of this devastating quake somehow became a harbinger of the delusion-based killings to come.

He was well-mannered and had tons of friends, was involved in all sorts of high school sports, and was even voted Most Likely to Succeed by his classmates. Sadly, success would never be his. Like many whose promising lives are derailed by mental illness, Mullin would soon join the sickest of the sick.

His parents were stern but not abnormally so, just a strict Roman Catholic family living life in the suburbs. In Mullin's early years, there were no signs of what was to come. This is often the case; some people don't begin presenting with mental illness until well into their late teens or twenties.

Several events later in his life appear to have pushed Mullin over the edge, starting with the death of his best friend in high school, Dean Richardson, in a car crash. Even thirty-four years later as he sat in prison speaking with me, the pain of that loss was palpable in the quivering of his wrinkled lips and the sheer agony that washed across his aging face as he recounted the tale.

It was September 1965. Mullin and Richardson had been close friends for two years, spending nearly every day together during their junior and senior years of high school.

"How did that happen to him? Was he drinking and driving or was it just bum luck?" I asked, prodding with calculation, knowing that this was a monumental moment in Mullin's life that would be the catalyst for what was to come.

Mullin spoke softly about the crash, his eyes wandering from ceiling to floor.

"What did he run into?"

"A whole mess of trees, bouncing off trees like ping-pong balls."

"Did that affect you?"

"Oh, it tore me apart. It just tore me apart.... As far as tears, I've never shed so many tears before or after that event. A flood. Personal flood."

He squeezed his lips together tightly as if fighting back the urge to shed even more tears, then rambled somewhat incoherently for a bit before coming around to the theme that permeated our talk: freedom.

"I've never been married, and so I want to have a second chance myself.... Even if they put those electric collars on my ankle and around my neck, if they give me a second chance, I'm pretty sure that I could prove that I'm a halfway decent citizen, and that I just literally at that time in my life stepped over a line into total insanity and was completely out of my mind at the time."

I listened and nodded, offering him affirmation, knowing I needed to placate him, however unrealistic his thoughts, if I was ever going to get at the heart of why I was there—to learn more about what exactly makes people like Herbert Mullin tick. Or Herb, as I called him.

But it would take some time.

"Perhaps you could walk me through how you think this all came about and walk me through the crimes?"

"I can't walk you through the crimes, because I'm not going in there anymore. You know, I mean that that part is over. Those people deserve more respect than talking about whatever happened. And I hope that they're okay today."

It was clear we were going to be there a while.

After Richardson's death, Mullin sank into depression and began experimenting with marijuana and extensively using LSD, things we now know can exacerbate and speed up the onset of psychosis in those who are already predisposed to mental illness. Tune in, turn on, drop out. Get high. Some just never come down.

He worked odd jobs and tried unsuccessfully to join the military. He also became sexually confused and dabbled in homosexuality with a friend. This, too, began to unravel Mullin's mind, as he couldn't really figure out who he was anymore or what the future held for him. Then came the voices in his head, voices he perceived to be real—of his parents, his friends, the community. He went in and out of mental institutions and would ritualistically burn his penis with a lit cigarette.

In September 1972, Mullin moved back in with his parents in the Santa Cruz area and stopped taking the medication that had partly been diminishing the crazy thoughts in his head. He took a job as a busboy a month later, but things quickly started to unravel. He heard his father's voice in his head commanding him to kill.

It was also around this time that an eccentric Bay Area scientist predicted to the world that a major earthquake would devastate California in the coming months. While most people just wrote it off as the wild ramblings of a self-proclaimed seismic expert, Mullin saw it as a call to action. He had to do something—in fact, the voices would command it. His first kill was just around the corner.

It was a dreary morning on Friday, October 13, 1972. Mullin would later claim that his father had been sending him messages telepathically in the days before, telling him that "if I didn't kill, it would bring shame to the family." He grabbed a baseball bat from the family garage and was driving along a winding road through the forest when he spotted a man walking alone on the side of the street. It was Lawrence White, a fifty-five-year-old homeless transient.

Mullin drove past him, then pulled off just ahead. He popped open the hood of his blue Chevrolet station wagon and acted as if he was having car troubles. White approached and offered to take a look at the engine. Mullin bashed his head in with the bat. He then shoved White's lifeless body off the road and drove away.

Mullin later said that White appeared to him as Jonah from the Bible and had sent him mind-to-mind messages, among them, "Kill me so that others will be saved." He called this the "Die Song," something he would recount almost incoherently to a psychiatrist after his arrest: "I'm telling you to die. I'm telling you to kill yourself or be killed so that my continent will not fall off into the ocean. See, it's all based on reincarnation. This dies to protect my strata."

During our talk years later, he explained to me that this first kill is what got everything started. And that more voices in his head, specifically from his father, told him that if he didn't kill, he would be considered a coward. "If you don't go and kill someone, then that's what you're going to be," he told me the voices said. "And this was nonverbal communication, so for all I know, it might not have existed. I mean, obviously it didn't exist, because telepathy and these types of psychic phenomenon [sic] are probably impossible."

"Might not have existed"? "Probably impossible"? Clearly, he still had not come to grips with reality even after nearly three decades behind bars.

His next kill would come eleven days later, on October 24, 1972. Mary Guilfoyle was late for a job interview, so—like many during those freewheeling hippie days in the Santa Cruz area—she started to walk with her thumb out, hoping to hitchhike, when Mullin pulled up.

The twenty-four-year-old woman didn't give him a second glance before hopping into his station wagon. He was quite handsome, soft-spoken, and nice, with a stature that wasn't much bigger than hers. Not threatening at all.

As she kicked back in the car relaxing, Mullin pulled off onto a side street, whipped out a hunting knife, and stabbed her repeatedly. He then proceeded to disembowel her, tearing out her organs and scattering them in the woods. Her body wouldn't be found for nearly a year.

Just over a week later, on Thursday, November 2, Mullin walked into the Saint Mary Catholic Church in the town of Los Gatos, about a half-hour's drive from Santa Cruz. He needed to confess his sins. It was All Souls' Day, a time for commemoration of all the faithful departed—those who have been baptized but were believed to be stuck in purgatory because they died with the guilt of lesser sins.

Mullin claimed the voice in his head once again began speaking to him, explaining that Father Henri Tomei, whom he met inside the church, was volunteering himself to be sacrificed for the greater good of humanity. The "Die Song" played again in his head.

He stabbed the sixty-five-year-old priest to death in the confessional booth.

Mullin would then take a three-month hiatus from killing. I can only surmise that maybe he was thinking that the deaths had been working to stave off the great earthquake. At the same time, it is also possible that he was aware that authorities were looking to catch whoever was doing these murders. You can be mentally ill and delusional and still know what you are doing and that others see it as wrong.

But the hiatus wouldn't last long. On January 25, 1973, Mullin got it into his head that he needed to kill James Gianera, the man who had introduced him to smoking marijuana and with whom he had taken considerable amounts of LSD. He drove to the home where he had last known Gianera to be living. He was greeted at the door by a woman named Kathy Francis, who told him Gianera had moved; she provided him with the address.

Mullin offered his polite thanks and left. But it wouldn't be the last Francis would see of him. Gianera let Mullin in without a second thought, a bad move. Mullin shot him and his wife, Joan, in the head before repeatedly stabbing them both in an enraged act of overkill. He then drove back to Kathy Francis' house, where he fatally shot her and her two young sons, then viciously stabbed all three of them after they were dead. Was it rage or more misperceptions and psychosis that mandated it? Given his refusal to "go there" during our prison interview, I wasn't able to delve into that with him.

Two weeks later, on February 6, 1973, Mullin came across four teenage boys camping in the woods. He says he telepathically asked them if they would allow themselves to be sacrificed and they agreed, again hearing the "Die Song." He shot all four to death on the spot.

And he wasn't done killing yet, and likely would have kept on killing had he not been caught. During his crime spree, as he liked to call it, he had become a multiple murderer, with two mass murders in less than two weeks. The next kill, however, would bring an end to the spree.

Mullin was out in his station wagon getting firewood for his family when he believed he heard yet another telepathic message from his father. "Don't deliver a stick of wood until you kill somebody," the voice in his head told him. At about that time, he saw a man named Fred Perez working in his driveway. Mullin casually pulled up and shot the man in the chest.

He'd been lucky so far. Even without much planning or calculation to the killings, he'd managed to get away clean. The cops hadn't even been close to narrowing in on him as a suspect. But on this day, his luck would run out. A neighbor heard the shot, caught a glimpse of Mullin's car and license plate, and called the police.

Mullin was stopped by a patrol officer at a red light a short time later and immediately arrested. He didn't even put up a fight. While he never said it at the time, or even later during interrogations or court proceedings, Mullin acknowledged to me that he was relieved.

"What was your reaction when the police got you?" I asked him during our 1999 prison interview.

He blew air out of his puckered lips, making a hollow whistling sound, and rolled his eyes. "I don't know.... I knew a big change was going to take place in my life.... I'd say that I was relieved that that part was over. I knew that they'd keep me out of society for a long time. And from there, you know, I can see now that I know that these places really do heal people. If you have a psychological illness and you come to prison, and if you are determined and you make up your mind to get healthy, these people will help you get your health."

Mullin didn't deny the killings, though he was charged with only ten of them in Santa Cruz County. The others had taken place elsewhere. The trial essentially came down to sanity. It was not a whodunit, it was a "whydunit." Clearly, Mullin wasn't firing on all cylinders and was the epitome of a delusional person. But none of that mattered. The case hinged on whether he was sane at the time of each of the killings, and it devolved into a battle of the experts.

The defense argued that he was clearly unhinged, suffering from paranoid schizophrenia and therefore not responsible for the crimes, that he should be locked away in a mental institution, not prison. The prosecution, however, contended that Mullin had made sane decisions both before and after each of the killings, and had even made some efforts to hide his involvement, which meant there was premeditation, criminal presence of mind, and forethought regarding his wicked plans.

Prosecutors pointed to his washing the blood off the baseball bat used in the first murder, taking shell casings from another crime scene, scrubbing the serial number from his gun, and getting rid of witnesses, like Kathy Francis—whom he would have had no reason to go back and murder had she not directed him to Gianera's home.

Those were tough facts for his defense to overcome, particularly the elimination of a witness. He could have just killed her first if she was indeed just another sacrificial soul in Mullin's grand plan to stave off the great quake. After all, the prosecution tried to explain, just because Mullin's delusions and the voices in his head were telling him to kill didn't mean that he didn't understand that what he was doing was wrong. You can be delusional and still know what you are doing and that it is wrong. And if he knew the killings were wrong at the time he was doing them, that would indicate sanity during those fleeting moments of the attacks.

One psychiatrist retained by the defense, Donald Lunde, testified that Mullin was indeed a paranoid schizophrenic. He played for the court a recording of an interview with Mullin during which Mullin tried to offer an explanation for his murder spree, rationalizing his crimes by again referencing the "Die Song."

"People like to sing the 'Die Song,' you know; people like to sing the 'Die Song.' If I am president of my class when I graduate from high school, I can tell two, possibly three young *Homo sapiens* to die. I can sing that song to them and they'll have to kill themselves or be killed…. They have to do that in order to protect the ground from an earthquake… because all the other people in the community had been dying all year long…. We have to chip in, so to speak, to the darkness. We have to die also. And people would rather sing the 'Die Song' than murder."[43]

Lunde later explained more regarding what Mullin rambled to him in a book called *The Die Song: A Journey Into the Mind of a Mass Murderer*: "He told me that if I would prepare a chronology of the world's wars and famines and compare it with a list of major earthquakes throughout history, I would see that when the death rate goes up, the number of earthquakes goes down."

Mullin clearly was fixated on this earthquake phenomenon, something obviously far from reality, but it didn't help at his trial. He was found to have been legally sane at the time of the killings and eventually was convicted on all ten counts, which delivered him multiple life sentences. He won't be eligible for parole until 2020. He has already been denied release several times. I suspect the jury members thought he might be insane but were so afraid that Mullin might one day be freed that they overlooked it as a minor detail in order to ensure he'd be locked away for life.

Some years later, renowned FBI profiler Robert Ressler would confirm what he believed was in the jury's mind, that Mullin was indeed insane, about as insane as it gets. He surmised that Mullin had suffered a great injustice by being sent to prison instead of a mental institution. Perhaps Ressler was right, but there's no point now in rewriting history. And it's tough to overcome the facts that argue for his *legal* sanity: He knew he was killing, and he took efforts to evade detection.

Mullin was and remains exactly where he needs to be, if only because he still won't take full responsibility, and the crack in his mental fault

---

[43] Donald T. Lunde and Jefferson Morgan, *The Die Song: A Journey into the Mind of a Mass Murderer*, (New York: W. W. Norton & Company, 1980).

line remains ever present, ready to shake the earth again through human aggression unleashed. "I've been in prison twenty-six years. I don't want to spend my whole life in prison, and I don't want to be the only one blamed for committing the crimes I committed," he told me with purpose.

"How did your family, friends, causing you to be gullible, naive, and immature, lead to the crimes?"

"I think as people mature mentally, they begin to see that there is a pecking order in society. If you go to a party, there's a pecking order. Certain people are more powerful than other people. And as you mature mentally, you begin to figure out how to deal with that pecking order so that sometimes you can put yourself in a more powerful position. And then at other times, you have to put yourself in a subordinate position so that you don't become ostracized, so that you don't become the whipping post…. I knew nothing about the pecking order."

He quickly brought the blame back around to his parents and appeared to sink into a deep sadness. "I think it may be, it's the most beautiful thing in the world, where parents teach their child how to live a good healthy life. And I wanted that so bad. And I kept hoping for it with words. But my parents didn't give it to me," he said in a low, raspy whisper.

Mullin then began to explain how his parents, not him, were the real criminals.

"What crimes did your parents commit?" I asked.

"It's probably along the lines of premeditated second-degree murder. Because they didn't know who was gonna kill me, just knew they were sending me out to go kill somebody…. I knew that during the crimes… that they knew what was going on. And so I figured that they prepared me to commit those crimes by keeping me in the state I was in and making it worse and worse and worse."

"So you felt they were controlling you?"

"You know, I'm fifty-one years old. I'm saying that now. My parents are dead. They're dead. So maybe God is making them suffer. Maybe God is punishing them."

This sort of external blaming is all part of the delusional thinking, at least for Mullin. More often, it's a component of an overall personality disorder. And people with delusions can also have a personality disorder, complicating things even further. Delusional people typically have a fixed or false belief, usually organized into some sort of conspiracy that is related to their mental illness—in Mullin's case, the supposed impending cataclysmic earthquake.

It's not a condition unto itself but a symptom that can be associated with a number of different mental disorders and certain types of intoxication, like the state of being on marijuana or hallucinogens. Extensive drug use doesn't necessarily cause mental illness but can exacerbate its onset. And unfortunately, some people who get high just never end up coming down because their drug use has flipped the switch of their vulnerability to that mental illness. So what started as a drug-induced condition becomes a permanently psychotic and delusional state.

But let me clear. Most mentally ill individuals, even those afflicted with severe delusions, do not go on to become violent. A very small percentage, in fact, act on their internal demons with outward rage or compulsion to complete a mandatory mission, and those are the scary ones, like Mullin.

Even something seen as so minor in the drug world, like marijuana, can have a massive impact on the mind. And the cannabis of today is rocket fuel compared to that of the '60s, '70s, and '80s. Breeding and other enhancements have resulted in a very potent, highly toxic substance for some, *without* some of the natural antipsychotic compounds that used to counteract destabilization.

Numerous research studies have shown—despite all the lobbying by pro-cannabis groups—that regular use of marijuana can actually speed up by an average of three years the onset of mental illness in youths who abuse it during their adolescence. This is an important fact, because the later the onset of the illness, the higher the baseline level of functioning for when they do get sick and the easier it can be to treat the disorder. Getting sick sooner means they are not going to get as well, even if they do finally get medicated.

Delusional people's fixed and false beliefs can be extremely bizarre, like the idea that one has been abducted by aliens, or less bizarre but still not rooted in reality, such as the notion that one has an illness like AIDS or cancer without actually having it. And despite clear evidence to the contrary, delusional people continue to believe the unbelievable.

Such was the case with Damascio Torres, who stormed the emergency room of the Los Angeles County+USC Medical Center. He shot three doctors and then took another one hostage; he finally surrendered after a five-hour standoff with authorities.

It was February 8, 1993. The forty-year-old transient had first visited the hospital in 1982, when he claimed to have been injected with a mysterious virus that was slowly killing him year after year. He felt he was rotting alive from the inside out. Incensed, Torres would make repeated visits to the facility complaining that he had a foul stench, couldn't digest his food, and had no control over his intestines.

Each time, he claimed, doctors refused to help him and instead kept insisting that he go to a mental hospital, that nothing was wrong with him physically. But he was convinced otherwise, though none of his thinking was based in reality. In his delusional mind, Torres believed he was the victim of a medical research conspiracy. Documents found in his hotel room after his arrest explained that he was being used as a guinea pig in a secret experiment.

"They are going to pay for treating me like a laboratory animal," Torres wrote. In his journal, he detailed the steps he was planning to get his revenge. They would all happen in meticulous order.

1. Walk to USC hospital.
2. Go to 5040.
3. Avoid metal detectors.
4. Surrender if caught by female deputy.
5. Surrender if caught by a group of deputies.
6. Shoot single male guard if possible.
7. Have a .44 Magnum in Army jacket pocket.
8. Have .380 inside belt.

9. Take .44 lever Magnum strapped to torso.
10. Cut off stock!
11. Get to the screeners table at 8:30 am.
12. Shoot all three screeners one shot to head, one shot to body.
13. If 4 screeners 2 shots each, if 3 shoot 2 in the ass empty gun put in poc.
14. Grab 2 nurse hostages take to inner ward.
15. Pull .44 Magnum pocket shoot all doctors.
16. Shoot anybody with a gun.
17. No talk, no dialogue that shit is for T.V.
18. Pull lever action from jacket.
19. Get more nurse hostages.
20. No men.
21. No black hostages.
22. Take hostages to door and close.
23. Go to lobby inside ward shoot doctors.
24. Put handcuffs on hostages also leg-cuffs.
25. Reload .380 .44 Magnum and .380 clip not reliable.
26. Practice cocking and trigger pull on .44 Magnum.
27. Return to a cubicle and stay there all day.
28. Make demands (no money, no getaway) make USC take responsibility for AIDS experiments in 79, 80, 81, 82.
29. Tie other hostages with string.
30. Make sure no doctors in wards if there are shoot them.
31. Yell out "Hostages I have hostages" "Back off."
32. Don't let guards delay you shoot if they hesitate.
33. Declare myself a human guinea pig infected with AIDS by USC.

It was striking how detailed the journal entry was, yet not much of the action went as planned. Although you can clearly see that his violence originated with delusion, his implementation and execution demonstrated organization, strong awareness of what he was doing, and awareness that the police would be trying to stop him. He knew his planned actions were wrong, delusional or not.

Various doctors opined that he suffered from a variety of ailments, including chronic borderline schizophrenia, paranoid schizophrenia, and a paranoid delusional disorder, and that he truly believed he was acting in self-defense. Prosecutors, however, argued that he simply wanted revenge and that he knew what he was doing was wrong, despite likely suffering from mental illness. His journal writings also didn't help the defense case that he just snapped, since he had taken great pains to plan out how he thought the day would go down.

He was convicted of attempted murder and false imprisonment, deemed sane, and sentenced to life in prison with the possibility of parole. He was last denied freedom in 2018 and won't become eligible again for parole until 2023.

In 1999, about six years after the attack, I visited with Torres at a California prison. He was just as delusional then as he had been at the time of the attack. He explained to me that "they're still conspiring against me. They're still doing it."

"What could have been done differently?" I asked.

"Nothing could have been done. It was a done deal. For some reason, they just kept at me and at me for ten years.... They kept at it, kept at it until I just struck back."

"Are you a religious man, then or now?"

"Well, that day I prayed that God would deliver my enemies to me, and they were there. They were there."

They were there simply because that is where they worked, but in his deluded mind, he drew a conclusion of special meaning, that God had delivered them to him. This is "referential thinking," something that commonly happens in psychosis.

"Have you figured out what they were up to?" I asked.

"Experimentation. They're using street people for experimentations.... I was their Frankenstein monster.... They created me, so it's all on them."

Delusions are frequently fueled and enhanced by false sensations, better known as hallucinations, that often co-occur in the most serious mental illness. So people might hear, as Herbert Mullin did, voices that are threatening or demeaning them or trying to convince them of a potential danger. These hallucinations become part of the evidence used to support their unrealistic beliefs and help propel them deeper into chaos, feeding the delusional system. I refer to it as a system because there are often highly detailed plot lines, explanations, backstories, and characters that are well-developed, particularly in longer-term delusions.

Take a delusional individual like Mark Hilbun, who helped popularize the phrase "going postal," now used in America to refer to the actions of any criminal who becomes extremely and uncontrollably violent, then carries out a killing rampage, typically in a workplace environment. Similar to Mullin's form of delusional thinking, Hilbun's thinking involved an impending apocalypse that was well beyond any sense of reality.

He was, and still is, just absolutely out of his mind.

Hilbun was born on May 9, 1954, and raised in a comfortable middle-class home in suburban Orange County, California. Throughout his school years, he was a quiet, introverted student whose main interests were reading books and listening to music. After high school, he joined the Air Force. As a member of the security police squadron at Edwards Air Force Base, he first showed signs of mental instability. Hilbun was hospitalized for a psychiatric evaluation and diagnosed as having a schizoid personality with depressive features.

This mental illness is characterized by a pattern of indifference to social relationships, and those who have it tend to avoid communal activities and interacting with others. They are not afraid of social interaction or necessarily anxious about it, just indifferent to it. By early adulthood, schizoid individuals start to emotionally detach from society, preventing them from having close relationships with other people.

The accuracy of mental health diagnoses is often an issue in these cases, with people such as Hilbun being frequently misdiagnosed. Then throw in the issue of corrupt hired-gun shrinks distorting their opinions in service of the retaining party in the criminal court proceedings, and diagnoses and opinions can become quite far-fetched. That's why I like to look at the data myself and arrive at my own opinions, with careful attention to the most objective information available.

In Hilbun's case, it is very unlikely that he would have been hospitalized for having a schizoid personality with depressive features. The usual reason for involuntary hospitalization is danger to self or others, among other things, and the usual culprits are an acute depressed state, a bipolar episode resulting in psychosis, or some other psychotic condition that causes the person to lose touch with reality.

Given that Hilbun was later diagnosed with bipolar disorder and clearly manifested psychotic symptoms, it seems most likely that something related to this state of mind was presenting itself. Certainly he may have been reclusive, but that is not why he was hospitalized.

The Air Force later took Hilbun's weapon away from him due to concerns about his well-being and safety, and in December 1980, he received an honorable discharge. A few years later, Hilbun took a job as a letter carrier with the United States Postal Service at a facility in Dana Point, California. He lived an almost reclusive home life alone in a tiny apartment, spending most of his days off from work kayaking, reading, watching MTV, and listening to his extensive music collection.

Things were pretty quiet and uneventful for Hilbun until the spring of 1992, when some of his coworkers began to notice alarming changes in his behavior and a deep sense of paranoia. His psychosis was beginning to take hold. A few months later, during a trip with colleagues to the Orange County Fair, Hilbun, who seldom had expressed any interest in women, took a liking to co-worker Kim Springer. He became obsessed with her over the ensuing weeks.

When she rebuffed his advances, Hilbun began stalking her everywhere she went. Springer ended up filing a complaint with police, but it was withdrawn after Hilbun agreed to stay away from her and undergo psychiatric treatment. That same month, Hilbun lost his job as his behavior became increasingly bizarre. He was soon committed to a psychiatric hospital, where he was given drugs that appeared to help stabilize his condition. Upon release, however, he quit taking them, and his erratic behavior returned.

Less than a year later, consuming heavy amounts of marijuana, he began to sink deeper into his own delusions. He came to the unwavering belief that an apocalyptic event was imminent and would soon bring the world to an end. He saw the signs everywhere—even, oddly, in a gangland peace accord that was being orchestrated at the time between the Crips and the Bloods, and in the migration of swallows that travel thousands of miles from Argentina to San Juan Capistrano, California, each year.

These were to Hilbun unquestionable evidence of the pending end of civilization as we knew it. The world was going to be rebooted, and he had been designated as the new Adam to repopulate the planet with Kim Springer, who would be his Eve. The apocalypse was coming, and coming soon. He now had a date: Mother's Day—Sunday, May 9, 1993.

"The world would end; all hell would break loose," Hilbun told me during our prison interview a few years after the incident. "I was committed…to the plan to survive the holocaust."

Now, reader, do you ever wonder why, when people are delusional, it seems to always be that they are the center of the most significant events, the main focus of a grandiose master plan? Or that they are related to some larger-than-life figure, or have been reincarnated from or are being persecuted by somebody important to popular or historic culture?

Well, I often find my mind wandering to these same questions. In the end, many people crave infamy or significance, and self-absorption adds to the equation. I cannot recall hearing of anyone delusional believing they were a slave forced to build the Pyramids in a prior life.

On May 6, 1993, a few days before he believed the world would come to an end, Hilbun fatally stabbed his sixty-three-year-old mother, then slashed the throat of her cocker spaniel. He claimed he had to kill them to spare them from the impending holocaust and postapocalyptic misery that he had been warned about by radio host Howard Stern through subliminal messages during one of Stern's programs.

He then headed to the Dana Point post office to get his Eve, Kim Springer. He was planning to kidnap her and take her with him to Baja, Mexico, where they would together repopulate the planet once everyone else had died in the worldwide calamity. He stormed the building armed with a gun, and when one of his friends and former colleagues tried to shield Springer, Hilbun shot him point blank between the eyes. In the hail of gunfire that followed, Hilbun shot and wounded another former co-worker.

Hilbun soon fled the scene without Springer and went on a two-day rampage, during which he shot and wounded several more people in three separate attacks before being arrested while drinking cocktails and watching television at a Huntington Beach, California, sports bar. Not quite Baja, and not entirely consistent with awaiting the pending apocalypse.

He is now serving life in prison with no chance of parole.

When I met with him a few years later, he was low-key, soft-spoken, and reserved. He absolutely loved music, and me being a rock-and-roller myself, we shared that interest and it helped get him to open up to me. So our conversation naturally segued into music—Led Zeppelin, Neil Young, the Rolling Stones, and Buffalo Springfield. He was excited about a boxed set soon to be released.

He told me that he had killed his mother as an act of love and that he had attacked at the behest of God: "God directed me. God actually did it. God gives life, takes life. I was God's instrument.... The world was going to hell, and a major change was going to happen."

"How did you come to believe that?"

"Somehow, I had been chosen to help restart the world, restart the human race.... It seemed like the entrenched power structure was determined to stay where it was and God had decided we would be swept right out of the way." His thinking was that he and Kim Springer would keep the world going even after the hell storm that would wipe the slate clean of humanity: "We'd get together, and it would be Adam and Eve all over again. Start from scratch.... The rest of the world would be reborn."

It was hard to determine whether he still believed these delusions, as he waffled back and forth between seeming to acknowledge that none of them were real and speaking of the incredible responsibility bestowed upon him to save the world.

"Do you believe this now?" I asked.

"No."

But that could just be because the apocalypse never came, and so now he was trying to reason away his unreasonable belief in the doomsday scenario.

"I look back and see that I went over the edge...when I decided to put the plan into action.... But it was my responsibility to make sure the human race survived," he said. That "but" was a pretty big qualification and underscored his continued lingering belief that this delusion might be true.

The tendency for people who are psychotic like Hilbun is to grossly misperceive that there are hidden messages in innocuous or normal events, and to see connections between events or occurrences that do not actually exist. For example, a delusional subject might watch a newscaster and believe that a certain movement or voice intonation has a meaning beyond its being just a movement or intonation. To the delusional individual who is experiencing this referential thinking, it may represent a signal that the end of the world is near and that only believers and a special few can detect these signs—in other words, the delusional person has been given some sort of special power.

As mentioned, he also may see connections between unrelated events, such as an eclipse and an earthquake in another country, and believe them to portend something to come. One guy I interviewed came to believe that the government was abducting people, substituting imposters in their place, then having trash trucks collect the victims, who were quickly killed and incinerated. He had gone off his medication, was smoking a lot of marijuana, and had stopped going to his treatment appointments.

During the process of trying to fight off the threat, which included fighting the government he no longer viewed as legitimate, he broke into a house, found a loaded shotgun, and ended up killing two innocent people before being arrested. No amount of attempted convincing could change his belief in this conspiracy. He was fixated, and his thinking would never change. He never believed the killings were wrong, illegal, or immoral.

Medication used to treat mental disorders, especially psychosis with delusions, may dampen some of the overt symptoms, like agitation, hallucinations, or voices in the head, but in many of the more serious cases I've seen, the individual still holds on to delusional beliefs. The violence is controlled, but the ideas persist.

With Herbert Mullin, his own mental illness actually seemed to frighten him. While still somewhat delusional, he knows he never wants to have those wicked thoughts again, those desires to kill. I prodded him about this during our final meeting in prison, trying to get at whether he even understood what his state of mind had been at the time of the killings, trying to understand more about whether he did indeed know, well, if he was mentally off. I'm not sure I ever got that answer, but clearly he knew that something had been—and still was—wrong with him.

"Would it be safe to say you were in Never Never Land?" I asked softly but pointedly toward the end of our talk. Mullin paused and looked surprised, almost worried at the thought of vanishing again into a world of terrors inside his mind.

"Well, whatever that really means, I bet it's a bad place. I don't ever want to go there."

CHAPTER 8

"I'll Be Watching You"

Stalkers and Their Prey

"I kissed thee ere I killed thee. No way but this,
Killing myself, to die upon a kiss."

—William Shakespeare, from *Othello*

It all began for Lenora Claire in the spring of 2011 as she was gaining some impressive exposure for her art and in her Hollywood career, with a spread in *LA Weekly*. There she was, in a striking photograph with her bright red hair draped over her shoulders, sitting in a chair holding a monkey in her lap.

"Lenora Claire is one of America's weirdos," the story began. "Weirdo," to Claire, is a term of endearment. She's no doubt eccentric, describing herself to the publication as "P.T. Barnum with boobs." *LA Weekly* isn't exactly *The New York Times*, but it's a cool, hip, free newspaper that reflects trends, reports on cutting-edge events, and covers interesting people.

As Claire mingled with guests at one of her art galleries that spring day, "weirdo" took on a whole new meaning. And it began for her an unimaginably terrifying years-long journey, one that is still ongoing. A man approached her wearing a Halloween space suit costume, helmet and all.

It didn't faze her at all at the time. As she explained to me recently, "I have a really high tolerance for funny people, so I didn't really think much of it." Quirky people surround her in her daily life. It's just her style. But things would soon get way beyond quirky, beyond eccentric, beyond uncomfortable to absolutely frightening.

Claire and I would become friends over the ensuing years as she tried to navigate her upended life. But we'll get to that later.

"So he comes up to me, engages me in conversation, and I can tell he's bright. I can tell he's quirky. I can tell something is off, but it's not quite alarming at the beginning," she told me a few months before the writing of this book, recalling in detail the day her life changed forever. "Then, like, you just snap your fingers; his eyes went crazy, and he looks at me and he says, 'You look like Jessica Rabbit. I'm going to stalk you.'"

It wasn't the first time she'd been compared to the character from the film *Who Framed Roger Rabbit*. The two both have flowing long red locks and, well, enormous breasts often accentuated by low-cut outfits. But, of course, the stalking comment spooked her, and she soon had the man ushered out of the gallery.

A few days later, things got really strange. Friends who had seen him there began calling her after recognizing him through numerous media reports as having been arrested multiple times for stalking Ivanka Trump, daughter of then-private citizen and businessman Donald Trump. Things were getting really weird, but they would get so much worse.

The man is Justin Massler, who apparently has been diagnosed with schizophrenia and who legally changed his name to Cloud Starchaser. Yes, Cloud Starchaser. It's not the first time a deranged stalker has altered his name. When I asked Madonna's stalker how I should refer to him during a prison interview, he exclaimed, "I am the fifth amoeba of God!" (Upon his declaration, I wondered to myself who the first four were.) Filmmaker Steven Spielberg's stalker asked that I call him "Mickey— Mickey Mouse," when I interviewed him in prison. At the time, he was in solitary confinement, reportedly for stalking another inmate.

Delusions can twist perceptions of self-identity. Cloud Starchaser, though, that says it all—the dark cloud, chasing the stars. Madonna's stalker, interestingly enough, had threatened that when he got out, he'd get a gun and that he'd be found literally shooting at the stars in the sky, trying to knock them down: "That's where I'll be, trying to knock your stars down."

Massler has been in and out of jail and psychiatric treatment facilities for years due to his stalking of Ivanka Trump and so many others, but he has always been released back onto the streets.

Claire went on with her life, eventually closing down her art gallery to focus on her career in film and TV in Los Angeles. But Cloud Starchaser wasn't done with her. He would make good on his promise to stalk her.

In subsequent months, Claire began receiving dozens of letters that she said "at first didn't make much sense, rambling incoherently." Yet, and importantly so, Massler had been able to find an address and get them to her. So despite whatever psychosis he had, he could still organize his behavior.

As she described the letters, they were "bizarre but at that point not too alarming." That quickly changed. As she began to receive more and more letters, emails, and correspondence via her website, sometimes hundreds of them a day from Massler, they went from bizarre to violent.

He believed the two were married. He believed it was his mission to save her. Claire was about to become among the hundreds of people in America who are stalked by complete strangers every single day. When a stalker believes that he is loved by or already has a relationship with a victim but there is no basis for that, the clinical term is "erotomania."

Madonna's stalker, for instance, Robert Hoskins, believes he married the star on a tour bus in Denver, when she was in *male* form, in a spiritual ceremony. Beliefs like these are understandably disturbing to victims.

Claire recalled: "The emails started getting hypersexual. He wrote a rape fantasy about me called 'Lord of the Rack'…I'm raped by a hobbit in a volcano. Some really sexually bizarre sci-fi things. It was nonstop. So that's the first time I went to police."

It was now early 2012. She was looking over her shoulder everywhere she went, petrified by the thought of coming face to face with this maniac, a complete lunatic living in some crazy fantasy world of rape and murder, in which she was the star. But police in Los Angeles, surprisingly, were no help. The LAPD had created the first domestic antistalking unit in the country in 1990, and was set up for cases just like this while also aiming to educate the entire department about options in pursing stalker cases.

But personnel change, priorities shift, and politics sometimes results in less-than-ideal staffing, which means mistakes are made. So the police officers whom Claire first reached out to told her they could issue a protective order, but they needed to know where he lived so he could be served with the paperwork. Their assistance at that point stopped there.

And Claire had no clue where he lived. She'd only seen him that one time at her gallery and had never replied to any of his correspondence. "They just told me they couldn't do anything for me and 'Good luck to you.'" You'd think they would want to take on such an over-the-top, creepy, and obvious stalking case, but there are, unfortunately, lazy cops. That was one of them for sure.

She walked out infuriated, depressed, anxious, and angry, with "victim blame and shame," as she called it.

Massler, or Cloud Starchaser, whatever you want to call him, carried on with his campaign of terror against Claire for several more years. The messages waffled between his being in love and in a relationship with her, and his wanting to murder and rape her. She never saw him, never had any physical contact with him, but for all she knew, he was watching her every move.

He sent a death threat to a friend and boss of Claire's at a casting office. She soon lost the job.

That's one of many problems victims experience. Everyone around them is scared shitless and doesn't want to take the risk. You can't necessarily blame those people, but once again, the victim suffers for something he or she didn't cause.

By early 2015, Claire had been stalked for nearly four years by Massler. "At that point, I now have stacks of physical letters, literally thousands of emails from him, rape fantasies, murder threats, you name it," Claire recalled. She went back to the cops, thinking now surely they could do something about this.

Nope. Their advice? "You can start by dying your hair. That will get you less attention. And you could go off the internet," Claire said she was told.

I cannot express enough how disappointed I was that some lazy, loser cop would outrageously infer that *she* needed to change her life to accommodate the stalker, and that he would impose his judgments about how her appearance somehow had brought this on. A Neanderthal cop like that does not deserve to wear a badge, let alone an LAPD badge. He tarnishes the hard work that most of them do to do the right thing, working the extra hours and putting in the effort to help people like Claire.

What a slacker, and he could get someone killed through his laziness. Down the road, I'm thinking now, this guy needs to be identified and dealt with.

Claire had to become her own fighter, her own protector. Police wouldn't do anything for her. Unlike Ivanka Trump, who can afford top-notch round-the-clock security, Claire was practically on her own.

"I needed law enforcement to give a damn," she said.

Doing her own research on her options, she discovered that Massler had more than two dozen protective orders against him from others he had been stalking around the country. Claire finally got a protective order of her own issued against him, but she was still in a pickle. It needed to be served. She needed to know where he was.

As luck would have it, a short time later, Massler showed up at a San Francisco Bay Area office building where a woman he went to high school with was working, apparently having found yet another victim to terrorize. But things didn't go as planned for him. Security was called, police arrived, and he was detained. Claire's protective order was served.

"I'm thinking, 'Finally! This is my first small victory,'" she told me, remembering that day as her having jumped over an enormous hurdle, offering a sense of relief for the first time in years. But not long after that day, she got another message from him.

"I know the LAPD has kidnapped you," it read. He ranted about their being married and how he would save her with his superpowers. Nothing had changed. She was still being bombarded with the same violent sexual emails and death threats.

"This is my life now," she told me she remembered thinking, and she sank into depression.

Protective orders are a great first step, but they're not going to stop a bullet. They're not going to stop someone from jumping out of the bushes with a knife. But if the contact persists, they do give law enforcement a reason to arrest the suspect, with the evidence that the person had been formally put on notice.

In fact, about 60 percent of the time, protective orders do help reduce the stalking behaviors of offenders, but we never tell people it's a bulletproof vest. They just often slow the offender down a bit and put the person in felony territory: Upon violating the order, the offender can be sentenced to a longer prison term. I tell victims a protective order is a test of what this guy is going to do, so hunker down and get a safety plan, but know that this only is a piece of paper. If it works, great. If it doesn't, we escalate the setting of more boundaries, which means the police and prosecutors can take a more aggressive stance. The protective order adds teeth.

But this was Claire's first big step starting to reclaim some of her power from the system that couldn't—or, rather, seemingly wouldn't—help her, the system that wanted to keep revictimizing her. She went on a media blitz, offering interviews about her experience, trying to educate others, helping them deal with their own stalkers, reaching out to government officials trying to get laws enacted to aid people like herself.

She agreed to appear on an episode of CBS's *48 Hours* detailing the horrifying lives of those who are stalked. In preparing for the show, host Erin Moriarty reached out to Massler via a web-based video chat. His incoherent rants showed just how disturbed he was. While such contact is not necessarily recommended, importantly, the video recording provided strong, tangible evidence of what Claire was up against. Moriarty compassionately and responsibly tried to intervene and it was clear that she got what the authorities had not until that point: Claire had a serious problem and she needed help.

"Can you tell me right now that you will stop sending emails, sending Facebook posts, to these women, including Lenora Claire? Will you stop right now?" Moriarty asked.

"You're just a news broadcaster! I'm not going to promise you anything. First of all, those restraining orders aren't legal, and second of all you're, like, a news broadcaster and you don't actually have any authority," he told her, his eyes wide with craziness. "Look, I'm Jesus Christ. I have authority over everyone.... So I'm going to tell you right now. I will not stop sending them, because those restraining orders are illegal and I will continue to defy this government's orders, and if they go against me, I will use the power of God to fuckin' destroy anyone who opposes me!... If you go against me, you're going against Jesus Christ and I will fuckin' destroy you! Try stopping me!"

Moriarty attempted to interrupt as Massler started becoming even more unhinged, screaming angrily into the camera, "You go against God, you die! If they try and stop me I will kill them all! I promise you! They! Will! Die! You will not stop me from sending these messages, and if you try, you! Will! Die!... I will not stop sending emails to Lenora Claire or Ivanka Trump, who is my baby mama! I will kill you! I will destroy you!"

I had been interviewed for the same TV program earlier in the week, and got a call shortly after the video chat with Massler. Erin Moriarty and the team at *48 Hours* were concerned and recognized something needed to be done, and asked for my input. I came in to review video and it wasn't a hard threat assessment. This guy needed to be dealt with. It was a Saturday, and we got hold of the new Threat Management Unit OIC (officer in charge). I couldn't believe what I was hearing from him, and immediately understood Claire's frustration.

He mentioned he was on a camping trip. *He can't be bothered? I thought. That's why the fuck you have detectives and this unit in the first place, to deal with guys like Massler.* I was absolutely blown away. But with the video, my input, and the looming threat of Erin Moriarty and the team of *48 Hours* blowing the lid off Claire's horrifying victimization and the OIC's inadequate response, the OIC was forced to take immediate action, as opposed to putting it off until Monday. The wheels of justice started to move, and Massler was now, finally, being tracked down.

The video chat did nothing to slow down Massler's pursuit behavior. The emails and messages kept coming to Claire, in fact a barrage of them immediately after that video chat. He told them he would not be stopped, and he was making good on his threats.

"It starts to very clearly indicate that we're in a relationship. Sometimes he's Roger Rabbit. I'm Jessica Rabbit. We're married. He's really starting to believe that we're connected," Claire told me. His communications fluctuated between sexual fantasies and death threats. Several times he told her he would kill her by pumping poisonous gas beneath her door while she slept.

"He would go between being in love with me to wanting to kill me," she said.

It was terrifying.

But a short time later, he finally got picked up by cops in Utah for menacing someone else and was locked away in a mental institution. It was the first fruit of the efforts from that Saturday video call. Finally, the boundaries were beginning to appear. And Massler needed them. In my view, someday he will kill someone if left unchecked.

Claire recalled experiencing an overwhelming feeling of relief. It was a roller coaster of emotions. "So finally, for the first time in years, I get a break. I'm feeling good about things. I'm not getting death and rape threats every day," she said.

It didn't last long. Massler escaped.

However, about three weeks later, Donald Trump won the election and became president of the United States. Again, Claire felt relief. After all, Massler also was stalking Ivanka Trump, and now her father was the leader of the free world.

A liberal to her core, no fan of Donald Trump, she told me she thought, "I've won the stalker lottery. I share my stalker with the now-president's daughter. I'm the only person to benefit from the Trump presidency, because now they really have to give a shit." Before that, she said, she had tried to reach out to Ivanka Trump on numerous occasions to share her experiences and seek out help from someone who obviously had the resources to do something, and who was facing the same horror from the same man. She said she never heard back.

But with Trump now president, maybe, just maybe, things would be different. "This is going to be a disaster for the country, but maybe I'll benefit," she half-jokingly recalled thinking at the time. And indeed, something did happen. Massler was soon arrested in New York.

"So now I'm thinking, 'Okay, he's going to go away for a long time now.' Nope, like six weeks later he's released." Massler was soon back in Los Angeles continuing to terrorize Claire. Absolutely nothing had changed. Her life was still in absolute turmoil.

Then in late 2017, Massler reached out and told her he was going to find her and kidnap her at L.A. Comic Con, a yearly festival that celebrates comics, horror shows, sci-fi, anime, and pop culture. And he was dead serious. When she showed up, he was ready to carry out his plan. Fortunately, a crowd of fans tackled him and held him down until police arrived on the scene and arrested him for violating the protective order. It would now be a felony.

"They had done absolutely nothing to help me," Claire recalled. "I caught my own stalker."

This wasn't the first time *that* had happened. Years ago, I worked the first cyberstalking case, in which a rejected suitor stalked his victim by going into S&M and BDSM chat rooms, posing as the victim, and inviting men on the sites to come over and enact rape fantasies.

He then posted the victim's address on the internet. Several times, potentially dangerous men showed up at her residence, interested in gang rape and other sadistic sexual acts. The victim's father went online, did some posing of his own, and found the guy in a chat room. He handed off the information to federal and local law enforcement officers, and they caught him. He was convicted and sentenced to seven years in prison.

In Claire's case, she once again got a reprieve from the constant fear, as Massler was now locked up awaiting trial. In early 2019, he pleaded guilty in a deal with prosecutors and was sentenced to four years in prison.

But it is far from over.

Many positive trends begin in California, but the Golden State also has had an abundance of high-profile stalking cases. Once upon a time there were no stalking laws, but the mass homicide by stalker Richard Farley in 1988, whom we will get to later, and the murder of actress Rebecca Schaeffer, who was fatally shot in 1989 by a stalker, both in California, led the state in 1990 to establish the very first antistalking penal code statute.

Now there's a federal antistalking statute, and all fifty states have since criminalized the behavior in one form or another. Most industrialized countries have done the same.

You know that rule that therapists have a "duty to warn" and break confidentiality when their patient is making threats? Well, the first example of that came from a 1969 stalking case in which a California university student who was seeing a therapist told her of his violent impulses and later ended up stabbing his victim to death, the culmination of his obsessive pursuit.

Prior to these laws, terrified victims would go the police, who would tell them, "Call me when there's a crime." Unfortunately, stalking-related crimes often involve violence, which cannot be reversed.

The typical legal definition of "stalking" mandates a course of repeated, unwanted contact that puts the victim in a state of fear. "Course of conduct" usually means more than one action, but in the real world, it's usually not just two times but an overwhelming number of contacts across multiple modalities.

These days, contact can occur in every universe and platform people have to communicate with, given our social-media-connected world. It is a good thing that we now do not have to wait for a stabbing, homicide, or mass murder in order to intervene as suspects become obsessive and threatening and pursue their victims.

But even with the laws, now three decades later, there are still road-blocks. These include lazy cops, police who do not understand the laws themselves, victims being too terrified to approach police for fear it will aggravate the situation, and victims not seeing the big picture that they are being stalked, because they are just trying to cope with the barrage of scary behavior moment to moment.

Victims also need to provide documentation to police so the cops have something to work with. Throw in overwhelmed and understaffed police agencies, and there still can be inertia.

Stalking laws might allow for a misdemeanor charge, which usually means the stalker will get out pretty quickly or receive summary proba-tion. At other times, at least in California, the best-case scenario on an aggravated felony stalking case is that the suspect gets about seven years in prison.

But what is seven years in prison? It includes time served while await-ing trial, and if it is state time behind bars, parole might cut that time in half. In other situations, a stalker might be deemed insane and instead sent to a mental institution, where the person might be detained longer or released even sooner if he can prove he is no longer a danger.

It's not a perfect system, but it's better than what we had before, which was nothing.

And stalkers can be extremely dangerous. Stalking is an old behav-ior, but stalking-related statutes are relatively new criminal statutes on the books, and even to this day the laws continue to evolve. The cyber-stalking case is a perfect example, representing a course of conduct that included proxies. Remember, that offender never went to the victim's home himself, but others did so, lured there by imposturing internet postings. Prosecutors managed to convict him anyway.

In the Steven Spielberg stalking case, the law evolved once again. The director, thankfully, wasn't home when his stalker showed up with duct tape, handcuffs, and the intent to rape Spielberg in front of his family. But as soon as the Hollywood director was alerted, he was terrified. So that fear upon notification or awareness of being stalked was now being con-sidered in the law as a part of the legal justification to arrest the suspect.

You might think there are a whole lot of nuances, and there are. But that's what happens with the law. And for good reason. Previously, the suspect could challenge an arrest, claiming how could it be considered stalking someone if the person wasn't even home? Or, in the cyberstalking case, how could the suspect be arrested if he himself never even went to the victim's residence?

So the law is an evolving thing, and necessarily must be.

While we hear mostly about celebrity stalking, it's a crime that harms the everyday person even more. Research I conducted on more than a thousand stalking cases found a 75 percent violence rate in cases in which the suspect stalks a private figure, which is usually a rejected former intimate, but only a 2 percent violence rate among instances involving a public figure or celebrity.

That is likely because, as noted in the case of Ivanka Trump, celebrities can hire entourages or private security to protect them before violence occurs. Ordinary citizens, however, usually don't have those kinds of resources and are left to fend for themselves. So that 2 percent doesn't necessarily mean the stalker isn't dangerous, but rather the data may be picking up the benefits of celebrities being able to surround themselves with protection, which fends off the suspect from being able to carry out violence.

I've come up with four categories of stalkers to help us better understand these violence rates.

Lenora Claire's stalker, Justin Massler, fits neatly into the category of Public Figure Stalker. This type fixates on people with some sort of celebrity status or widespread notoriety.

The Intimate Stalker is a criminal who pursues a current or former intimate partner. The most infamous case, one I worked closely on with law enforcement, is that of O.J. Simpson. This type is usually the most ominous menace.

The Acquaintance Stalker hunts someone who could be a co-worker or perhaps a caregiver or a classmate at school. This type can also be quite dangerous. We found a 50 percent violence rate in this group.

Lastly, the Private Stranger Stalker harasses victims he knows from his circle of life but has never met or with whom he has had only passing contact. This type may be that peculiar person who lives down the street or hangs out at the mall who for some reason becomes fixated on an individual he doesn't really know.

Dr. J. Reid Meloy uses the broader term "obsessional following." This term captures the dynamic of individuals who engage in an abnormal or repeated pattern of threats or harassment directed toward an individual, and engage in more than one overt act of unwanted pursuit perceived by the victim as harassing. Stalkers obsess and pursue.

They create terror and distress in their victims in many different ways, including but not limited to telephone calls and texts, in-person approach attempts at the victim's residence, workplace encounters, and sending letters, packages, and unsolicited gifts. All this can eventually lead to extreme violence and even murder.

Stalkers are thin-skinned, narcissistic people with a set of grandiose and demanding expectations and feelings of entitlement. Their perceived connection to their victim becomes like an addiction and provides an external, unquenchable fix for their inadequate sense of self or their insatiable grandiosity. But when they are disappointed by rejection, idealization quickly turns into devaluation, shame, and humiliation, which is then converted into outright rage. They soon seek out ways to punish their victims or teach them a lesson, and this is where things can begin to escalate toward violence.

Victims often perceive that the stalker's desire to control or instill fear is the primary motivation for the stalking behavior, but there can be many convoluted factors. In terms of their mental state, most stalkers who pursue a victim they've known do not have a psychotic illness like delusions or hallucinations, while those who pursue a celebrity or someone they've never met yet, but believe they do have a relationship with, are more likely to have a serious illness like psychosis.

So what *is* wrong with the prior relationship stalkers? They usually have some sort of personality disorder—borderline, narcissism, and dependency issues. I've talked about narcissism already, but the borderline issue warrants a bit of discussion. Think Glenn Close in the movie *Fatal Attraction*, the bunny-boiling lover who cannot tolerate feelings of abandonment.

Drinking and drug use also are common across all these groups of stalkers. So when you start thinking about what it might take to treat or "fix" a stalker, there usually is no easy answer, as every case is often different. That's why we always start by simply trying to keep the victim safe.

There is no better, more well-known example of an intimate stalker than O.J. Simpson. Sure, most people today think of him as just a thug who got away with murder, but it's what led up to the crime that is often overlooked in history. Simpson was the epitome of a stalker, whether you believe he killed his ex-wife and her friend or not.

O.J. and Nicole Brown Simpson had divorced in the early 1990s after he pleaded no contest to a domestic battery charge. Nicole sought out police at the time, saying Simpson had hit her, kicked her, and threatened to kill her. She said she had suffered beatings and emotional abuse for years at the hands of the former football great. It was finally enough, just all that she could take.

But over the ensuing years, Simpson couldn't let the relationship go. Everything culminated on the night of June 12, 1994.

Nicole's friend, Ronald Lyle Goldman, had just arrived at her home to return glasses that had been left at the restaurant he worked at, when an unknown assailant ambushed them. Both were stabbed to death viciously and repeatedly outside her Brentwood, California, condominium. A passerby found the bloodied body of Nicole sprawled out on the steps of a walkway leading up to her apartment. Goldman's body was discovered just a few feet away in some nearby bushes. You know the tragic story.

Given the documented history of abuse by O.J. Simpson against his ex-wife, police quickly zeroed in on him, first noting that they just wanted to speak with him as a potential witness. By that time, Simpson was in Chicago, having apparently caught a late flight out of Los Angeles sometime after the killings. Reached on the telephone by police, who alerted him of what had occurred, Simpson hopped the first flight home, and upon arrival was immediately handcuffed.

He adamantly denied any involvement in the killings. Soon the cuffs were removed and Simpson headed to the police station to be questioned. He was released a few hours later.

As the investigation took on an intense urgency, cops eventually came to the conclusion that they had their man less than a week after the killings. Simpson was the perpetrator. They were certain.

At 8:30 in the morning on Friday, June 17, 1994, police called Robert Shapiro, one of Simpson's attorneys. They said his client needed to surrender by 11:00 a.m. to face murder charges. His arraignment had already been set for later that afternoon.

But Simpson wasn't ready to turn himself in. The time came and went, and he was now labeled a fugitive. What happened next is among the most surreal moments in criminal history: the white Bronco chase, broadcast live on television stations around the world as news helicopters followed Simpson's car on a wild ride across Los Angeles' sprawling freeways, with police cars with flashing lights close behind.

Simpson had left his home with Al "A.C." Cowlings, a former college and pro football teammate of Simpson's. Amidst the chase, District Attorney Gil Garcetti said at a news conference that anyone helping Simpson flee would be prosecuted as a felon.

"We will find Mr. Simpson and bring him to justice," Garcetti told the media, noting that it hadn't yet been decided whether the death penalty would be sought.

Come 5:00 p.m., Shapiro, Simpson's lawyer, held his own press conference, at which a longtime friend of Simpson's read a letter penned by Simpson as he was still trying to evade capture. It sounded like a suicide note: "Don't feel sorry for me...I've had a great life, great friends. Please think of the real O.J. and not this lost person. Thanks for making my life special. I hope I helped yours. Peace and love. O.J."[44]

---

[44] Times Staff, "'The Juice is loose': How the O.J. Simpson white Bronco chase mesmerized the world," *Los Angeles Times*, June 17, 2019, https://www.latimes.com/local/lanow/la-me-oj-simpson-white-bronco-chase-timeline-20190617-story.html.

Within an hour, Simpson called 911 from the road where he and his friend were driving along in the white Bronco. Authorities traced the call to his location, and the pursuit began. Crowds gathered on overpasses and along freeways, cheering on the football star as this slow-speed chase continued.

By about 5:00 p.m., Simpson and Cowlings pulled up to Simpson's Brentwood home, police still right on their tail, and negotiations began for his surrender. Simpson was eventually taken into custody.

I was the on-call psychologist for the LAPD tasked with responding to barricades and consulting with the negotiation team but was unaware of what was happening at the time. At home in Pasadena when it was all going down, I was aggravated that the rock-and-roll music I was listening to on the radio kept being interrupted by news of some freeway pursuit.

In my mind, it was bad enough that pursuits were now being constantly broadcast and interrupting television programming. And now they were on the radio? Then I realized the news was about O.J. Simpson.

I called the SWAT headquarters and asked if we were being called in to help. I was told to go to Simpson's home. Detectives had spoken with Simpson, and he was supposed to surrender soon. It took me about twenty minutes to get from Pasadena to Brentwood. At the base of the street, a crowd of about five hundred people had gathered. It was surreal. Media trucks lined the sides of the road.

I parked my car, and when I got out, there was my old friend SWAT supervisor, Sergeant Michael Albanese. He introduced me to Robert Kardashian, Simpson's attorney and friend, who gave us the rundown of what was going on.

Simpson was despondent, armed with a handgun, and threatening suicide in the Bronco. I slipped on a bulletproof vest and was escorted through the backyard past two full-size statues of Simpson. Inside the house, the walls were adorned with self-aggrandizing photographs. I do not recall seeing any photographs of family. They were all Simpson, all the time.

It was not hard to profile him: narcissistic—his way, his needs, all about him.

SWAT officer Pete Weireter was already negotiating with Simpson from the doorway of the residence. I slipped in beside him and validated the themes. Simpson was worried about his reputation being damaged, his loss of status. I could see the shiny gun held to his head, and something in his other hand that we later learned were photographs. I suggested that we use what we had, the crowds: "Look at all these people. They still love you."

A short time later he surrendered, collapsing safely into an officer's arms, deflated. He wanted to use the restroom, call his mom, and get something to drink. All of which happened. But it took some time to get him the drink. I learned a short time later that was because one of the cops was looking through the fridge for orange juice.

"O.J., have some orange juice." Juice for "The Juice." Cop humor. Gotta love it.

This was all such a tragedy, the epitome of an intimate stalking case with the worst outcome. What came next has been described as the trial of the century, broadcast live around the world. It would come to a shocking conclusion 474 days after Simpson's arrest: not guilty. Simpson was acquitted of two counts of murder and walked away a free man.

The stalking aspect would play a key role at his trial, however. Again, despite what you believe about his guilt or innocence in the killings, there is no doubt he had been stalking Nicole ever since they split. Even before.

Deputy District Attorney Christopher Darden made that clear in his opening statements at trial, describing Simpson's jealous, ugly side that he hid from the public, noting that he murdered his ex-wife "because he couldn't have her," then killed her friend when "he got in the way."[45]

As Darden continued to hammer home the repeated instances of Simpson's stalking and intimidating Nicole, Simpson would shake his head in disagreement. At one point he leaned over to his attorney and whispered, "That's a lie." Typical denial and minimization. A stalker never

---

[45] "The O.J. Simpson Murder Trial: Excerpts of Opening Statements by Simpson Prosecutors," *Los Angeles Times*, January 25, 1995, https://www.latimes.com/archives/la-xpm-1995-01-25-mn-24229-story.html.

believes he has done anything wrong. He is smart and ever ready with an explanation for everything—all the encounters are just coincidental.

"He killed Nicole for a single reason," Darden told jurors. "Not because he hated her.... He didn't kill her because he didn't love her anymore, because in his mind he did.... He killed her because he couldn't have her, and if he couldn't have her, he didn't want anyone else to."

Darden added: "By killing her, he committed the ultimate act of control." This is also typical stalking behavior—the overwhelming desire for control over the victim's life and, in this case, death. Darden detailed for the jury several instances of Simpson's abuse and stalking. Among them was an incident in 1985 when Simpson used a baseball bat to smash the windshield of the couple's Mercedes-Benz after a fight between the two of them. Darden also referenced a 911 call in 1993 during which Simpson could be heard yelling at a terrified Nicole in the background. It was later played in court.

"Can you get someone over here now to 321 Gretna Green? He's back. Please," Nicole Brown Simpson is heard telling the dispatcher.

"Okay, what does he look like?" the dispatcher asked.

"He's O.J. Simpson. I think you know his record," Nicole replied.

"What is he saying?"

"Oh, something about some guys I know and hookers and Keith.... I started this shit before and it's all my fault.... I just don't want my kids exposed to this."

The prosecutor also would detail yet another instance of stalking when Simpson went to his estranged wife's home and watched her through the window having sex with another man. Ironically, Simpson himself would later describe that episode in a 2006 interview on Fox that wasn't aired until more than a decade later. He said he had been out with some friends and decided to swing by Nicole's house "to see if she's still up. I don't know how late she stayed out and, you know, maybe I can get some."

He laughed and slapped his hand down on his chair, acting like just a charming guy with a glib explanation for simply being in the wrong place at the wrong time. Simpson then went on to explain how as he approached the front door, he could hear movement and voices inside the home. He peered through the window.

"And when I looked, I could obviously see that she was involved in something. I don't know who it was with. And I hit the door and left," he continued. "I wanted them to be aware that somebody's around and maybe they'd move or something. I didn't even look. I just hit the door twice and left." In his own words, he admitted he was there. It was classic stalking behavior, and he was still trying to explain it away as no big deal—typical of a stalker.

The Keith that Nicole had referred to in that 911 call in 1993 was Keith Zlomsowitch, a man she had been seeing on and off since leaving Simpson. Years later, in an interview with Dr. Drew Pinsky on the HLN television network, Zlomsowitch recalled his interactions with Simpson, specifically a passive-aggressive message that Simpson left on his answering machine after he learned that Zlomsowitch had been seeing Nicole.

"It was sort of a sarcastic, 'Hey, this is your old pal O.J.; I'm here with a friend of yours,'" Zlomsowitch said. The underlying message was, *I know what you are doing, I don't approve, and you should be frightened.*

As much as Simpson denied ever stalking Nicole, Zlomsowitch said there was no question that it had occurred. "We witnessed the stalking firsthand. He followed us everywhere. He watched us through windows, showed up at every restaurant and bar we ever went to. He made it absolutely difficult, impossible for us to be together," Zlomsowitch recalled. "I know she was beaten on a pretty consistent basis, and she was abused consistently by him. I mean, she told me of numerous accounts of him beating her and abusing her and treating her just horribly. I witnessed a lot of it myself. It was just frightening to be around."

This behavior by the sports star O.J. Simpson is no different from that of the common intimate stalker. Kathleen Baty's terrifying ordeal with a stalker began in 1982. At the time, prior to her marriage to NFL football player Greg Baty, she was Kathleen Gallagher.

During high school in the late 1970s in Redwood City, California, south of San Francisco, Gallagher didn't pay much attention to a classmate named Larry Stagner. They ran track together, but she never recalled having any sort of meaningful contact or conversations with him. She did recall, however, that he had a speech impediment.

About a decade later, Stagner would become Gallagher's worst nightmare, fitting into the category of Private Stranger Stalker. Arguably, one might consider him an Acquaintance Stalker, but there really wasn't any significant contact between the two of them. They just happened to be at the same school, in the same environment.

It was Thanksgiving Day 1982. Gallagher, a junior at the University of California, Los Angeles, was home with her family for the holidays when the telephone rang. It was an unwanted blast from the past. While she hadn't seen Stagner since high school graduation, she immediately recognized his voice and speech impediment.

Strangely, he wanted her to go on a trip with him, just out of the blue. She politely declined and wrote it off as just an odd occurrence. But the following day, the phone kept ringing. It was Stagner. He was not giving up, and the harassment and stalking would continue for another eight disturbing years.

Gallagher finally got a protective order against him and hoped it would all end, but that only provoked Stagner even more. In 1987, he tracked her down in Southern California, where she was strolling on the beach not far from her Marina del Rey condominium. She ran back home and called police immediately as she watched him from her patio getting a pistol from his car. She was terrified.

Stagner ended up getting arrested for violating the protective order and was sentenced to two months in jail.

Eventually, Gallagher married Greg Baty and got a job as a realtor in Menlo Park, California, but Stagner's presence was constant. He popped up in all sorts of random locations. This would go on for years; Stagner would be picked up by police and serve a few months in jail, then be released to take up his fixation with Gallagher, now Kathleen Baty, again and again. One time he was arrested near her house with a semiautomatic rifle and 180 rounds of ammunition. Hard to believe he was jailed for only 48 hours for that.

Like many Private Stranger Stalkers and other stalkers who never really had a prior relationship with their victims, he had a major mental illness. Stagner had been diagnosed with paranoid schizophrenia in the past. He believed if he could be with her, all his problems would vanish.

Then came what was supposed to be a quiet afternoon for Baty in 1990 when she returned home from her job to relax. It was the beginning of a harrowing experience for her, one she narrowly escaped with her life. Stagner was there waiting, armed with a hunting knife and other weapons. At some point, she was able to call her mother, who reached out to police before Stagner tied her up and told her he was taking her away.

As he attempted to drag her outside to his car, police swarmed in and Baty managed to escape. Stagner ran back into the house and whipped out a gun, and a nearly twelve-hour standoff ensued. Negotiators attempted suicide intervention and even delivered wine coolers.

At one point, Stagner went into the garage to drink some of Baty's wine. When he put the gun down, he was tackled by officers, and a flash bang went off, damaging his cornea, before he was taken into custody.

He was convicted of attempted kidnapping and sentenced to nearly nine years in prison. Here's where the nuances of the law are so frustrating. It was called "attempted" because he had not managed to take her far enough for it to qualify as a kidnapping.

"The day his sentence ends, mine begins," Baty said at the time. "I have no doubt he'll be right back on my doorstep."

Stagner was paroled in late 1994. He had served four years. "I don't have nothing to do with her. I'm a total stranger," Stagner said in an interview with *The Mercury News* (formerly *The San Jose Mercury News*) upon his release, regarding having any more involvement with Baty. "I affected her life in a very negative way. I have no reason to talk to her. I'm going to approach girls in a totally different way."[46]

About a month later, he was arrested again for violating the conditions of his release and sent back to prison for a year. He had disabled his

[46] "Man who sparked stalking law released," *Associated Press*, https://www.recordnet.com/article/19960127/a_news/301279992.

electronic monitoring ankle bracelet and skipped town for six days. And yet today he is a free man—no parole, no control.

Kathleen and Greg Baty have since lived a somewhat private life, trying to keep their home address secret. She won't discuss where her stalker is today. She has since become an amazing advocate for victims. She helped lobby with Congressman Ed Royce for the first California antistalking statute, regularly helps other victims, and consults about private security. She even wrote a book, *A Girl's Gotta Do What a Girl's Gotta Do: The Ultimate Guide to Living Safe & Smart*. It is a personal safety handbook for women. She has reclaimed the power her stalker tried to steal from her through terror.

But he's still out there. Somewhere. And I can assure you based on my years of research into these sorts that he is likely stalking someone else by now. This kind of behavior is often episodic and reflects a lifelong pattern of obsession, fixation, and pursuit.

Richard Farley was another egotistical and entitled pursuer. He is an Acquaintance Stalker but could also very easily be considered a work-place shooter and even a mass casualty shooter, as he ended up murdering seven people and wounding several others.

Farley met his stalking victim at work in the mid-1980s at a Northern California technology firm. Laura Black, age twenty-two at the time, wanted nothing to do with him, but Farley was fixated and would have none of that. "Rejection" wasn't in his vocabulary, as he was the quint-essential narcissist. Despite having a girlfriend at home, he decided that Black was to be his, and that he would help her with a personal improve-ment plan. In his mind, "She didn't want it, but she needed it."

He would proceed to stalk her for four years, even after getting fired from his job for his continued harassment of Black. He sent her hun-dreds of letters and would show up at her apartment and health club, repeatedly demanding that she date him. Black finally sought a protec-tive order, and a hearing in the case was set for February 17, 1988.

It was time to strike. He had to stop her from obtaining any protec-tion against him. So the day before his court date, he packed up his motor home with nearly one hundred pounds of ammunition and firearms and headed to his former workplace. He intended to kidnap Black and take seminude photographs of her that he would use to counter her attempt to obtain the protective order—a convoluted plan of intimidation.

In his mind, he imagined a judge would rule in his favor, reasoning something to the effect of arguing, "How could she think I'm a danger if she would pose for such pictures?"

Upon arriving at the firm, he waited for her. But he couldn't find her immediately, and so he stormed the building with guns blazing, killing seven people and wounding several others, including Black, during the rampage.

As he was holed up inside, police surrounded the facility and negotiations began to get him to surrender. Farley contemplated suicide, concerned about what life would be like behind bars if he gave himself up. He wondered whether he would get to do fun things, and if he might have computer access.

He was extremely self-absorbed, lacked any empathy for the victims, and remained acutely focused on how Black had driven him to do this and how she needed to pay. At the same time, during negotiations he told police he had no desire to kill anyone but himself. He expressed great interest in how Black was faring after being shot, wanting her to survive and suffer with the memory of what she had caused him to do, of the brutal deaths of her colleagues. This was all her fault in his mind.

Ultimately, Farley lost interest in killing himself and got hungry as the negotiations dragged on. He surrendered hours later after being delivered a sandwich from Togo's restaurant—turkey, ham and cheddar with no tomatoes—and a Diet Pepsi.

As of this writing, Farley is on death row at San Quentin State Prison in California. That's where psychologist Chris Hatcher, my former mentor who is now deceased, and I met with him in March 1998.

When we asked him to tell us the story of what happened, he started off with his bullshit excuse about having a "dissociative disorder," but then never mentioned that again. He went on to tell us his tale with details and recollections that had no trace of dissociation whatsoever.

Dissociation is often used as a "designer defense" by lawyers and their clients trying to elude criminal responsibility. In the *Diagnostic and Statistical Manual of Mental Disorders*, fifth edition, commonly known as the DSM-5—a diagnostic handbook for mental health professionals—it says that in a person with dissociative disorder, reality testing is intact, meaning the person knows exactly what he or she is doing. Right or wrong.

Farley still blamed Laura Black for what had occurred. He went on to tell us about how he "basically fell head over heels in love with her," calling it "an infatuation at the time" that he didn't immediately express to her.

"I have as much right as anybody else to go up and say, 'Would you like to come to dinner with me?'" he told us defiantly, even though we know Black had repeatedly rejected his advances. "Initially she was polite and says, 'Well, I'm busy; I just can't do it today.' I read that as, 'Well, we'll try some other time,' rather than, 'I don't want to have anything to do with you,'" he continued. He was, and clearly still is, infatuated with her and just isn't able to see the signs that she has no interest in him whatsoever.

"At some times she's angry. She's really running hot and cold," he said, trying to again place the blame on Black for giving him mixed signals. He recalled how she had once waited for him, or so he thought, as they both came out of an aerobics class at work. He perceived it as a friendly gesture and an inkling that she was becoming interested in him.

"I probably came across as cold, because the next day she didn't wait for me," Farley said, before going on to not only cast some more blame on her but continue to express his love. "Now, she'll deny every bit of it. She doesn't have as good a memory about events that happened at this time as I did. She was my life—my hobby, life, my existence essentially, when I wasn't doing anything else."

Seven people had died, and Farley did not express a single bit of remorse for them. In his mind, his actions were justified. *How dare she?* He remained one scary guy, full of bravado and big words, excuses and contradictions. Even other inmates, truly violent ones serving life terms, thought Farley was "off."

On a break during our interview with him in the prison, one of the inmates summoned Dr. Hatcher and me over. I thought, *Here we go. He's going to hit us up for something.* But that wasn't it all. He had been listening to Farley tell his story, his unapologetic tale of cold-blooded, narcissism-infused stalking and mass homicide.

"That guy, man, there is something really wrong with him," the inmate told us.

Even within the prison, by another murderer, Farley was seen as something different, something more—immensely bad, truly evil. He disturbed the other lifers. And with good reason.

As long as people have formed relationships, stalking behavior has existed. In the past, with limited technology, perhaps it was easier to track stalkers. But now, with billions of people using social media, they don't even have to get close to terrorize and disrupt the lives of their victims, and it is much easier to find information about their targets using online sources.

Virtual stalking has exploded as the internet has become the new normative communication highway. Millions of people are being stalked every year in America. In fact, 10 percent of people in the U.S. will be stalked at some point in their lives, the vast majority of them women.

Are you being stalked? Is someone repeatedly pursuing you, or is someone you care about making you feel uncomfortable or afraid? There are a few basic things to be aware of. First, recognize that there might be a problem. Listen to your intuition, gut, and feelings of discomfort. Our bodies often tell us what our minds don't want to believe.

Second, despite being repulsed by and wanting to trash anything that reminds you of the person, document and save everything—letters, recordings, any materials that could be used as evidence against the person. These are critical to establishing the course of conduct when it comes to trying to get the person locked up. While I was initially concerned that the journalists working for CBS's *48 Hours* program reached out to Lenora Claire's stalker, in the end, that video with him making threats became the most powerful piece of evidence against him, finally getting law enforcement to give a damn.

You must also seek help. If you encounter inertia or a weak response from cops, keep seeking help until someone listens. Do whatever you can legally do to keep yourself safe—personal security enhancements, relocation, whatever—and recognize that you have to take an active role managing your case. Seek out emotional support. These days, there are stalking support networks and informational clearinghouses, and people like Claire and Baty, who have survived, can offer helpful tips and lessons from their experiences.

Last, never give up. There is hope, and there are people who care. But just know that there is regrettably no magic bullet, no one-size-fits-all way to end the horror. For Lenora Claire, nothing stopped the day Massler was sentenced to four years in prison. Yes, it is a reprieve, but her trauma reminds her that someday he will be free. Every day is still as frightening as the day before. That's because, as it turns out, four years doesn't really mean four years.

Not only had Massler already been locked up for about a year while awaiting trial, but under California law, stalking is categorized as a non-violent offense, meaning four years is really about two years, minus another year for the time he has already served. Victims can thank former Governor Jerry Brown and his cronies for that one.

Massler is set to be released in late 2019.

"That's it. All of this for that," Claire recalled with a heavy sigh, saying it felt like a gut punch when she learned he would be getting out that soon. "It's not done. It's just a small break. I don't feel relieved. It doesn't mean shit. It's once again just sitting and waiting for it to start back up."

Unfortunately, she is right. But she is an amazing person, smart and strong, and she can survive. Know that you can, too.

There's a saying in law enforcement when dealing with these offenders. We never close a case until the stalker is dead.

"For me, it's pretty simple," Claire said. "I was just living my life until a fuckin' lunatic saw me."

A Whole Lotta Lies

False Victims

"Thou shalt not bear false witness."

—Exodus 20:16

CNN headline on January 30, 2019: "'Empire' star Jussie Smollett attacked in possible hate crime." The first news of this alleged attack came early January 29. Smollett claimed he was attacked by two people who were "yelling out racial and homophobic slurs" and who "poured an unknown chemical substance on the victim," police said.[47] One of Smollett's alleged attackers also put a rope around his neck, according to police. Both fled the scene. He was shaken and angry that an attack like this could happen. Smollett told CNN he fought the attackers. He also claimed that the attackers yelled he was in "MAGA country," a reference to the Make America Great Again slogan of the Trump campaign. Immediate statements of outrage and support came from the actor's employer,

---

[47] Sandra Gonzalez, "'Empire' star Jussie Smollett attacked in possible hate crime," CNN, January 30, 2019, https://www.cnn.com/2019/01/29/entertainment/jussie-smollett-attack/index.html.

Twentieth Century Fox, as well as from GLAAD, offering assistance and support.

The plot then thickened, as it was subsequently reported that a letter containing a white powder later determined to be aspirin was sent to the Chicago set of *Empire* days before Smollett was allegedly attacked by those two men on January 29. Chicago police told CNN that the letter, received on January 22 at Cinespace Chicago Film Studios, where the show is filmed, prompted a response from the HAZMAT unit. Chicago police spokesman Anthony Guglielmi said authorities determined the powder to be aspirin, but declined to give details on the content of the letter.

Smollett's family came out the day after the initial report with a statement: "We want to be clear, this was a racial and homophobic hate crime." Smollett himself took to social media and wrote a letter to *Essence* magazine, thanking fans, reassuring them he was okay, and stating, "My body is strong but my soul is stronger." He also attempted to quell the growing rumors that there was something wrong with the integrity of his story.

> I am working with authorities and have been 100% factual and consistent on every level. Despite my frustrations and deep concern with certain inaccuracies and misrepresentations that have been spread, I still believe that justice will be served.
>
> As my family stated, these types of cowardly attacks are happening to my sisters, brothers and non-gender conforming siblings daily. I am not and should not be looked upon as an isolated incident. We will talk soon and I will address all details of this horrific incident, but I need a moment to process.... Most importantly, during times of trauma, grief and pain, there is still a responsibility to lead with love. It's all I know. And that can't be kicked out of me.[48]

---

[48] Dory Jackson, "Jussie Smollett Slams Conspiracy Theories About Attack: I've Been '100% Factual and Consistent On Every Level,'" *Newsweek*, February 1, 2019, https://www.newsweek.com/jussie-smollett-conspiracy-theories-slams-factual-responds-attack-1314807.

Unfortunately for Smollett, the area where this alleged attack occurred has a very high density of private and public surveillance cameras. More than one hundred people were interviewed, fifty search warrants were executed, and hundreds of hours of video surveillance were reviewed by the tenacious and determined Chicago police department. Two brothers were identified from that investigation, but they had departed to their home country of Nigeria. When they returned, it was determined during an interview that they were witnesses, not suspects. A grand jury was convened. It was determined that Smollett had staged himself to be a victim of a hate crime, and he was charged with sixteen disorderly conduct charges. The Chicago police believe he sent the threatening letter to himself, inflicted the minor scratches and bruises upon himself, and paid these two men—who were African—$3,500 to stage the attack against him. He faced up to three years of prison and was written out of the series he starred in.

Who would do such a thing? And why? It was reported that he staged his own victimization because he was dissatisfied with his salary and wanted to boost his career.

Then the plot became *really* thick. On March 26, 2019, prosecutors dropped all charges and made the following statement: "After reviewing all of the facts and circumstances of the case, including Mr. Smollett's volunteer service in the community and agreement to forfeit his bond [ten thousand dollars] to the City of Chicago, we believe this outcome is a just disposition and appropriate resolution to this case."[49]

The prosecutors implied that somehow volunteer service and the forfeiture of a minimal bond counterbalanced whatever had occurred in this case.

Chicago Mayor Rahm Emanuel expressed understandable outrage: "This is without a doubt a whitewash of justice and sends a clear message that if you're in a position of influence and power, you'll get treated one

---

[49] Julie Bosman and Sopan Deb, "Jussie Smollett's Charges Are Dropped, Angering Mayor and Police," *The New York Times*, March 26, 2019, https://www.nytimes.com/2019/03/26/arts/television/jussie-smollett-charges-dropped.html.

way. Other people will be treated another way," Emanuel said. "There is no accountability then in the system. It is wrong, full stop."[50]

Police Superintendent Eddie Johnson said he stood by his detectives' conclusions and reaffirmed his belief that Smollett staged the attack. "If you want to say you're innocent of the situation, then you take your day in court."

The forfeited bond did not even come close to making a dent in the material costs of this investigation: twenty-four detectives removed from their regular cases, one thousand hours of time not including overtime, interviews of over one hundred individuals, review of fifty-five cameras' surveillance, and fifty search warrants executed. The damage to actual victims of hate crimes, the disruption to our world, and the intensification of intergroup polarization: incalculable. Mayor Emanuel said it best, that the city saw its reputation "dragged through the mud" by Smollett's plan to promote his career.[51] The hoax also could endanger other gay people who report hate crimes: "Now this casts a shadow of whether they're telling the truth, and he did this all in the name of self-promotion," he said. On March 28, 2019, a lawyer for the City of Chicago demanded $130,000 from Smollett as reimbursement for investigative costs, and gave him a one-week deadline to pay restitution. The city announced an intent to sue when the week passed with the demand and deadline unanswered. Simultaneously, President Trump tweeted that the FBI and the Justice Department would be reviewing the "outrageous" case further. On top of that, the Illinois attorney general was also reviewing the matter.

So many unanswered questions, and Smollett and his legal team doubled down, claiming that he had been 100 percent truthful with the police. Really? So two guys—who are African, who happen to be his

---

[50] Colin Dwyer, "Making Sense Of The Smollett Legal Drama: What's Going On Here?," NPR, March 27, 2019, https://www.npr.org/2019/03/27/707247716/making-sense-of-the-smollett-legal-drama-whats-going-on-here.

[51] Chicago Tribune Staff, "Read Mayor Emanuel, Chicago top cop's comments about Jussie Smollett charges being dropped," *Chicago Tribune*, March 26, 2019, https://www.chicagotribune.com/news/breaking/ct-met-jussie-smollett-emanuel-johnson-transcript-20190326-story.html.

associates—yelled out racial and homophobic slurs, assaulted him, and made a MAGA comment? In the days prior, letters had been sent with a white substance that happened to be aspirin? The Smollett case highlights the challenges and dangers to those raising questions about the veracity of a person's claims of victimization. Things get ugly really fast. But let's get back to the question of who would make false allegations and why.

Let's go back. Way back. I'm no Bible thumper, but I've read my fair share of the Old and New Testaments—these days usually in the context of some case in which the offender is making biblical references. I know the Ten Commandments, and the ninth is "Thou shalt not bear false witness." There is something immoral and evil about falsely accusing someone of something the person did not do. And it was biblically recognized in the earliest recorded history with the creation of a rule for human conduct as we became more "civilized."

There's even a story about it in Genesis, Chapter 39. Potiphar is a captain of the pharaoh's guard, and had employed Joseph to take care of his household. Joseph is an attractive man, and Potiphar's wife tries to seduce him day after day, to no avail. Upset over his refusal to have sex with her, she cries rape. She tells her husband that when she screamed for help, Joseph ran off, leaving his cloak behind. Potiphar is furious and locks up Joseph in the king's prison, where he spends two years before the pharaoh eventually releases him, based upon Joseph's ability to interpret dreams (as opposed to a finding of factual innocence).

Hell hath no fury!

False claims of criminal victimization have been noted in a variety of cultures for many centuries. We have a lot of fancy names and explanations for people who falsely claim to be victims. One is false victimization syndrome, and in a chapter in the awesome 1998 book *The Psychology of Stalking*, edited by Dr. J. Reid Meloy, we laid out our best thinking on it. I say "we" because it was my mentor Dr. Chris Hatcher and Detective Doug Raymond who put out the most thoughtful insight into understanding this phenomenon, from a ton of case experiences. And not just our own case experiences. I was able to talk with the handful of others who had written about it, including the late Roy Hazelwood, the amazing John Douglas, and the late Dr. John Macdonald. Some of their experience was with false rape complaints, as well as false claims of other crimes such as stalking.

We traced the different types of false victimization experiences, noting similarities between false crime complainants and those who reported medical symptoms for which there is no known physical cause, as well as others who have Munchausen syndrome or Munchausen syndrome by proxy.

In the nineteenth century, for example, physicians encountered patients who claimed their arms or legs were paralyzed—yet there was no basis for paralysis. With hypnosis, the patients were cured. It seemed that the loss of function served a purpose in their lives and was unconsciously expressed through these experiences.

Munchausen syndrome derived its name from the fictional character Baron Munchausen, who traveled the world telling wild and untruthful stories. Patients with this label doctor-shop, with complicated and sophisticated medical complaints. Many end up getting operations. The motivation in these individuals seems to stem from the benefits of being sick, such as avoidance of responsibility and conflict.

Munchausen by proxy is similar, except it is the caregiver for a dependent, often a child, who falsely claims the dependent is ill. These individuals seem to also enjoy attention from the medical establishment. The most disturbing part of this manifestation is that some parents will even do something to their children, like give them medication or even poison them, in order to add legitimacy to their claims. Think about Richard Angelo, the "Angel of Death" from the serial killer chapter. That's kind of what he wanted to do: induce a medical emergency so he could play the hero.

An unusual variant of false victimization is when a person falsely claims that he or she is a missing person, having escaped captors. One famous case involves Frédéric Bourdin, nicknamed "The Chameleon," a French serial imposter, who may have assumed up to five hundred different identities; he began his impersonations as a child. In 1997, he assumed the identity of Nicholas Barclay, a child who was thirteen when he disappeared from his home in San Antonio, Texas, in June 1994. Although Bourdin has brown eyes and a French accent, he convinced the family he was their blue-eyed son, saying he had escaped from a child prostitution ring and that the ring had altered his eye color. Bourdin lived with the family for almost five months until March 1998, when inconsistencies were noted that led to DNA testing, the discovery of his true identity, and criminal charges. He did it again in Spain in 2004, claiming to be a teenager whose mother had been killed in the Madrid bombing attacks. Bourdin indicated that his motivation was getting "love and affection" and the attention he had never received as a child.

More recently, in 2019, a man came forward claiming to be a boy who disappeared in 2011, and that he had also been a victim of child sex trafficking. His charade was discovered through DNA testing as well, and he admitted that he'd learned about the case by watching a *20/20* special about it, that he sought to get away from his family, and that he desired a father like the missing boy's. He was charged with lying to federal agents.

Another new phenomenon is "swatting," the act of making a bogus police report—usually regarding an urgent or violent crime—to lure law enforcement or SWAT teams to a location. In one case, a man was charged with sending the police to a location in Wichita, Kansas, 1,400 miles away from the caller, on the claim of an urgent hostage situation, which ultimately led to the shooting death of an innocent man at the target location. The Los Angeles–based offender reportedly did it within the context of anger that had evolved during an online multiplayer Call of Duty game, to punish one of the gamers in a dispute over a $1.50 bet. He ultimately pled guilty to fifty-one federal charges related to fake calls and threats, and was sentenced to twenty years. Many swatting cases have involved teenagers who were online gamers and had disputes within those matches against gaming rivals, who then used calling apps that masked their identity to make the false crime reports.

Then of course there are those who claim they are ill, or exaggerate their illness in order to win a lawsuit, evade criminal responsibility, or get out of the military. We have a word for that in my profession: malin-gering, which refers to falsely claiming or exaggerating an illness for an obvious secondary gain. I've seen a lot of that in the criminal cases I work on—criminals pretend to be sick with psychosis or some condition like dissociation, to mitigate their responsibility for serious crimes like homicide.

And finally, there are those who claim they are ill or crime victims because they are psychotic and delusional. These are typically not diffi-cult to spot. They genuinely believe they are ill, thus I do not consider them to be having a true false victimization event. As noted earlier, Damascio Torres shot three doctors and took hostages at a hospital because he falsely believed he'd been a victim of medical experimenta-tion there, and that he was dying after being infected with an AIDS-like virus. I recall that another woman filed a report claiming the police had stolen her ovaries.

The journey to understanding those who falsely claim they are ill or crime victims, to say the least, was a fascinating one. It was as twisted as the stories the fake victims create—often elaborate stories derived from TV, movies, and popular notions of the crimes, but overplayed and not quite fitting the real world of criminal behavior. And they typically pick current issues that are very much in the public view, such as hate crimes and political turmoil and conflict. Sound familiar?

But there is one important point to note here. Most victims *are legitimate*, and it is only after the appearance of evidence that leads to suspicion that a false-report investigative case should be launched. In stalking cases, the rate of false claims is about 2 percent. Thus, I think it is more harmful to accuse a true victim of making things up than to be fooled initially and then redirect. Yes, these cases waste a ton of resources that otherwise could be used to address real crimes. And they tend to be politically quite loaded—there is much indignation and hostility when a victim is revealed to be false. Things can get ugly really quickly as investigators are accused of mistreating the individual, groups posture, and glory-seeking self-anointed advocates hurl accusations—and some advocates are quite litigious. These groups and advocates can also fuel intergroup tensions and destabilize communities.

For example, in 1987, the infamous Tawana Brawley case in New York evidenced many of these dynamics. The fifteen-year-old African-American girl claimed that six Caucasian males, including a man with a badge, had abducted her for four days and raped and tortured her. When she was found, apparently disoriented, she wrote "White cop" on a piece of paper. Mike Tyson, Bill Cosby, and others jumped on the bandwagon. Tyson gave her his Rolex watch and offered her a fifty-thousand-dollar scholarship. Seven months later, a grand jury determined she had faked the whole thing. But it didn't stop there. Brawley's advisers, including the Reverend Al Sharpton, went so far as to point the finger at a local prosecutor, who went on to become an assistant state attorney general, Steven Pagones. Pagones ended up winning a defamation case against Sharpton, Brawley, and others in 1998, after filing a $170 million suit against them.

In reviewing what was known about false victimization, we came across a number of faked hate crimes. Given the sympathetic media attention, such claims are a surefire way to receive support—at least until the deception is discovered. A lot of the cases we came across, though, had at their center simple greed, such as insurance fraud and other kinds of fraud. A pastor in Iowa, for example, filed a report that someone had vandalized his Mercedes-Benz with spray-painted racial epithets. He took his case to the media, appealing to *The Oprah Winfrey Show* after the insurance company refused to pay; he claimed racism. Interestingly, it was discovered that he had sought paint estimates at different body shops *prior* to the "vandalism." The local police chief jokingly explained the pastor's motivation for the false claim: "My best guess is that he wanted his car painted very badly."[52]

If I were to do my research all over again, though, I would have avoided the whole "false victimization syndrome" label. I'd have called

---

[52] K. Mohandie, C. Hatcher, and D. Raymond, "False Victimization Syndromes in Stalking," in R. Meloy (ed.), *The Psychology of Stalking: Clinical and Forensic Perspectives* (San Diego: Academic Press, 1998).

it what it really is: crime-scene staging. A person is staging the crime to make it falsely look like he or she is the victim.

What do we know about crime-scene staging? It's intentionally manufacturing a crime scene or false report to misdirect the attention from the true and most likely culprit. And how do we detect crime-scene staging? We identify a number of clues or indicators, such as atypical victim presentations, obvious secondary gain, psychological disorders (especially personality disorders), history of lying, attraction to the victim role, suspect profile problems, and obvious motives.

What are the usual motives? Sometimes people need an alibi or an excuse to cover up for something they shouldn't have done. It can be as simple as having sex with someone they weren't supposed to, all the way up to murder. Other times they may be playing the victim to reconcile a relationship, playing on a partner's need to rescue them. Of course there is also straight-up revenge. These are usually cases in which the "victim" points the finger and names somebody. When you name a suspect, it forces the "victim's" hand, giving the accused an opportunity to refute and expose the falsehood, which is why in a number of these cases, there is no suspect identified or the description is ambiguous. That keeps the game going.

Usually there's an obvious ax to grind. And of course there is always the old standby of seeking attention and sympathy. Being a victim gets a person a lot of understanding and sympathy. False claims are also very common in family law court, as warring parents seek leverage for custody issues as well as favorable rulings on issues such as who gets to stay in the residence until the case is finalized.

Other indicators include the report of a crime coinciding with life stressors or family dynamics, and sometimes there is just a gut reaction that something isn't right. But at the top of the list is forensic and scientific evidence that proves something couldn't have happened the way the person is claiming it did. And sometimes, the person has done it before.

When I was at the LAPD, I saw a lot of cops for therapy. After all, it was Los Angeles, right? Lots of shrinks, and it seems everyone has one, even the cops. Therapy took place at a satellite office, for confidentiality reasons, in a bank building in Chinatown. I had an awesome office over-looking the city, comfortable couches, and a bookshelf, on one of which was Dr. Meloy's 1998 stalking book, complete with my chapter on false victimization.

I'd see cops for marital problems, everyday problems with anxiety and depression and loss, the trauma of a shooting, frustrations with a super-visor, and sometimes stress from a disciplinary complaint. I was stuck in that office with a cop threatening suicide and cops threatening me, and had cops bring duffel bags full of guns because they were afraid of killing their supervisor. A lot happened in my Chinatown office. But hey, it was my home away from home.

One day a guy came to see me, stressed out by the LAPD disciplinary process he found himself in, and started to tell me a story about how his ex-girlfriend had set him up. He'd broken it off with her because she was so dramatic and demanding. Now I've heard this story a hundred times; as they say, booze, bad relationships, and bad debt are the downfall of many a cop. But there was something different about this guy's story. He told me how she'd invited him over and had a negligee on, and the next thing he knew, he was being accused of having assaulted her. He was arrested and made bail, but was now mandated off work, accused of a serious crime, and facing jail and job termination.

I thought of my chapter, and for some reason I pulled Reid's book off the shelf and gave it to him to read. To my surprise, he said, "That's her." I was thinking the comment was metaphorical, but the woman who was accusing him of domestic assault was actually one of the people in my chapter!

Around this time, I was reading the book *The Celestine Prophecy*. Its principal theme is, there are no accidents, no coincidences. And here was a prime example.

So he tried to inform LAPD brass and Internal Affairs of the fact that this person had a track record of doing the same thing, which even included self-injury. Unfortunately, the political climate at the department at the time included a horrible police chief who opened personnel investigations on everything and investigated the most ridiculous complaints, including that ovary-stealing complaint I mentioned earlier. In a department with some ten thousand officers, there were more than three thousand personnel complaints. Some called that officious chief, derisively, Darth Vader. So the department didn't seem to care about the impact of all these investigations, in fact it doubled down. This led to lawsuits, and it took some time until this officer's reputation was cleared up.

But that's not the end of it. The accuser ended up suing me for defamation, because I had written about her prior false complaint—something she discovered in the context of all this dizzying litigation! Fortunately, I had fact-checked the case directly with the investigating agency, and much of what I wrote about existed in the public domain. Remember the First Amendment! The accuser tried to silence me due to all the litigation surrounding her false complaint. Ultimately I countersued her, her lawsuit was dismissed, and she had to pay my attorney's fees and costs.

No good deed goes unpunished.

There have been so many cases. Here's another twisted one. Gina, a twentysomething woman attending a Los Angeles-area university, reported an attempted sexual assault to the university's Department of Public Safety. She claimed that the suspect had grabbed her from the rear, pushed her head into a door, then pulled her backward into another dormitory room across the hall. She described in great detail how the alleged attacker had torn her clothing and scratched her body. She showed scratches on her body as well as tears in both her outer clothing and undergarments. When she finally gave her statement to the police, certain details were very specific, like, "He looked at me in the eyes and smiled," but she was unable to describe his general facial features.

Shortly thereafter, she told the police that the attacker had left an envelope underneath the doormat of her dormitory room, containing a poem and half of her bra that had been torn during the attack. She had been visiting her boyfriend nearby and experienced a "bad feeling," which had resulted in her going to her room and finding these items.

She claimed she recognized the voice of her assailant while walking on campus. The student was identified, but because she could not provide certain eyewitness identification, no further investigative information could be developed. The young man was not arrested, but he was expelled from the university.

Gina told family members and others that she had started to receive hang-up phone calls, threatening calls, and cards, and that she had been followed for six months after the initial incident. She received a special parking space at the school due to security considerations. Six months later, she received a mutilated and dismembered Barbie doll, covered in a red substance, with a threatening letter.

Due to the concerns about stalking behavior, the LAPD's Threat Management Unit (TMU) detectives were brought in on the case by the initial sexual assault detectives. A meeting was scheduled. Special security officers escorted Gina to and from her classes. The day before the scheduled meeting with TMU detectives, Gina went to the student lounge after an early class dismissal. Prior to the security officers' coming to get her, she was discovered by a classmate near the bathroom. She had long scratches on her back and superficial lacerations, and her clothing was disheveled. It looked awful, like some Ted Bundy sort had attacked her.

Gina claimed she had been attacked from behind while in the student lounge listening to music, and that when she awoke, she was tied to a desk, on her stomach, with her wrists bound. Her jeans were pulled down to her ankles. She was transported to a rape crisis center. Photographs of her in the emergency room captured almost a smile or smirk on her face, as if she was halfway enjoying the attention.

The incident became a local media event, hysteria erupted on campus, and warning flyers were distributed.

Detectives interviewed her the next day, and subtle inconsistencies began to emerge: This was not a typical stalking case, in which the offender would usually be known or make himself known, and there were two distinctly different types of rapist being described (pseudo unselfish and sexual sadist). Gina's mother was an advocate for rape victim rights who herself had experienced a sexual assault. Further investigation indicated that the complainant had been having academic problems in

school, was confused about her career direction heading toward graduation, and had started dating another guy. Her ex-boyfriend had been
physically abusive with her, but became less violent when she started
reporting her "victimization." The ex indicated that she had once falsely
claimed being pregnant.

She claimed she had chewed her way out of the shoelaces that she had
been bound with—but the cuts to the shoelaces were clean. All of the
lacerations she had experienced were consistent with her reach.

After detectives reviewed all the evidence and the behavioral history,
with consultation and a review by myself, it was determined that this
was a false case. Now it was time to bring her in, hopefully gain her confession, and close the case. Several appointments were scheduled, then
canceled by her. Finally, she arrived for the interview with Detective
Doug Raymond, Detective Gary Van Esch, and myself.

I collected my thoughts, going through my private ritual to mentally
prepare and center myself. With every sense alive, electric focus, every
cell of my being laser sharp and directed to this purpose, I entered the
interview room.

In the room were several large envelopes and file folders with the
name of her case and descriptions in bold, easily viewed with labels like
"forensic evidence," "lab results," and "surveillance." I'm not going to tell
you there was little or nothing in those envelopes and folders.

I did a deposition recently, and the lawyers had thick binders with
my name on them. They had theatrically asked in front of me that the
binders be brought into the room. It did not concern me one bit. There
could have been nothing relevant to anything in there; likely they were
stuffed with blank paper or the materials from another case. I was there
to tell the truth, and what was in there mattered not.

It is the guilty conscience that is curious. *What do they know? Do
they have a smoking gun? I know I've been lying, and it seems they might
know, too.*

And so the folders and envelopes beckoned Gina hypnotically. They
were part of the chess game that underlies many relationships, and certainly part of the cat-and-mouse endeavor of an investigation unfolding.

Raymond started it off: "One of the reasons we're here today is, we've got a problem with your descriptions. I went to Dr. Mohandie, and I had him look at the information and independently review it. And Gina, he comes up with the same conclusion."

Leaning forward, at the edge of her seat, across the desk from Raymond and me, in the otherwise barren room with towering, empty bookshelves—a surreal, Kafka-worthy room—she immediately responded: "Um…are we talking about…I mean, the whole thing?"

No "What are you talking about?" or exclamatory "I don't know what you mean." Her response already revealed that she knew we were questioning the truthfulness of her allegations.

Raymond continued, as I sat quietly, half prop, half team member waiting for the opportunity to play "good shrink." "One of the reasons we're here today is because of those inconsistencies, and to go over those inconsistencies, or more importantly to put this thing to rest."

She began to babble: "I really don't understand what's going on.… I don't understand, because this happened. I don't understand why." Her hands were on the table, palms up, expressing her pseudo perplexity.

Raymond firmly and quietly responded, "It didn't happen, Gina."

Gina half protested: "I woke up in the bathroom, and that's it. The next thing I know—"

Raymond stopped her. "Let's look at the first incident that happened, in July of last year…"

Gina continued to protest. "All I know is, what happened, happened."

Raymond again stopped her. "That's not what happened. It isn't what happened. And you have to first of all understand there are three people here who want to believe you, and started to believe you. And the physical evidence shows us it didn't happen." He was calm and firm, and Gina moved her left hand nervously to her face, and I could see the emotional buildup just beneath the surface. She touched her eye, almost as if to turn off her activating tear ducts. She was breaking, and I moved in.

"I think the reason we are here, Gina, is because a lot of people put a lot of time and resources into investigating this. As Detective Raymond has been saying and Detective Gary Van Esch has been saying here. The three of us are the people here to talk with you and sort out what really happened. And I go to prisons and I talk to people who have done these things. I talk to people who have really had these things happen. I know what those people can recall. I know what those people can see. And it's just like night…and day."

She moved her hands to cover her eyes. She wanted it to go away. She did not want us to see her emotion and that she was caving in. The truth was behind a thin, fragile veneer. And it was about to burst forth.

Raymond picked it up. "Gina, I've given you an opportunity here. We can sit here and go back and forth. You still are trying—and I can see it on your face—you're trying to figure out a way to explain all of this and make it fit. And the only way it's going to fit is if you tell us the truth. Because that's the only path we are going to follow."

She began to cry, her two hands still shielding her eyes, and in a choked-up voice said, "Yeah," nodding. Raymond and I sat forward, and she practically cradled her head in her hands. She began to sob as the truth got ready to burst out.

I reinforced it with, "You don't have to keep this dirty little secret anymore."

Sobbing, she tearfully released it: "I don't like myself very much… and I don't…. I feel like such a terrible person…and it's not about that. It's not about anyone else."

Raymond coaxed her along: "I don't see a terrible person. I see a person reaching for help."

"I don't even know how to explain."

Now I encouraged her: "Just do the best you can. That's good enough."

"I don't like myself. I don't know why…. My family and everybody, they all look at me as this person who is strong and takes control. But I'm, like, not this person. I didn't want to be alive anymore. I didn't want anything. I didn't want to deal with any of it. I couldn't go through with anything. So what am I supposed to do? Everyone's asking me what happened. You know. And the thing is, I didn't even say anything; everyone just assumed things…"

Gina was making references to her injuries, to the facts that she had engaged in self-injury and let others assume she had been victimized.

"And what was I supposed to do then? Come out and say, "Okay, sure, I really did this to myself. Or something. You know. So I didn't say anything." She was sobbing.

I reflected. "So you were trying to hurt yourself, and you couldn't finish it, and you needed to have a reason to tell people what happened. And they kind of made it up, and you went with it. Is that what happened?"

She sobbed. "Pretty much."

Raymond pushed: "Did you try to mutilate yourself in that room?" She nodded. "Was that the first time?"

"Yeah."

Raymond went in for some factual confirmations: "You didn't chew through the laces, did you?"

Gina repeated his question, "Did I chew through them?" She was buying herself some time. Then she said, "I came down there, and there were people out there and I didn't want to be found. And I thought if I could just get home. I didn't realize I had hit my head so hard, and I was really dizzy.... I just can't take it all." She had just admitted banging her own head.

Raymond reflected, "That's a lot of plates to keep balancing." At that point, we wanted to close the deal, lay this case to rest.

We brought in her parents—who had filed a lawsuit against the college for having a dangerous environment that had allowed Gina to be "victimized"—so they could hear, firsthand, that none of it was true. We broke the news to her dad out in the hallway after her tearful confession.

In the room with Gina, her father said: "What they told me was that none of this happened. That you had done this to yourself. Is that true?"

She could not make eye contact with her father and was sobbing, her face buried in her hands. Even without her affirmation, her guilt was palpable.

The case was over. She had staged her own victimization, including making false claims of rape and stalking. Why? Because she hated herself, engaged in self-injury she needed to explain, was at a crossroads in her life, was juggling a boyfriend and an ex-boyfriend (gaining a reprieve from probable aggression from the latter), and because she got a whole lot of secondary gain from it, including attention, special parking spaces, and notoriety.

One student was expelled before the truth came out, thousands of dollars were spent, a false perception of the university being an unsafe place was created, and the university was sued. Gina was later expelled, too. That's a high price tag for a whole lot of lies. But that's what happens in cases of false victimization.

The Aftermath

Where Do We Go From Here?

"To live is to suffer, to survive is to find some
meaning in the suffering."

—Friedrich Nietzsche

"They must be crazy. Absolutely nuts. Insane. Out of their minds."
This is a common refrain we hear from the general public in the
aftermath of murder and mayhem. I mean, how could the person not be
crazy? Who does these things unless he or she is absolutely insane?

The answer is much more complicated than you might think. Sure,
there can be an element of mental illness in many violent offenders,
but oftentimes no such condition exists. And even when it does, to the
average person, insanity is far different from its narrow definition in the
criminal justice system.

For instance, many serial killers do present with various diagnosable
mental conditions, but by and large are found competent to stand trial
and ultimately criminally responsible by the conclusion of legal proceedings. That is because the legal standard requires only that perpetrators
have an understanding of what they are doing and know that it is wrong

at the time of the crime. Diagnosable mental conditions or not, they can be held accountable for their actions.

While the rules of court procedure vary from state to state, the defense team members can first seek a competency hearing before a judge if they are trying to assert that their client is too sick to stand trial because of mental illness. The main issue is if the person's illness prevents him from participating in his own defense. Maybe the person is so delusional, he thinks his lawyer is part of the conspiracy, or he doesn't even think he is in a courtroom. Madonna's stalker, Robert Hoskins, believed he was in a "heavenly courtroom," and that Madonna was there to "save him." He was still found competent, because he had a keen enough understanding of the role of the judge, that there were crimes charged, what various pleadings meant, and that his freedom was on the line, but you get the point.

Typically, there's a court-approved mental health professional hired separately by the defense and another one hired by the prosecution to evaluate the suspect. They appear before the judge in what is called a bench trial, or a typical jury trial, to testify as to their opinions on the individual's state of mind. If the person is determined to be competent, the trial goes on. If not, the suspect is sent to a medical facility for treatment until deemed fit to go to trial.

Trials begin with what is called the "guilt phase," during which both sides present their cases before a jury. Keep in mind that the defense team members can seek a separate competency hearing at any time during the proceedings if they believe their client is melting down. Sometimes these hearings are even held *after* the guilt phase but before the jury is set to determine a sentence or a separate "sanity phase" of the trial is held.

To prove guilt in criminal cases, prosecutors must meet the rigorous standard of "beyond a reasonable doubt," meaning there can be no reasonable uncertainty by the jury of the person's culpability in the crime. The burden to prove this rests solely on the prosecution. The presumption is always that the person is innocent. Remember that the premise of our criminal justice system is "innocent until proven guilty."

Sanity hearings are a bit different, during which there is a lower standard of proof, referred to as a "preponderance of the evidence," which basically means "more likely than not." Furthermore, in most jurisdictions, including California, the burden of proof in the sanity phase shifts to the defense to prove the client is insane. This is what is referred to as an "affirmative defense." It is the defense team's job to prove it once they claim it. The presumption in this scenario is "sane until proven otherwise."

But I have also testified in a couple of states, like Colorado and New Mexico, where it is the other way around. The prosecution, if the issue is raised by defense, must prove the person *is* sane. I guess people in those states are presumed insane until proven otherwise. One would think that would be the case in California, of all places!

The judicial process can be quite convoluted, but these procedures are part of what ensures that the American justice system is objective, and that suspects receive a fair trial. Take Herbert Mullin, for example, a clearly mentally ill individual who believed voices in his head commanded him to kill in order to save California from a cataclysmic earthquake. No doubt he was delusional, but he also made perfectly sane decisions before and after each of his thirteen murders, as well as efforts to hide his involvement in the crimes, cover his tracks, and take out at least one witness. It was too difficult a hurdle for his defense to overcome, and clearly indicated he had known precisely what he was doing with each murder and understood it was wrong, at least legally.

And keep in mind, in so many cases, one person's crazy is another person's ideology. That is why we don't use the term "crazy" in the legal realm—because it really doesn't mean anything.

During sanity trial proceedings, the process of holding these offenders accountable, in a just manner, often turns into a battle of the experts on the witness stand, with one or more mental health professionals working for the defense and others for the prosecution, each seemingly trying to prove their own theory. Ideally, they should simply be objective, basing their conclusions and opinions on verifiable data. There are often different findings, diagnoses, and opinions between the two sides, and the evidence is presented to the jury for the ultimate decision. It often really comes down to which side's expert is more believable.

The problem is that a lot of these mental health professionals allow themselves to be corrupted, and payment and personal biases tend to distort their opinions. It's disheartening to see. I once testified for the prosecution opposite a defense-hired psychiatrist who, in a different high-profile case, had admitted that he deleted twenty-four statements and rewrote ten pages of his notes at the request of the defense attorney. It really undermined his credibility in front of the jury when he had to answer questions about this prior case, something referred to as "impeachment." In tandem with some questionable data interpretation and shifting opinions in the current case, it appeared that he was again distorting his work to support the defense's theory and not being objective. It showed a pattern of bias and a lack of intellectual integrity. The suspect was found guilty and sane.

In another case, I was retained to testify for the prosecution in the trial of a young man who was accused of killing a gay classmate with a bullet to the head when both were teens. The defense expert's opinions oozed with strong personal views against homosexuality. He essentially blamed this struggling teen for the bullet fired by the hateful perpetrator, who murdered him in cold blood. In essence, he was saying that *the victim* was responsible for his own death because he was gay. The jury ended up being unable to come to a verdict at all, after a contentious trial in which the victim was blamed by the defense and at least one juror, believe it or not. The panelist later said, outrageously, that the offender "was just solving a problem." In the end, the killer pled guilty to second-degree murder and voluntary manslaughter, agreeing to twenty-one years in prison.

Thankfully, much has changed since that 1949 case of Howard Unruh, who killed thirteen innocent people in what is believed to be the first mass casualty shooting in America. He was simply locked away in a mental institution for sixty years until his death; he never had to face trial, because a judge deemed him incompetent. Only one psychologist at the time claimed he *should* stand trial, noting that locking him away in an institution without having to be held accountable for his crimes "would be regarded as psychiatrists coming to the rescue."[53]

It is not up to mental health professionals in these matters to come to the rescue, though I do think some, consciously or subconsciously, feel that it is. Our jobs are simply to determine—based on our expertise, not emotion—the suspect's mental state and how that relates to the legal issues at hand.

Fortunately, there are ethical guidelines and rules that most forensic psychologists and psychiatrists abide by now, something that was not even a consideration back when Unruh carried out his killings.

However complicated, this is all part of the process of putting a suspect on trial with rigorous debates in courts about what crimes to charge, what mitigating circumstances may exist that affect those decisions, and ultimately the proper sentence. These factors can include an abusive childhood, for instance, and even mental capacity and IQ level.

But there are much larger questions to consider in the realm of criminality. What are we to do about the world we live in today? Can we effect change? Can we prevent or interrupt the next crime?

Let me spoil one answer right now. The term I use out of necessity and humility is that what I and my colleagues do is threat management, not threat prevention. We want to prevent, divert, and interrupt all the threats, but the reality is that we probably can't. Given the necessary constraints of living in a free society, we just can't stop them all. The cost would be too great. And I'm not talking about the financial costs, but the costs to our freedoms.

Roughly 75 percent of school shooters and mass casualty offenders, in particular, evidence leakage—telling friends or family of their plans, for example, or posting messages on social media in advance of the crime. That allows for identification, assessment, and ultimately threat management. Then professionals, after someone has seen something disturbing and said something about it to others, can assess for variables such as

---

[53] Joseph A. Gambardello, "Inside the Mind of the Philadelphia Area's Worst Mass Killer," *The Philadelphia Inquirer*, October 2, 2017, https://www.inquirer.com/philly/news/breaking/inside-the-mind-of-the-philadelphia-areas-worst-mass-killer-20171002.html.

whether there is evidence that the person is on a violent pathway, preparing weapons and the like to carry out carnage.[54]

We would also then look for any increasingly pathological fixation on a person or agenda, a deviant identification with a past perpetrator or violent events, and an energy burst of behavior related to potential targets or violent actions, such as repeated visits to a gun range or preparing manifesto videos, among other factors.

I don't want to sound too "doom and gloom," but we are no doubt living in a more dangerous world than ever before. We are engulfed in a war of words and opinions, two parallel lines that never converge and that never really go anywhere. One line bemoans gun violence that is raging out of control. The other declares we must protect Second Amendment rights to bear arms even if it includes easy access to military-grade assault weapons that are constantly being used to carry out mass killings across America.

The American Civil Liberties Union defends personal freedoms to the point of permitting delusional ticking time bombs to walk the streets until they explode. The group fights against laws that could safely contain, maybe even treat, these potential perpetrators by involuntarily committing them to a mental institution if they show any signs of instability that could lead to impending violence against themselves or others. Meanwhile, the members of the National Rifle Association have politicians wrapped around their fingers; meaningful gun control laws remain but a pipe dream while legislators sell their votes to the firearms lobby in exchange for reelection.

Perhaps we might be able to actually prevent the next mass shooting or school attack if we had some sort of call-center hotline to report individuals we have concerns about, before the next killing. And if we had some laws with teeth that provide police with the authority to take them off the streets until they are no longer deemed a threat.

---

[54] J.R. Meloy, A.G. Hempel, T.B. Gray, K. Mohandie, A. Shiva, and T.C. Richards, "A Comparative Analysis of North American Adolescent and Adult Mass Murderers," *Behavioral Sciences and the Law* 22 (2004), 291-309.

We require automobile drivers to renew their licenses, yet we don't do the same for gun owners? How does this make any sense at all? Maybe it shouldn't be easier to obtain a licensed firearm, particularly assault weapons, than a license to drive a car.

We are ever enmeshed in back-and-forth bickering that leaves us at a standstill in our efforts to stem the scourge of school and mass casualty shootings. The discussion has now turned toward arming teachers in classrooms and posting more police officers at schools. And arming pilots. So the solution is more guns? The firearms lobbyists and companies that produce the weapons must be thrilled.

Do we really want to put the guns in exactly the environment they shouldn't be in, handled by people whose job is customarily not to handle them, who have other important priorities, such as educating students or flying a plane? If this happens, would-be offenders would not even have to worry about obtaining or bringing a gun prior to their attack. Rather, their plan can simply be to capitalize on the inevitable sloppy handling of that firearm so that it can find its way into their hands. Yes, it is a terrifying proposition.

Firearms should be regulated more strictly, people should periodically have to requalify for their gun licenses, and background checks should be much more in depth. And if anyone in the home where the gun is to be stored has mental issues, or known anger or impulse control problems, well then, guess what? No one in that house gets a gun.

If there is a gun in the home, there needs to be a hotline for people to call when they have concerns that a person with easy access to firearms is becoming unhinged. These kinds of calls should trigger a reopening and reexamination of the legal process used to get the weapon, followed by an investigation into whether the person still should have one. And if not, the gun needs to be taken away.

Doing this would mean more manpower, more personnel, more money, and changes in our laws. It would be costly and challenging, and people with lots of money would fight it. But how much money is one life worth? Or two or three or dozens of lives?

I am no gun grabber. I own guns, but I know how to use them and, well, I am not a dangerous individual. But there are too many people who have them who shouldn't.

We *should* have more trained police officers, air marshals, and undercover highly trained professionals on campuses and in malls, airports, and other transportation locations, like train stations. Artificial intelligence also can aid in this through high-tech surveillance and biometric screening. There also should be a centralized federal database filled with the names of potentially violent or mentally unstable individuals, so that this information does not get lost between states and is shared among all law enforcement agencies right down to the local sheriff.

Some states have enacted "red flag" laws, which are increasingly being adopted. They empower family members and law enforcement to seek an Extreme Risk Protection Order that would restrict someone's access to guns when that person poses a danger to himself or others. The provisions vary by state, but generally these laws are triggered when a person is in crisis and loved ones or law enforcement see signs that the person poses a threat.

Red flag laws allow people to seek help from a court to remove guns from dangerous situations. A full hearing would then take place before a judge, during which the court would determine whether the person in question poses a significant danger of injuring himself or others with a firearm. If that is found to be the case, that individual would then be temporarily prohibited from purchasing and possessing guns, and would be required to turn over any weapons while the order is in effect.

There are obviously state-by-state variations. For example, Connecticut, Indiana, and Florida allow only law enforcement to petition the court in such a circumstance, while California, Washington, and Oregon also allow petitions from family and household members. Connecticut was the first to get a red flag law on the books; it happened in 1999 after a disgruntled accountant at the state lottery killed four of his supervisors. California accomplished getting one on the books in 2014, after Elliot Rodger's rampage and killing of six people near the campus of the University of California, Santa Barbara.

Florida was one of the most recent states to enact one. The 2018 mass shooting at Marjory Stoneman Douglas High School in Parkland, Florida, that left seventeen people dead mobilized a grassroots movement of teens that shows no signs of stopping. It has impacted local, state, and federal politics, helping to counter the traditionally powerful NRA and gun lobby.

The Florida red flag law was courageously enacted on March 9, 2018, by Governor Rick Scott, who risked the wrath of the gun lobby, less than a month after the tragic Parkland shooting. The law gives police the power to ask judges for temporary orders to take guns away from dangerous people, without any input from that person. If the judge rules favorably, police take the guns and a final hearing, during which the person can argue his case, is scheduled within fourteen days. Judges are given fifteen criteria to determine whether someone is a danger, including whether the person has made any threats toward himself or others or committed any acts of violence (such as being arrested for a violent crime), or has a serious mental illness or a past conviction for domestic violence.

An important point is that the law does not require that the person qualify for an involuntarily commitment as an *immediate* danger to self or others. That is a much higher threshold to meet. It is helpful to not have to reach that immediacy threshold because many people are not going to be imminently dangerous. Some are ticking time bombs whose danger peiod extends beyond the window required under the state's involuntary-commitment laws.

Of course, there were unhappy gun rights advocates after these red flag laws went into effect. Florida attorney Eric Friday whined that "every legislator that voted for it and every police department that uses it should be ashamed to call themselves an American."[55]

You go ahead, Eric, and keep sending thoughts and prayers to the victims of these murders and their families, instead of doing anything to figure out real solutions that balance the Second Amendment with

---

[55] Jessica Lipscomb, "Florida's Post-Parkland 'Red Flag' Law Has Taken Guns From Dozens of Dangerous People," *Miami New Times*, August 7, 2018, https://www.miaminew-times.com/news/floridas-red-flag-law-has-taken-guns-from-dangerous-people-10602359.

common sense. Red flag laws work and so does grassroots activism, though it takes time to put immediate, meaningful pressure on lawmakers to do the right thing and be accountable to the communities they serve. How much they receive from the gun lobby, and what actions they take to make the community safe, should become solid criteria for whether they remain in public office or have their heads put on the voters' chopping block.

Other countries do not seem to have the same gun violence problem we have here in America. And when they do have mass killings, they are quick to enact laws aimed at stopping another one. In March 2019 in New Zealand, an Australian man attacked two mosques, killing fifty-one people with high-powered assault weapons. Less than a week later, New Zealand Prime Minister Jacinda Ardern announced that all military-style semiautomatic and automatic weapons would be banned in that country.

Historically in America, shooting after shooting occurs with little meaningful legislation to follow. I think times are changing, though, with the growing grassroots movement by credible stakeholders—the very kids who actually suffer the most when a school shooter attacks. Our future leaders! It is getting harder and harder for the gun groups to hunker down, deflect, and buy off change until the next crisis.

These are what I refer to as macrolevel strategies for managing the problem. At the individual level, on campuses, at workplaces, in communities, and at home, "See something, say something" continues to be critical, with an acceptance that the responsibility for safety is shared by all of us. We cannot assume that someone else is addressing the problem. We each have to do something. And that takes courage.

My son was a freshman in high school in the aftermath of the Parkland shooting when I assisted in a school violence threat management training program at his institution. Another trainer in the active-shooter training drill was a parent and former cop with the LAPD's elite metropolitan unit. The director of the school put together a safety committee to identify areas to improve, including adding more surveillance cameras and gaining better control over access to the campus. All of this was very well-received by the staff *and* students.

About a month later, I received a call from the principal. She indicated that everything was okay but wanted to let me know that my son had been involved in an incident at school. My heart dropped. *Uh-oh*, I thought. *Some teenage angst.* I braced myself.

"Your son did the right thing and brought forward a concern about a student who was making threats at the school," the principal said.

I was floored. My son had not told me, even though he knows what I do and we had been having discussions since he was in elementary school about what actions to take if a shooter were to come onto campus. Apparently, he had used his cell phone to capture video of this kid making threats.

The student was investigated and thankfully deemed to not be a danger, but given his problems, he was removed from the school.

Schools, businesses, government offices, and any publicly accessible places need to consider their vulnerability to attacks and violence, have physical security appropriate to the setting, and conduct training with their employees about what to do in different scenarios that are relevant to that setting. Schools, universities, and workplaces of all kinds should strongly consider having an in-house threat assessment team that includes mental health professionals. The primary task for these teams would be to investigate threats of violence and separate false alarms from potential or impending danger. Such an investigation could include interviewing not only the person of concern but also family members, peers, teachers, or coworkers. Police are sometimes the first people called, and certainly should be, if there are obvious signs of potentially imminent danger. Cops might be able obtain a warrant to search homes, cars, rooms, and computers.

Depending on the situation, the intervention could involve mental health services or law enforcement action such as arrest or detention. Members of threat assessment teams vary by setting. In general, the teams are multidisciplinary and include administration, faculty, law enforcement, mental health professionals, and attorneys. Mental health professionals often play an important role, whether they are directly evaluating a subject of concern or indirectly reviewing material, all the while considering the information to determine the presence of variables associated with the potential for violence.

Parents and family members need to keep an open line of communication with their kids, reinforce the importance of speaking up and reporting concerns when something doesn't seem right, and need to keep tabs on the stability of their own kids. Above all, they had better make sure that any firearms or other weapons in the home are stored safely.

Now let's talk about some culture and value shifts that we need to move toward. Many common behavioral themes can be found across the criminal spectrum. Key is the need for notoriety, for fame, for immortality. This can be found in just about every type, including the school shooter, the mass casualty shooter, the serial killer, and so on. A humble friend of mine, a man with no advanced degrees but who was strongly grounded and clear-thinking, once said it best to me as we sat down together years ago.

"An unmarked grave, Kris," he told me, referring to mass shooters. "Bury them in an unmarked grave outside of town and forget about them. Never mention their name again. Wipe out every trace of their existence."

I agree to a point. Let's stop making them heroes. We can still learn from them, but maybe we can stop using their names and instead just refer to them as suspects or offenders. The fact pattern and motives can be shared in order to learn the lessons that might help prevent another crime, but the killer's name is really not essential. We need to learn what we can from these perpetrators, but we don't need to show their glorified gun-filled pictures or homicidal videos.

The Columbine effect continues to pollute the minds of wannabe offenders, recently in yet another country. In Brazil in March 2019, two young men stormed their former school with hatchets, crossbows, and guns trying to emulate the Columbine killers. They murdered five children and two adults, then killed themselves. The message needs to become, "If you kill, you will be forgotten," and that there is no glory whatsoever in gunning down defenseless people who are essentially being blitzed and ambushed with no way to protect themselves. The message should be that it is a coward's act.

But so many issues and questions remain. Do movies and violent video games make our society less safe? Which malleable, unstable, or violent-fantasy-obsessed minds react to what stimuli? What influence does popular culture in general have on people imagining evil deeds? Does "aggression immersion," or wallowing in movie screen violence, indulge or exacerbate these fantasies? The answer is that violent movies and video games do not create the violent impulse but are sought by the person *already* interested in it.

I do not believe aggression immersion directly causes violence, but for a mentally ill, angry, or violently inclined person already fantasizing about committing a crime, such outside influences will further allow him to indulge those fantasies through repeated exposure to the material. And the person may even seek to replicate scenes from that media. Research shows, for example, that some people do get more accurate in their shooting skills by playing first-person war games, and they can get desensitized to shooting a living human being by such repeated conditioning.

As previously discussed, Jeffrey Cox, who stormed his California high school in 1988 armed with an AR-15 rifle, was institutionalized for a time before the attack after having contemplated suicide. At the facility, a nurse gave him a book about an angry student who holds a classroom hostage at gunpoint. Huge mistake.

While Cox later admitted the book fueled his own ideas and violent impulses, it did not make him into something he was not already. It did, however, serve to embolden him. He told me he didn't blame books or movies, but added an important thought: "Ideas, you know, they come from everywhere. So I had the idea, I read the book. I thought this is pretty good stuff, you know, truth through osmosis...." It resonated and gave form to his existing inclination to do something.

And the Columbine shooters were impressed by the movie *Natural Born Killers*. But their impulses and violent fantasies were already in full swing. When I teach threat assessment, aggression immersion is definitely on the radar screen, because when you see it, it is surface evidence of an underlying violent fantasy and deviant interests.

I'm not talking about someone who saw Stanley Kubrick's *A Clockwork Orange* once or twice, or *Terminator 2* a couple of times, but rather someone who shows evidence of an obsessive, highly repetitive, idiosyncratic relationship to the movie, video game, or book, and the item is watched, played, or read repeatedly.

Evan Ramsey, who in 1997 fatally shot his principal and another student at his Alaska high school, told me he played the violent first-person shooter video game Doom five hours a day. Five hours every day! So obviously, while I've made it clear that a movie or a TV show on its own isn't going to cause violence, it can exacerbate the wrong mindset if that person is already going down a lethal path. If you want a romantic evening with that special someone, you might put on some Barry White to set the mood. But the violently inclined tend to choose something more menacing, with themes and scenes that help maintain, reinforce, or even escalate their negative and violent state of mind.

As for serial killers, there are a few things that can be done to help prevent the next killing or at least cut down on the body count, such as (obviously) identifying and catching them earlier. But prevention techniques also include actions that can be taken prior to any killings, like addressing the budding deviance as the person is arrested repeatedly for offenses carrying a lesser sentence, such as sex crimes or the killing of animals.

Mental health professionals who deal with adolescents may need to become better at directly evaluating their fantasy lives. And when sex and violence are the mainstays, or power-laden fantasies the foundation of their internal homeostasis, methods and interventions to prevent these impulses from becoming permanently imprinted need to be further developed and implemented.

Some of those with these fantasies had rough childhoods, so anything we can do as a society to protect kids from being victimized—which can fuel an insatiable need for omnipotent power—will likely be helpful.

But we will never know for sure how many we have stopped from ever becoming killers. We just have to try.

Keep in mind that most people who have experienced abuse and difficult childhood upbringings do not become serial murderers. Indeed, more research would certainly be helpful to see just what it is about this vast majority that makes the difference. But make no mistake about it, there are those who are simply born bad, and no outside influences technically contributed to their violent fantasies. They just want to kill. They are just evil.

Prisons exist to protect us, and in some cases, I do not have a problem with the death penalty. Is the world a better place without the Nazi war criminals executed after the Nuremberg Trials? Absolutely. Is the world a better place for the multitude of victims of Timothy McVeigh after he was executed for the Oklahoma federal building bombing? I believe so. Is the world a little bit safer with one less serial killer roaming the streets? Of course.

That may sound harsh coming from a psychologist, and I have been on both sides of the issue. In court, I have testified for prosecution and defense teams in capital punishment cases. The issues are what they are, and I lend my expertise to assist. I have known people who were later executed, including the bigoted serial killer Joseph Paul Franklin. He deserved exactly what he got.

I've met multiple death row inmates in several states, learned about the victims of their crimes, and the effect the crimes have had on the survivors. The acceptability of the death penalty is a matter of personal moral conviction. I remember talking about capital punishment with someone who had hired me to do a school violence threat management workshop. She told me she was against it. Good enough. I respect that. Then she felt the need to add a reason.

"Because it doesn't have a deterrent effect."

It was good enough to say she was against it, that she didn't believe in it, but I couldn't resist. "How can you say that? Because he'll never kill again," I retorted. Not being able to kill again absolutely has a deterrent effect.

The argument that an innocent person could be executed is certainly a good one. But was that *really* the reason California governor Gavin Newsom issued an executive order in February 2019 putting a temporary halt to all executions in the state? Are you telling me there isn't a solid group of offenders on death row that we know with 100 percent certainty are guilty as sin of the crimes they were convicted of? I say let's just set aside the questionable cases for further review to be sure we are not executing an innocent person, but let's expedite the death penalty for the ones we know are stone-cold killers.

Serial murderer Richard Ramirez, "The Night Stalker," faced mountains of indisputable evidence proving his guilt, then died of natural causes on death row. Richard Farley, the stalker and workplace shooter who viciously killed seven people, also is without a doubt guilty. There are plenty of cases where there is literally no risk of executing an innocent person. Let's just get on with it.

But how can there be harm in simply keeping these killers in prison? We don't really have to take their lives, do we? They're already locked away for life. Well, ask the average family member of a deceased victim who lives every day with the loss what it is like knowing that while the loved one is no longer around, the killer stills breathes air and lives.

And here's a particularly horrendous scenario to really think about. Imagine your young son or daughter has been tortured, sexually assaulted, and murdered by a monster—you weren't there to protect your child. And that offender continues to enjoy and relive that memory, sometimes even masturbating to it while sitting in jail. I would say that certainly isn't justice.

The explosion of social media and easy access to the internet has fed the surge of violence around the world as killers not only learn from one another but leave behind their manifestos for all to see. Again, they leave their stamp on the world, and in their minds this is a pathway to immortality. We saw this in the 2019 New Zealand mass killings at two mosques. The gunman streamed live on Facebook the first sixteen minutes or so of the shooting. The video lived for hours online, on YouTube and other sites, before the companies took them down.

Social media sites like Facebook and YouTube are not being responsible enough to police their own sites and prevent the exchange of violent ideas. The law is pretty clear that the First Amendment does *not* cover speech that is dangerous and beyond hyperbole. The tech companies need to step up their efforts and use some of that bundle of money they get from the literally billions of people who use their platforms. They need to hire more threat-savvy professionals and develop better algorithms to search proactively for problems in real time.

These tech companies, like all of us, must bear some responsibility and act accordingly. In the aftermath of the fanatically driven Islamic terrorist attack in San Bernardino that left fourteen people dead and wounded twenty-two others, Apple refused to cooperate with the FBI's investigation by assisting in unlocking the suspects' iPhones. The feds ultimately had to use an outside source to crack the codes.

Are you fucking kidding me? These powerful tech companies need to step up to the plate and own up to their responsibilities as members of the world community.

We also live in a world that is growing more intolerant by the day, with attacks on houses of worship becoming disturbingly commonplace as hatred is fueled by more hatred and fanatical bigotry. In 2012, six members of a Sikh temple in Oak Creek, Wisconsin, were fatally shot by a white supremacist. About three years later, nine black worshippers including a pastor were killed by yet another white supremacist at a church in Charleston, South Carolina.

In 2017, a gunman killed six men during evening prayers at the Islamic Cultural Centre of Quebec City in Canada. And in 2018, a gunman known to have spewed anti-Semitic slurs online stormed the Tree of Life Congregation synagogue in Pittsburgh and opened fire, killing eleven Jewish worshippers.

There is a strong belief among many that the rise in these hate crimes has a correlation to the election of President Donald Trump and the intense political rhetoric that followed, with his constant posts on Twitter regularly degrading and demeaning those who speak against him. However, this nastiness is not limited to the president, but is seen in politicians and leaders on both sides of the political spectrum. Again, we all bear some responsibility.

We Americans as a culture have lost our civility. It's evident in talk shows, highway road rage, and especially on social media. This palpable and increasing interpersonal hostility and quickness to counterattack seem to be on the rise. It is time for a return to the basic parameters of civility in relationships, even among adversaries.

One of my favorite movies of all time is David Fincher's masterpiece, *Seven,* based upon a serial killer who uses the seven deadly sins as the organizing theme of his homicidal series. All violence, especially extreme violence, has its origins arguably in sin. And is not criminal law, in many respects, the secular codification of so-called sin? Sins against society. Pride, greed, lust, envy, gluttony, wrath, and sloth.

Fame without achievement, such as with a school or mass casualty shooter—someone who converts seething anger into a cold-blooded plan for revenge—usually comes after some injury to ego and pride. An unwillingness to earn true recognition is sloth. Killing for money is greed. Sexual homicide is lust. Hostility to authority, outrage over powerlessness, and an unquenchable thirst for omnipotence—do these not have envy at their very core? Nothing's ever being enough to satisfy whatever dark impulse someone has is metaphorical gluttony.

But at the head of the procession, arguably, are ego and pride. So much of what killers do is out of this insatiable desire to build upon both.

I take great relief in being just one minor speck of a human among nearly eight billion on a small living planet in an ever-expanding infinite universe. It is a relief from the bondage of the self that can otherwise overcome each of us. To those with dark impulses, I suggest there are solutions.

You are not alone. There are people who do and will care about you. Someone is capable of understanding you and helping steer you away from despair. You are important, but you are not the center of the universe. Do not give up, and do not give in to your darkest impulses. There is no victory there, nothing important to be remembered, and any memory of it will eventually disappear. Be a person among people and know that the greatest acts are those that occur in relative anonymity—when someone has a need and you fulfill it, perhaps by offering a kind word or gesture that no one besides that person knows about or will ever see.

We should never allow ourselves to become numb and accept this violence as our new and everlasting reality. We can all effect change and insist that those we have elected to see it through are held accountable.

We do need our leaders to step up their efforts and behave better. But even if they do not, each and every one of us can. We can greet people with a smile and genuinely be glad to see them. We can be sincere in finding out how they are doing and proactively do what we might be able to do to make their life a little bit better, at least for a moment.

We can let a driver with his or her turn signal on into our lane instead of speeding up and cutting the person off because we are in a hurry. We can refrain from reacting with instant hostility. Such goodwill is free, is infinitely powerful, and is something within the grasp of each and every one of us every day we draw breath. We can get back to the basics of our humanity and love, and maybe even notice the larger world around us, of which we are all a part.

Martin Luther King Jr. had a vision of global belonging he expressed in his 1967 Christmas Sermon on Peace: "If we are to have peace on Earth, our loyalties must become ecumenical rather than sectional. Our loyalties must transcend our race, our tribe, our class, and our nation; and this means we must develop a world perspective."

In California, the drought is over, and the hills of my youth are once again green. Yesterday the clouds hovered in beautiful pieces with the sun's shimmering beams shining down acceptingly upon all creation. The rays burned in brilliant reds and oranges like they did when I was a child. But everything in the world of humanity now seems different, and the eyes of my childhood have been replaced by a much darker vision. But I refuse to allow that vision to blind me.

The world is different, but in many ways, it is still the same.

EPILOGUE

Sometimes I reflect on what I used to be like and where I started. It's easy just to slide into who you are now, with no appreciation of where you've been. But there are definite signposts that announce where you are.

I was locked in the room with him, the camera was recording, and he was sitting, unshackled, on the opposite side of the table. The deputies were supposed to be watching the live feed, and his attorney was on the other side of the door, with the ability to see and hear what was going on.

He had killed a man in what appeared to be cold blood. He had been walking down a highway, likely angry. The victim had refused to sell him more booze, so the man shot him with a rifle. But now he was claiming some mental defense. Voluntary intoxication and an anger problem are not mitigating factors in California for criminal responsibility.

I had read everything and gone to the scene, and he had told me his version of the story. Now, it was time to confront him about the inconsistencies between his story of a "blackout" and what he told the police and actually did that argued strongly against his blacking out. I guess he must have figured I didn't read any of the police reports, or that he could simply substitute his self-serving version of events—the version the shrink on the other side apparently had bought without question.

I started to gently confront him about the inconsistencies, the facts that were indisputable that argued against his ridiculous defense. A man had died and he wanted a pass. Well, if it was the truth, I would have called it as such, but there were questions, and it wasn't going well for him. Confrontation doesn't have to be ugly; in my approach, it is simply asking, "What about the fact you told police this?" or "What about when you did this?"

He stopped responding for a minute. I looked up from my laptop and saw that he had started to get out of his seat and was glaring at me.

"Fuck you. You fucking preppie asshole. You think you know so much. You tell me, since you seem to know."

I looked at the table, moved the pencils to my side without drawing attention to the action, and waited for the troops to come in, or a voice on the intercom. Nothing. Nothing from his attorney either.

He said something else to the effect of, "Fuck you. I should kick your ass right fucking now!"

In my mind, everything seemed to slow down a bit, which gave me time to scan the room for any obvious weapons besides the pencils and generate plans A, B, and C. Plan A: I wear my shrink hat and talk him down hopefully. Plan B: He continues escalating and tries to hit me, to attack me with his fists or an object, and I grab the back of his hand with my left hand, use my right hand to push his elbow in, breaking it if I have to, and subdue him. Plan C: I use my laptop on his head after I sidestep his attack. Then pin him down, hard.

The shrink thinking kicked in, and I began analyzing this anger projected onto me—the rage quickly rising, on top of years of oppression by the system, and his casting it upon me, someone with the appearance of the white oppressor. Unbeknownst to him, and it didn't really matter, we probably shared more than he knew.

"Mr. Jones, please sit down. I meant you no disrespect. Please sit down." My voice was low, calm, controlled. My eyes softened and I lowered the intensity of my gaze.

He continued glaring.

I repeated myself.

After a tense few minutes, he sat down and we resumed. I continued asking questions. Ultimately, I finished the interview. The video camera recorded the whole thing, destroying the contention that he was angry and violent only during blackouts or while drunk. His anger and hostility were part of who he was. He later pled out—that several-minute scene during our jail interview obliterated the defense of being mentally ill.

The defense attorney had been terrified during the recorded scene. It must have appeared like one of those movie scenes in which someone is trapped in a room with a monster or killer, and those safely on the outside can only watch as someone is injured or killed.

The only difference was, I knew who was coming out of that room.

ABOUT THE AUTHOR

Dr. Kris Mohandie is a clinical, police, and forensic psychologist with over thirty years of experience in the psychology of violence. He has consulted in field responses and case investigations for local, state, and federal law enforcement organizations including the LAPD and the FBI. He has consulted on and testified in numerous extreme violence and homicide cases, including single, mass, and serial homicide cases. Dr. Mohandie has conducted extensive trial pending and prison interviews of violent offenders, including a number of stalkers, hostage takers, workplace and school violence perpetrators, and serial and multiple murderers. His work has been featured in *The New York Times*, *USA Today*, and *LA Times*, and he has appeared in the news programs of CNN, ABC-*20/20*, CBS, NBC-*48 Hours*, BBC, and Fox, as well as programs on Investigative Discovery, A&E, History, and the Discovery Channel. He was the host and a producer on the Investigative Discovery show, *Most Evil*, and the 2018 series *Breaking Homicide*.